Library of
Davidson College

ORGANIZATIONAL MANAGEMENT THROUGH COMMUNICATION

Library of
Davidson College

ORGANIZATIONAL MANAGEMENT THROUGH COMMUNICATION

Richard K. Allen

Central Michigan University

Harper & Row, Publishers
New York   Hagerstown   San Francisco   London

To Jean, Steve, and Scott

Sponsoring Editor: Larry Sifford
Project Editor: Pamela Landau
Designer: Andrea C. Goodman
Production Supervisor: Kewal K. Sharma
Compositor: Bi-Comp, Incorporated
Printer and Binder: Halliday Lithograph Corporation
Art Studio: Vantage Art Inc.

ORGANIZATIONAL MANAGEMENT THROUGH COMMUNICATION

Copyright © 1977 by Richard K. Allen
All rights reserved. Printed in the United States of America. No part of this book may be used or reproduced in any manner whatsoever without written permission except in the case of brief quotations embodied in critical articles and reviews. For information address Harper & Row, Publishers, Inc., 10 East 53rd Street, New York, N.Y. 10022.

Library of Congress Cataloging in Publication Data
Allen, Richard K. 1931–
   Organizational management through communication.

  Bibliography: p.
  Includes index.
  1. Communication in management. I. Title.
HF5718.A45   658.4′5   76-27310
ISBN 0-06-040206-7

contents

preface viii

I Organizational Management and Communication 1

1 management and organizational structure: a behavioral approach 3

Organizational Theory 5
Organizations Defined 7
Organizational Goals 9
Classification of Organizations 9
Formal and Informal Organizations 11
The Systems Approach 17
System Openness and the Organization 20
The Managerial Role in an Organization 25
Summary 33

2 the role of communication in management 36

The Significance of Communication 37
The Communication Process 41
The Significance of Communication to Management 48
The Manager as a Communicator 51
Communication Settings for the Manager 56
Summary 59

3 the management and control of information flows 61

Communication Networks 63
Information Flow and Directionality 71
Information Overloads 80
Summary 86

4 the changing organization   89

The Formal Organization and Change   92
Barriers to Organizational Change   94
Organizational Resistance to Change   100
The Communication of Change   104
Heterophily and Communicative Uniqueness   105
Types of Organizational Change   106
Planning Change   111
Summary   114

5 communication as a management tool   117

Developing a Communication Plan   121
Diagnosing Organizational Communication
    Problems   123
Research Utilization   125
The Designation of Communication Roles   129
Communication of Change as a Management Tool   135
Motivation as a Management Tool   137
Group Leadership as a Management Tool   139
The Ethical Side of Communication   140
Summary   141

II The Manager as a Communication Strategist   143

6 the change agent   146

Managers as Communicators of Change   148
Skills Necessary for the Change Agent Role   150
Management Strategies and the Decision to Change   153
Change Agents, Opinion Leaders, and the
    Two-Step Flow   157
Strategies to Overcome Change Resistance   160
Consequences: The Ethical Side   163
A Strategic Case in Point   165
Summary   172

7 the interpersonal motivator   174

Persuasion, Belief, and Attitude   176
Interpersonal Trust and Morale   180
Attitude Management   184
Summary   196

8 the small-group leader   200

Small Groups and the Organization   201
Group Dynamics   204
Norms, Power, and Roles   210
Effective Leadership   215
The Effects of Leadership   224
Summary   227

9 the total organizational communicator   230

Internal Communication and Total Communication   231
External Communication   232
Write It or Say It?   234
Reporting   236
Interviewing   238
Managing the Conference   249
Public Communication   257
Advertising, Promotion, and Public Relations   259
Summary   261

10 the analyst and teacher   263

Recapitulation   265
Communication of a Training Program   267
Analysis of Organizational Training Needs   270
Selection and Design of a Training Program   275
Administration and Communication of the
   Training Program   287
Evaluation of the Training Program   292
Summary   293

appendix case situations   295

bibliography   301

index   307

preface

It has been a common and continuous charge against many, if not most, programs of management education that theory and practice have rarely supported each other. Few schools, courses, or even textbooks have been designed around any general theory of managerial action, certainly not upon any theory of action reflecting the world in which the manager must live. These are the basic demands which would normally be placed upon any respectable theory in, say, the physical sciences.

Organizational Management Through Communication is an attempt to answer these charges with a pragmatic and highly readable link between the behavioral research of organizational and communication theory, and the real world needs of today's manager on the firing line. This book is written for students. It presents a strategy- and solution-oriented interdisciplinary approach which utilizes real management experiences as much as possible. The author's years of sales management experience combined with a background in communication research are the bases for this book, a book that provides an interface between organizational theory, management theory, communication theories, and change strategies.

Of particular interest, and central to the theme of this book, are observations pointing to the fact that a manager is an executor of hierarchical plans and a communication link between the home office and the client system. These observations lead us to a categorical label, or set of labels, for a manager. A manager could quite logically be described in communication parlance as a *gatekeeper* and/or *change agent*. In this context, the term *gatekeeper* refers to a person who filters messages as they come over the channel, with control over which messages are passed over the channel and the best method for presenting them. The term *change agent* is defined as a "professional who influences innovation-decisions in a direction deemed desirable by a change agency."[1] For instance, every waking, working hour a manager is at-

[1] Everett M. Rogers and F. Floyd Shoemaker, *Communication of Innovations: A Cross-Cultural Approach,* New York, Free Press, 1971.

tempting to gain maximum support, acceptance, and eventually commitment from the subordinates, whether he or she is introducing a new product or communicating a change in company policy.

In the following pages I have undertaken an examination of the relationship between these separate but related bodies of knowledge and the development of an integrated, practical set of useful management communication tools. In Part I, "Organizational Management and Communication," a close look is taken at the needs of management in an organizational structure and the behavioral science approach to management. These sections lead naturally to an examination of the role of communication in management, the control of information flows in the organization, and an in-depth evaluation of communication as a management tool. In Part II we deal with management through communication strategies by looking at the manager as a communication strategist.

Of particular interest to students and the pragmatically oriented classroom teacher is an appendix which provides a sampling of short case situations to which students may apply the newly learned communication strategies.

Spurred by a personal management background and a belief in the value of studying communication as a key to learned and controlled management success, I have attempted to provide the student and teacher alike with a practical and readable, as well as substantive, text. In short, the book is written for today's students and future organizational managers.

The deliberate intent of this book, then, is to promote professional management through the process of communication. It develops strategies which should be used in goal setting, planning, organizing, controlling, problem solving, and so on. Professional management, especially as it is achieved through improved communication, is the aim of the book.

I would like to express thanks to God for the strength and will to complete this task and deepest gratitude to the people who guided my thinking and really made this book possible: to people-manager Norm Dietz, and inspirational friend Malcolm Brown; to Everett M. Rogers, mentor and inspiration; to all the outstanding friends and colleagues at Central Michigan University who provided a creative work climate, exchanged important notions, and, most of all, kept asking about the book's progress; to the undergraduate students who have continually challenged me to be a quality teacher and, hopefully, a quality human being; to the stimulating graduate students; to my parents; and, finally, to my loving and understanding wife, Jean, and sons, Steve and Scott, who continually helped and encouraged me in this endeavor.

R.K.A.

 ORGANIZATIONAL MANAGEMENT AND COMMUNICATION

Although the voice of the people cannot be taken as the Voice of God, the soundness of their judgment and their willingness to be led is impressive. George Gallup

The days ahead are going to demand a management competency unparalleled in the history of organizational management. The strengthening of labor organizations and the increasing quest for individual rights and human dignity has led to an enlightened era of organizational management, a management era that realizes it must communicate more often, more accurately, and more strategically if it is to survive.

In an era marked by such rapid change, managers must create a new social climate in which innovative work can flourish. This social climate must be a working climate that will encourage a free flow of ideas and, at the same time, control the inundatory flow of information to which an organization and its members are exposed.

Before such an effective management system can become a reality its members, present and future, must understand that individual attitudes and the management of these attitudes are the fabric from which organizational behavior is created. Strategies must be developed, then, to manage properly the communication of these attitudes.

We can never hope to develop these strategies without first understanding individual attitudes because it is very difficult to manage persons we cannot understand. Such understanding can best be reached through improved knowledge of the communication process and the communication behaviors that are so inextricably a part of each individual and each system. Our primary tool for providing the necessary management insight and understanding, then, is a broader knowledge of organizational communication problems; this is the objective of Part I.

1 management and organizational structure: a behavioral approach

> Complex organizations . . . manufacturing firms, hospitals, schools, armies, community agencies . . . are ubiquitous in modern societies, but our understanding of them is limited and segmented.
>
> *James D. Thompson*

OBJECTIVES for Chapter 1

After reading the chapter you should be able to:

1. Give your own definition of a formal organization and be able to describe potential effects of informal organizations upon their respective formal organizations.

2. Compare and contrast the three major organizational theories.

3. Describe in detail the entire principle of systems theory and give at least two practical applications of the theory as examples.

4. Discuss the characteristics that distinguish an open system from a closed system.

5. Detail the assumptions of theory X and theory Y management and, by analyzing the management of several different organizations, place them on a theory X to Y continuum.

6. Describe in detail the additional management dilemma in which a manager is placed by decentralization.

7. Identify 12 decentralized organizations, further identify the reason or reasons for their original decentralization, and analyze the success of the decentralization.

8. Describe the principle of organizational entropy and identify six examples of organizational management that have enhanced organizational stability and thwarted the entropic process.

BECAUSE this text is basically dedicated to an examination of communication as it applies to organizational management, it will be necessary first to examine the nature of organizations and their management. In Chapter 1, then, we will be laying the groundwork for the entire book by introducing the conceptual basis for the study of the management of organizational structures.

As indicated in the opening quote of this chapter, there is a paucity of data on the functioning of complex organizations. There is, at the same time, a rapidly growing interest in and need for accurate and useful information related to organizations, their internal mechanisms, and the executives who manage them. Many outside people, such as suppliers and clients who deal with large complex organizations, have exaggerated, almost caricatured, impressions of executives at work in their complex organizations.

One such caricature pictures executives as top mystics who wear their ulcers like a hair shirt and are quietly attended in their air-conditioned retreats by secretaries who whisper low rituals and occasionally give them some paper fetish to contemplate. The paper fetish is usually some ritualized art form such as the annual report of some corporation. Such a report symbolically represents the expenditures of the energy and life of some whole universe, which will show assets of $29,261,834.08 and liabilities of miraculously and precisely the same amount, $29,261,834.08. These figures are drawn together by the accounting priesthood, a group of highly trained specialists in selection, emphasis, and understatement. The assets and liabilities, of course, must rhyme like the final couplet of an Elizabethan sonnet. And so it goes, on and on. The foregoing is an amusing characterization of what goes on in our complex organizations; however, there is considerably more to the management of a large, complex organization than we find portrayed in this bit of fun.

ORGANIZATIONAL THEORY

Perhaps a brief look at the evolutionary history of organization theory would help our understanding of organizations in general. The early search for greater efficiency in organizational management produced what has come to be known as the *classical theory* of administration, sometimes known as scientific management. Out of this tradition came the entity described as the formal organization providing the structural format on which organizations normally pattern themselves. Arising as a sort of reaction to the rigid structure which is characteristic of classical theory was the school of organizational thought known as *human relations,* which emphasized the informal organization and its emotional, unplanned behaviors. There followed a third tradition that attempted to unite the best of the classical and the human relations approaches known as the *structuralist* approach.

The classical or scientific approach, founded mainly by Max Weber, recognized no conflict between people and the organization, assuming instead that what was good for management was good for the workers. In other words, the classical theory assumed that harder work and higher productivity would produce higher profits which would lead, theoretically, to higher wages and, still more theoretically, to greater satisfaction among workers. The classical administrators used a combination of time and motion studies and a physical capacity assumption that humans are driven by a fear of hunger and a desire for economic gain which will make them respond maximally to financial reward. Such a rational, economic orientation gave rise to such management techniques as bonus systems. The basic problem with the classical approach is the high concern for structure and unconcern for people.

The human relations approach, as stated earlier, was basically a reaction to the classical school. Elton Mayo, John Dewey, and Kurt Lewin were the chief contributors to this school of organizational thought. Human relations research discovered, among other things, that the amount of work done by workers is determined at least in part by their "social" capacities.

Human relations research findings began mainly with the findings of a classic set of studies known as the Hawthorne studies,[1] which were conducted at the Hawthorne plant of Western Electric in Chicago from about 1927 to 1932. Prior to the studies, the scientific management predictions of the classicists hypothesized that more physical illumination in the work area and its accompanying improved working conditions would increase production. The study actually rejected this hypothesis but revealed the following specific major findings:

1. The level of production is set by social norms, not by physiological capacities.
2. Noneconomic rewards and sanctions significantly affect the behavior of the workers and largely limit the effect of economic incentive plans.
3. Workers often do not act or react as individuals but as members of groups.
4. The importance of leadership for setting and enforcing group norms and the difference between informal and formal leadership.

The Hawthorne studies revealed the need for the inclusion of at least some social and humanistic thought in organizational theory and analysis. Researchers began, at this point, to be concerned about such variables as morale, social relations, worker attitudes, and the human relations approach to organizational analysis was born. But just as the classical approach was too concerned only with structure and function, the human relations approach has often been too concerned only with people.

The structuralist approach, in its effort to synthesize the classical and human relations approaches to organizational analysis, began to recognize the organizational dilemma. This dilemma encompasses such things as strains between organizational needs and personal needs, between discipline and autonomy, and between management and workers. The structuralists see the organization as a complex social unit with many smaller social subgroups constantly interacting. The synthesis is not necessarily complete since there are still some pure human relations advocates and even some pure classicists; however, the structuralist movement has brought about a broadening of the general approach to organizational analysis. According to Amitai Etzioni, this broader approach to organizational analysis includes:

1. both formal and informal elements of the organization and their articulation;
2. the scope of informal groups and the relations between such groups inside and outside the organization;
3. both lower and higher ranks;

4. both social and material rewards and their effects on each other;
5. the interaction between the organization and its environment;
6. both work and non-work organizations.[2]

Our continued examination of the organization in this chapter will follow the broadened general approach suggested by the structuralists.

ORGANIZATIONS DEFINED

What is an organization? Theoretically at least, an organization is a collective group of individuals capable of accomplishments beyond the capacity of individuals acting alone. Because of this notion our society has become highly organized. Most of us now spend most of our waking hours dealing with some type of organization. We work for organizations, we play in organizations, we pray in organizations, we go to organizations when we are sick and even when we die. Obviously then, we consider schools, clubs, churches, and businesses to be examples of organizations, but it is still not easy to pinpoint an exact definition.

Let us reconsider the notion that potentially an organization can accomplish feats not possible for a single human. The implication in such a statement is that an organization, a group of humans acting in concert and pooling their resources and abilities, is potentially capable of more than any single human member of that group would be. The term *potentially capable* as it is used here can be defined simply as "may be capable but not necessarily." In other words, if individuals band together in a group and then do not work up to their individual capabilities, the effectiveness of this group or organization will certainly be seriously hampered. Of course, the commitment and character of the individuals involved play a part in how fully they each maximize their capabilities.

In the main, then, a group working in concert can be, and often is, more efficient than any of its individual members working alone. Further substantiation for this point of view is pointed out by Jay Hall in his *Psychology Today* article "Decisions, Decisions, Decisions."[3]

We have acknowledged that an organization is certainly a kind of group because of its collective nature. We have also looked at some simple concepts of the comparative effectiveness and capabilities of groups and individuals. But our purpose here is to deal with organizations, so it is imperative that we examine the differences between a group and an *organized group*. Therein should be a workable definition of an organization.

A group is normally composed of three or more persons having something in common and each person interacting at some time with one or all of the others. The organized group, on the other hand, is based on repetitive interaction among members. As a result, the relationships are more permanent and the group has continuity. An organized group can recess or disperse and when reassembled it will repeat the relationships originally established between its individual members. In contrast, when an unorganized group disperses and is reassembled, the similarity between the original group and the reassembled group is often negligible.

An important organizational factor, then, is the repetition of social situations. An apparent prerequisite for this is a definite roster of members because, at the minimum, the members of an organized group must be identifiable to each other. The single most important factor in such identification is a common reference to an entity or a group name. For instance, as an outsider you distinguish one organized group from another by its official name. The members of the group likewise identify with that official name.

It is becoming apparent that an organization is a group of humans bound together by some formal structure. According to almost every organizational psychologist except the classicists, organization means more than just structure. Consensus seems to point to the inclusion of such factors an managerial controls, leadership, technology, and communication networks. An organization is seen by many researchers to be an intricate set of human strategies designed to achieve certain objectives or goals. We might say, then, that organizations are human groupings deliberately constructed to achieve specific and general goals. Such units as corporations, armies, schools, hospitals, churches, and prisons would fit this description very well.

According to Amitai Etzioni,[4] organizations are characterized by (1) deliberately planned *divisions of labor, power and communication responsibilities;* (2) one or more *power centers* which control, evaluate and, where necessary, restructure; and (3) *substitution of personnel* through hiring, termination, transfer, and promotion. In other words, an organization is much more in control of its own nature and destiny than is any other social group.

Perhaps the definition of an organization which best answers the needs we have thus far delineated is the definition set down by organizational psychologist Edgar Schein. Schein says that an organization is "the rational coordination of the activities of a number of people for the achievement of some common, explicit purpose or goal, through a division of labor and function and through a hierarchy of authority and responsibility."[5]

ORGANIZATIONAL GOALS

Because specific purposes and goals seem to be so much a part of any description of an organization, perhaps we should take a closer look at these goals. An organizational goal is a future state which the organization is attempting to achieve. Organizational goals serve a variety of functions. They provide orientation, guidelines, legitimacy, and evaluative standards, to name but a few functions. Organizations not only have specific goals, but these goals often become the entire reason for the existence of the organization. Many organizations develop *real* goals which differ greatly from the original or *stated* goals. Real goals, in this case, refer to goals that develop along the way as a result of organizational needs, and that command so much of the means, commitment, and resources of an organization that they are definitely of a higher priority than the stated goals. Etzioni points out that the distinction between real and stated goals has nothing to do with intended and unintended consequences.[6] Goals are always intended when they are formulated; however, there is a difference between stated intentions and real intentions. The stated goals often take on the role of the public image of an organization. They become, then, front or public goals, and may or may not be the actual sociological or economic goals of the organization.

In most organizations the goals are set by some designated body such as stockholders, members (i.e., labor unions), a board of trustees or, in smaller organizations, by an individual owner. Key roles in the establishment of goals are played by various organizational departments or divisions, by personalities such as a strong leader, and by outside forces from the environment in which the organization exists. An excellent example of environmentally originated organizational goals is the recent addition, by most major industries, of pollution control as a stated and real organizational goal.

CLASSIFICATION OF ORGANIZATIONS

The classification of organizations according to such factors as size or purpose will help us to define what an organization actually is. There are, of course, many ways to classify or type organizations. One of the most obvious ways is simply to examine the goals of the organization. For instance, what we might call a *mutual benefit association* would be exemplified by such organizations as political parties, unions, fraternal clubs, religious sects, and professional associations. Another goal-oriented organizational type would be *business concerns* such as industries, mail order houses, wholesale and retail stores, banks, and insurance companies. Under this system of typologies we could classify social work agencies, hospitals, schools, legal aid societies, and mental health clinics as *service organizations*. Finally, what we will call *commonwealth organizations,* public benefit organizations, would be organizations such as the State Department, I.R.S., the military, police and fire, and the research functions of a university or hospital.

A general typology of organizations has been worked out by Warren Bennis[7] in the chart below.

Type of organization	Major function	Examples	Effectiveness criterion
Habit	Replicating standard and uniform products	Highly mechanized factories, etc.	Number of products
Problem solving	Creating new ideas	Research organizations, design and engineering divisions, consulting organizations, etc.	Number of ideas
Indoctrination	Changing people's habits, attitudes, intellect, behavior (physical and mental)	Universities, prisons, hospitals, etc.	Number of "clients" leaving
Service	Distributing services either directly to consumer or to above types	Military, government, advertising, taxi companies, etc.	Extent of services performed

Etzioni presents still another interesting way to classify organizations when he describes them as being predominantly *coercive, utilitarian,* or *normative*.[8] A *coercive* organization is one in which coercion is the major means of control over participants as in concentration camps, prisons, and custodial mental hospitals. A *utilitarian* organization is one in which remuneration is the major means of control as in industries, business unions, and farmer cooperatives. A *normative* organization is described as one in which compliance with norms or normative power is the major source of control as in religious organizations, political organizations, and voluntary associations. Hospitals, colleges, and universities also fall into this category.

It is possible under this typology to have dual organizations that are combinations of the foregoing types. Some examples are a combat unit which would be *normative-coercive,* or most unions which would be *Utilitarian-normative.* Organizations such as early industries, farms, and ships might be classified as *utilitarian-coercive.*

Regardless of the method or typology used, it is important in the study of an organization to begin with some sort of method of classifying that organization.

FORMAL AND INFORMAL ORGANIZATIONS

The highly structured organization we have been defining and discussing has as its raison d'être the attainment of objectives or goals through the preplanned, efficient use of available resources. The ensembles of individuals who perform distinct but interrelated and coordinated functions within such structures are really the *formal* organizations. The implication of the designation "formal" is that there is also such an entity as an "informal" organization. We will examine the latter in a moment, but first we can benefit from a closer look at the formal organization.

The structure of a formal organization is based upon the classical, scientific management principles mentioned earlier. Briefly, these principles assume that a formal organization has:

1. *Task Specialization.* Because a concentrated effort on a limited number of endeavors increases the quality and quantity of output, organizational and administrative efficiency should be increased by specialization of tasks assigned to the participants. A quick look about us shows that this specialization has reached an all-time high, sometimes to the detriment of the individual who is well trained in one narrow field or task and suddenly finds that such jobs no longer exist.
2. *Unity of Direction.* If the tasks of every person in a unit are specialized, the objective or purpose of the unit would then be specialized. The unity of direction notion states that organizational efficiency increases when each unit has a single activity (or homogeneous set of activities) under the direction of one leader.

3. *Span of Control.* The principle of control points out that efficiency is increased by limiting the scope of control of a leader. In other words, the narrower the management responsibilities, either in diversity of tasks or the number of people to be managed, the greater the efficiency. The application of this control principle accounts for what sometimes appears to the outsider to be a top-heavy organizational structure (i.e. "Too many chiefs," etc.).
4. *Chain of Command.* Task specialization naturally creates many separate but related tasks. However, such a group of individual tasks being performed does not constitute an organization. The actual organization is created by forming these individual tasks into an interdependent and related pattern. The assumption is made that administrative and organizational efficiency is increased by arranging the individuals in a hierarchy of authority with the individual on top directing and controlling the individual on the bottom.

Such hierarchical patterns, referred to in the army as the chain of command, are what we often call a table of organization or, more frequently, an organization chart. Such a chart often hangs on the office wall proclaiming to all who pass by just what the formal hierarchical structure is supposed to be; a sort of pecking order. The chart is usually the pyramidal structure suggested by the classicists, which might look like the structure in Figure 1.1. Another format for a formal orga-

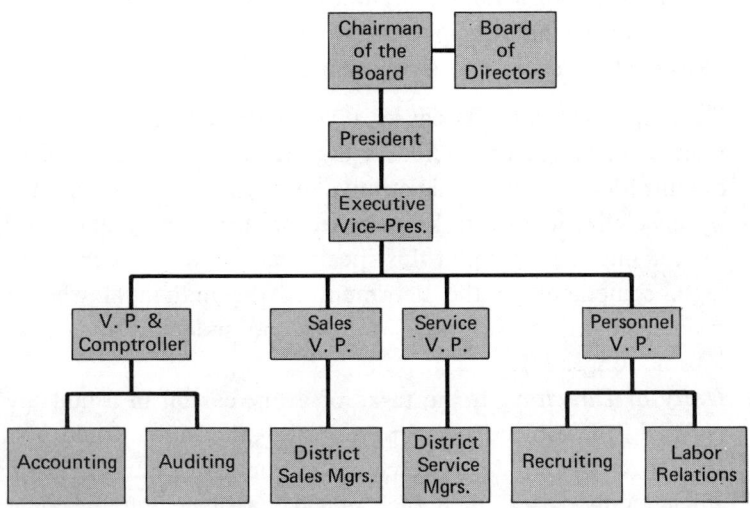

Figure 1-1 Pyramidal organization chart.

nization chart is a circle, shown in Figure 1.2. This particular circular chart is a chart from a middle-sized university. Job responsibilities (including who reports to whom) are very clear. It is even possible to show shared responsibilities such as data processing and budget direction on the circular chart shown in Figure 1.2.

One factor that determines the type of structure and how formal and well defined the structure must be is organizational size. Clearly, the larger the size, the more formal the structure must be in order to maintain the necessary control. Theodore Caplow in his book *Principles of Organizations* does a good job of approximating some divisions in organizational size. These divisions are as follows:

1. *Small Organizations.* A small organization ranges from about three to thirty members and is small enough to permit them to become a primary group within themselves. A family is an example.
2. *Medium-size Organizations.* These organizations are too large for the development of all possible pair relationships but still small enough that any member, including a leader, would interact with any other member. The medium-size organization ranges from about thirty to about a thousand. An average industrial firm might be an example.
3. *Large Organizations.* A large organization is too large for many members to know each other well but not too large for one or more leaders to be recognized by all other members. These leaders will be recognized by many more people than they are able to recognize. Such an organization ranges from about one thousand to about fifty thousand. Most universities are large organizations.
4. *Giant Organizations.* The giant organization has too many members which are too widely scattered to permit the direct interaction of any individual with all of the others. The range of the giant organizations is from about fifty thousand to infinity. Political parties and business conglomerates are good examples.[9]

One can readily see that the size of an organization does make a great deal of difference, particularly concerning how that organization will be managed. While a formally structured organization has many of the advantages already discussed, it is also faced with certain dilemmas. These dilemmas are, of course, magnified as organizational size increases. Some of the dilemmas of a formal organization are:

1. *Bureaucratic discipline.* It is highly desirable but not always possible to keep everyone operating from a "company" point of view.
2. *Professional expertise.* It is most difficult to find promotable people from within (or sometimes even from outside) to fill all the vital hierarchical slots.

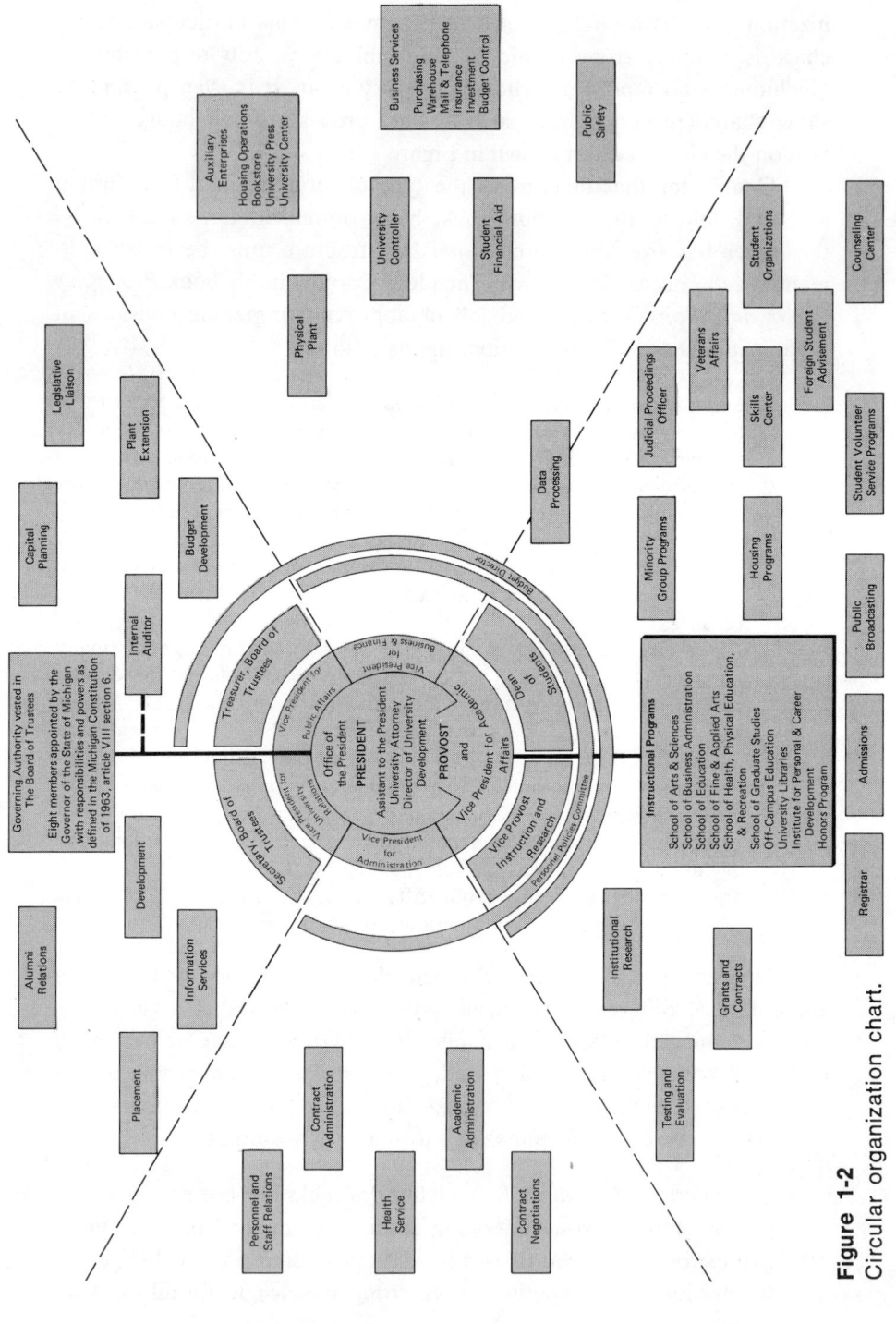

Figure 1-2
Circular organization chart.

3. *Coordination and Control.* The large formal organization can very easily become awkward and unwieldy.
4. *Managerial planning and initiative.* The formal organization requires an inordinate amount of ability on the part of its managers to plan carefully and then take the initiative in implementation.
5. *Communication.* Last, but certainly far from least, communication is too often hampered. Without communication and constant open interaction, the organization cannot survive and, as was pointed out in the foregoing breakdown by size, communication is far more difficult in a large formal organization than in a smaller organization.

Because of dilemmas such as these, there arise in every formal organization one or more informal organizational structures. A few paragraphs ago we took the opportunity to describe the components found in most formal organizations to illustrate what a typical formal organization chart might look like. If we plan so carefully and control so well how, then, do we find ourselves involved in the chaotic dilemmas just described?

A part of the chaos that may exist in an organization, as the human relations school has pointed out, is the failure to see any dimensions of the organization other than those implied by the formal organization chart on the executive office wall. The formal organization chart is, of course, an important structural factor simply because organizations are traditionally described by organization charts. An organization chart specifies the authority or reportorial structure of the system. The organization chart communicates some of the most important formal attributes of the system. Cyert and March point out that, "The organization chart still provides a lot of information conveniently—partly because the organization usually has come to consider relationships in terms of the dimensions of the chart."[10]

When we study a diagram of the structure of an organization, we learn something about the operation and about the communication patterns which accompany the operation of that organization. Yet when we place human beings into the slots on that organizational chart, we find ourselves with a second, but equally important, structural pattern, a sort of *informal organizational chart.*

The formal organization has already been described as a conventional methodical structure, a set of rules, and generally refers to the organizational pattern designed by management; a blueprint of the division of labor and the power of control. The informal organization, on the other hand, is a nonconventional methodological structure and often refers to the social relationships that develop among the staff or workers above and beyond the formal one determined by the organization; for example, they do not work on the same team but are friends. The formal aspect of an organization, then, is the classical hierarchical structure which the organization itself recognizes as its structure, that is, who reports to whom. The informal organizations are the less obvious human relations factors within each formal organization which, although not always recognized, are nonetheless present and must be dealt with for example, "the grapevine" or "rumor mill." More will be said about the grapevine in later chapters. Because of the relative obscurity and the lack of recognizable structure, any kind of informal structure is extremely difficult to deal with; however, it still must be dealt with.

The high degree of rigidity of the formal structure may account for the frequently reported growth of informal, and sometimes unidentified, communication channels in organizations. The growth stems from the fact that the informal structure is often better able to meet the changing, fluctuating, and dynamic needs of the organization, whereas the formal structure has a tendency to be more static. Too often the formal structure no longer describes what is, in fact, going on dynamically in an organization. Even more important, if formal organizations more nearly matched the informal organization structurally, the organizations would probably be highly productive, highly cohesive, and enjoy considerably more communication efficiency than they do. Since the informal and formal often do not match structurally, the recognition and understanding of the informal organizational hierarchy within the formal organization is an absolute necessity for an examination of the whole.

Keith Davis tells of a manager who had a formal organization chart on the wall which was a neat, logical document clearly showing the official lines of authority and communication.[11] But in a desk drawer this manager kept another organization chart. Although the same people were listed, the relationships were quite different and the communication lines took different routes. This second chart was a view of the informal organization. Like some other managers, this one could have pretended that the informal organization did not exist or hoped that it would go away. Instead, the manager accepted it as a fact of life and did everything possible to make it a positive force that could be utilized and a force that could contribute to organizational morale and efficiency.

So while the organization chart on the executive's wall is necessary and vital to the operation of the organization, smart executives will keep a second chart, the informal one in their heads or, better yet, in their desk drawers for quick reference at all times. That chart in the desk drawer may, at times, better describe what is happening in the organization than the one on the wall. At the very least, there will be a frequent need to lay one chart over the other to get a total picture of the organization.

THE SYSTEMS APPROACH

Some references have already been made to an organization as being a *system* or a *social system*. For our purposes in this book we will define a system as an organized, complex whole; an assemblage or combination of parts forming a complex whole. We will define a social system as a bounded collection of interdependent parts devoted to the accomplishment of some goal or goals.

The foregoing definition of a social system is closely tied in with our earlier goal-oriented definition of an organization. But why use a systems approach to studying organizations at all? Fundamental to systems theory is the concept of input, throughput, and output. James D. Thompson points out: "Complex organizations exist ultimately as agencies of their environment, acquiring resources in exchange for outputs and, in the final analysis, obtaining technologies from environments."[12] The concepts basic to systems theory, then, do a good job of describing what is going on in an organization and, therefore, provide a useful look at these organizations.

Systems theory itself certainly bears further examination for our purposes here. As stated earlier a system is made up of a series of *inputs, throughputs,* and *outputs*. To clarify these concepts it would be helpful to examine the system in an industrial plant for a moment. In the industrial setting, such factors as raw materials, workers, capital, and so on, are considered inputs. The manufacturing process conducted in that plant is the throughput and the finished marketable product is considered to be the output.

Ideally a system should be *self-corrective;* that is, the system has a *cybernetic* control mechanism which will tell it when adjustments need to be made. For instance, in a modern heating system the cybernetic device is the thermostat and in a human system the cybernetic device is the brain. But how is that self-corrective? If your human system, your body, is driving a car down the highway and a child darts out in front of you, what do you do? Your eye sees the child and flashes a message to your cybernetic device, the brain, which says, in effect, "Danger ahead—correct at once." Your brain says swerve to the left or right and you will miss the child and so you do. Now if you have overcorrected and are heading for the ditch the same process occurs and you are back on course as shown in Figure 1.3.

This simplified description of a system and its cybernetic is really not any different from the very complex functions of a large social system such as a formal organization. The principles pointed out in this simple example are that, through feedback from the environment, a system may adapt and adjust in a self-corrective fashion and, not only survive, but ultimately reach its original goal. The simple illustration of the child and the car also points to another principle of systems theory known as the *law of equifinality*. The law of equifinality simply says that there are many ways to get to an ultimate goal, not just by the single course originally planned.

If we return to our industrial example, we will see that the reading of feedback from the environment by the cybernetic portion of the system ultimately becomes important in the profit and loss statement. Basically in our industrial example the sale of the product or output provides the capital necessary to buy the raw material inputs to make more products (output) and on and on continuously. However, in order for the system to continue, it must be under control at all times by its cybernetic and must constantly be adjusting and self-correcting. For example, it would be as unprofitable to have too much unused raw material lying around as it would be to have the throughput ready to operate and have no raw material on hand. On the other hand, it is not profitable to produce a greater output than the market can handle at any given time. It is necessary, then, for the cybernetic—in this case management—to keep correcting the system to maintain a steady process of input, throughput, output, input, throughput, output, etc. What is really involved here is another concept in systems theory known as the *principle of optimization*.

The principle of optimization means that a system attempts to reach a point at which it is getting the maximum output in return for the minimum input. The business of the cost accountant, for instance, is one of optimization. Obviously, one of the main functions of any modern

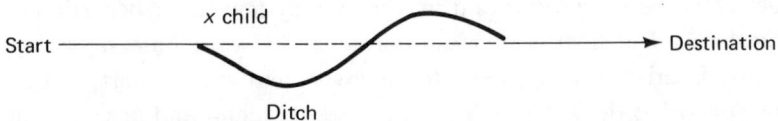

Figure 1-3 Systems Theory model.

manager is continually to correct flows in the system until it reaches, or at least nears, that point of optimization.

Organizational multiplicity

The subject of interrelatedness, one organization to another or of subparts within organizations, has already been mentioned in this chapter. Most organizations are related to other organizations in one of the following ways:

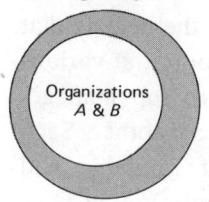

1. *As a congruent organization.* Congruence in this sense refers to an organization where the membership of organization A is identical with the membership of organization B, but the two organizations have completely separate goals and purposes.

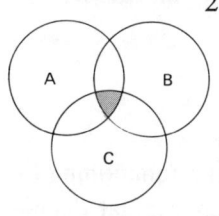

2. *As linked to another organization.* Here we have a situation more of overlapping membership than of congruency. We find that certain members of organization A belong to organization B, and perhaps even to organization C, but still these organizations do not have the same purposes. As the diagram shows, there are three two-way organizational interfaces and one three-way interface.

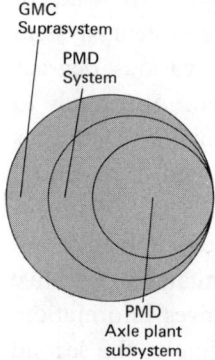

As a component of another larger organization. Our concern here is with a relationship of subsystems, systems and suprasystems which, in a complex structure, seems to go on almost to infinity. An example of such a component structure would be General Motors Corporation in which all the employees of the Pontiac Motor Division are at the same time employees of the corporation. Conversely, however, all employees of the corporation are definitely not employees of Pontiac Motor.

According to Daniel Katz and Robert Kahn, most formal organizations function through five basic subsystems:

1. *productive subsystems* concerned with the work that gets done;
2. *supportive subsystems* of procurement, disposal, and institutional relations;
3. *maintenance subsystems* for tying people into their functional roles;
4. *adaptive subsystems* concerned with organizational change;
5. *managerial systems* for the direction, adjudication, and control of the many subsystems and activities of the structure."[13]

Also, in most organizations such subsystems are not equally powerful in their influence over one another and over the total system. An interesting phenomenon then, which occurs in some organizations, is a *leading system*. There is an almost infinite number of reasons why one subsystem might lead the other subsystems and exert the greatest influence over the organization. These reasons may range widely from the fact that the chairman of the board came up through that particular subsystem, to the fact that a subsystem possesses technologies that are particularly vital to the total organization, and even to the fact that a certain subsystem such as the sales department provides the income that keeps the blood flowing in the organizational vein. Of course, at various times and for various situationally appropriate reasons, top management may be influenced first by one subsystem and then another. Such multidirectional influence is unquestionably the most equitable and technologically sound way to manage for, and achieve, optimization.

SYSTEM OPENNESS AND THE ORGANIZATION

Before we can examine the effects of openness upon the functioning of an organization, we must provide at least a limited conceptual definition of *system openness*. System openness is the degree to which a system exchanges information with sources outside the system. System openness includes open and closed systems and the various degrees found along a continuum stretching between the two. According to Matthew Miles, "An open system is related to and makes exchanges with its environment, while a closed system is not related to and does not make exchanges with its environment."[14]

Basically, then, a *closed system* is an isolated, self-contained system or at least a system that has fallen into a self-contained operative pattern. In contrast, an *open system* constantly exchanges information, ideas, energy, and so on with its environment. According to the second law of thermodynamics, the physical world is directed toward chaos, maximum disorder, and disequilibrium. This thermodynamic law applies specifically to a closed system. In other words, where there is no open exchange with the outside environment, a system will stagnate and wither. This stagnating, withering, perishing process is known in systems theory, just as it is in the thermodynamic sense, as *entropy*. Biologically speaking, entropy is the principle which states that when we are born we begin to die. Entropy in an organizational context may be defined as the tendency for a system to move to a random and chaotic state in which there is no longer a potential for throughput or work.

We have just seen that an open system is a system that is related to and makes exchanges with its environment and that the opposite is true of a closed system. If information is the lifeblood of any organization, then we might expect a closed system to experience a rapidly increasing state of entropy. Conversely, an open system with a steady flow of information at its disposal should experience what we call a *steady state*. A steady state can be defined as a state where the composition of the system remains constant, or in a state of equilibrium.

Recall that earlier in Chapter 1 we spoke of general systems theory and the concepts of inputs, throughputs, and output. The systems theory option of input and output in an organization is really the maintenance of a steady state or a state of equilibrium between the input and output of that organization.

Because open systems, unlike closed systems, are constantly exchanging energy, materials, and/or information with their environments, these open systems take in (input), process (throughput), and give off (output) in relation to the environment. Of course, open systems experience some entropic tendency toward disorder, randomness, and a loss of energy that goes on in a closed system. But the open system can restore order, cut down on randomness, and replenish energy by adjusting and taking on inputs of greater energy or a higher order than their own outputs.

Besides this organizational life-giving characteristic of an open exchange with the environment and the consequent steady state, there are other characteristics that distinguish an open system from a closed system:

1. Open systems are examples of the *law of equifinality* already discussed; that is, there is more than one path that may be followed to obtain identical results.
2. An open system is *self-regulating*. In other words, such a system is able to adjust to adversity and unexpected barriers and still arrive at its original destination with the mission accomplished. It is flexible enough to roll with the punches and correct itself as it goes along and then return to the steady state.
3. Open systems are able to maintain a steady state and regulate or self-correct through *feedback*. Whether the feedback refers to materials, information, or whatever, the principle still remains that

a system must have a portion of its output fed back into the inputs which will ultimately affect future outputs. It is the ability of a system to adjust future behaviors and outputs by reference to past behaviors and outputs through a proper reading of the feedback portion of the inputs. One basic fact related to this type of feedback is that normally it is negative feedback. It should be clear that the need for self-regulation or self-correction in the systems can only really be pointed out by negative feedback. When negative feedback vanishes, the very reason for correction or regulation also vanishes.

4. Just as we have shown the communication process within a system to be cyclical and constantly in motion, so can we view an open system as a *cycle of events*. An open system with its input–throughput–output and its self-regulatory feedback is certainly a dynamic rather than a static concept. A simple linear stimulus-response exchange between two entities does not constitute social structure; however, two entities stimulating and responding to each other in a cyclical fashion form the basic dynamic unit in a system. Such a single cycle of events gives us the simple form of structure. A typical complex organization is a system of event cycles made up of many such single cycles, both in and out of the organization, most of which are interrelated.

5. Because of the foregoing features found in an open system, another feature of such systems is *negative entropy,* sometimes called negentropy. Since an open system, in addition to the foregoing features, can store the imported energic inputs, it can acquire negative entropy. The acquisition of energy, its storage, and subsequent use at the times when it is most needed is one of the main functions of management. When we manage our systems best, we manage for negative entropy and an ultimate state of organizational equilibrium.

6. The culmination of all features found in open systems is contained in the ultimate goal of any success-seeking organization, the achievement of a *dynamic equilibrium*. On the surface there seems to be some confusion as to whether an open system provides the impetus for constant change or provides a steady system which resists change. Many people feel that an open system produces stability and infrequent change because of the stable, mechanical system necessary to keep information flowing in and out of an organization. Others feel conversely that the major impetus for change in an organization comes from outside the organization

because of the fresh approaches that exogenous information brings with it.

The notion of a dynamic equilibrium, because it is not a motionless or true equilibrium, is the key to this dilemma. Basically, a dynamic equilibrium, with its flexibility, allows for growth and change without loss of the overall steady state. In other words, growth and change are possible in an open system because its self-adjustive factors prevent any extended state of disequilibrium. Such a system reacts to change or anticipates change through growth which assimilates the change into the existing structure. A new operational level is thus established and the organization adjusts and functions around this new level but with the same old internal balance and equilibrium.

Effective management and organizational health

The mere survival of a formal organization such as a business or industrial firm in today's competitive world is almost in itself a tribute to management. What we are talking about when we say survival, is a sort of organizational health or well-being. That healthy state will no more take care of itself than our bodies will survive in a healthy state without sleep, a balanced diet, and proper overall care. The business of taking care of the overall health of organizations is the main function of management.

We have already pointed out that systems, be they biological or social systems, are subject to a force known as *entropy*. Recall further that the tendency of a system toward maximum entropy is the movement of a system toward disorder, complete lack of resource transformation, and ultimate death. Entropy increases in a system until eventually the entire system stops; if the system is left unattended, the total entropic state and the accompanying system stoppage happens much sooner than one might anticipate. Just as we eat three balanced meals a day, brush our teeth, get plenty of sleep, and so on, in order to prolong life and hold off biological entropy, so must the manager continually be searching for and applying remedial steps to hold social entropy to a minimum in the organization. Clearly, a biological system can only slow down or temporarily arrest the inevitability of the total entropic state. A social system, on the other hand, may be capable of offsetting entropy indefinitely through proper management. However, the principle remains that when a human organism or a social organization is born it begins to die, and everything possible must be done if we are to hold off this process and maintain a healthy state as long as possible. A great deal more will be said about the managerial maintenance of an organization in a healthy state throughout the remainder of this book.

Organizational health would seem to be a prerequisite to organizational effectiveness no matter how effectiveness is measured. There are, of course, many ways to measure organizational effectiveness; however, any evaluation of organizational effectiveness is ultimately a measure of managerial effectiveness.

There are some evaluative factors which should be included in a framework for predicting the effectiveness of any organization. One such factor is *stability*. In this case stability refers to the ability of the organization to maintain its own hierarchical structure as well as the maintenance of stable input-output relationships. Implicit in such stability is the ability of an organization to remain flexible and maintain itself as a self-corrective system throughout its many internal changes and pressures as well as the external influences by which it is constantly bombarded.

Another criterion of organizational effectiveness is *integration*, which in this case refers to the level of interaction and the internal flow of information. In other words, what we are really dealing with here is communication integration; who talks to whom, about what, how often, and so on. Integration, then, is affected by such factors as physical proximity of organizational members, by the degree of formality in the organization, and by organizational size.

Morale is yet another important measure of organizational effectiveness. Morale, in this case, means roughly the ability of the organization to provide satisfaction to its individuals and to maintain a desire within those individuals to continue their organizational participation. High morale is apt to cause individuals to conform to organizational norms with a minimum of pressure or coercion. The importance of the morale and integration factors is pointed out by Katz and Kahn when they assert:

> Three categories of behavior are required to achieve high levels of organizational effectiveness. People must join and remain in the organization; they must perform dependably the roles assigned to them; and they must engage in occasional innovative and cooperative behavior beyond the requirements of role but in the service of organizational objectives.[15]

One final effectiveness criterion which is probably the most obvious of all is *goal achievement*. Goal achievement is the result of the total organizational activity and is, of course, a highly objective, results-oriented measure. Such yardsticks usually take the form of productive output, the profit and loss statement or corporate earnings, all of which are undeniably objective and "cold" to a fault.

The best total measure of organizational effectiveness is all of these yardsticks drawn together as a composite measure in addition to each of them individually. This composite approach is necessary because each of these effectiveness factors seem to be interdependent.

There are many other variations and choices for organizational effectiveness criteria but the foregoing seem to be the basic ones. For instance, we have only been discussing the effectiveness of an organization and its management against a predetermined criteria. Another effective evaluative procedure is to compare one organization with another similar organization.

In summary, we can say that a system will prevail if the management of that organizational system:

1. maintains an openness to its environment and to its own suprasystem and subsystems.
2. watches for and utilizes the existing feedback in a self-corrective manner.
3. constantly strives to manage toward negative entropy.
4. constantly strives to manage toward a point of optimization.

THE MANAGERIAL ROLE IN AN ORGANIZATION

So the managers, in these various ways, are guardians of organizational health and well-being. But how do managers effect such controls? What is the manager's functional role in the organization? One obvious role is that of a task-oriented motivator and mobilizer of the competencies and human resources under the manager's control. If the task-oriented goals of the organization are to be achieved, they will be achieved through the efforts of individuals who ultimately are directed and mobilized into an efficiently functioning team by some manager.

The strong need for managers to assume a task-oriented role cannot be denied; however, it is becoming more and more important to consider carefully another managerial role. According to Warren Bennis:

> This is the paradigm: bureaucratic values tend to stress the rational, task aspects of the work and to ignore the basic human factors which

relate to the task and which, if ignored, tend to reduce task competence. Managers brought up under this system of values are badly cast to play the intricate human roles now required of them. Their ineptitude and anxieties lead to systems of discord and defense which interfere with the problem-solving capacity of the organization.[16]

In other words, a managerial role equal in importance to the task role is the role of creating a social climate and work environment in which the task is most likely to be accomplished.

It should already be evident that the total management role and the leadership required to be a good manager are much easier to talk about than to accomplish or possess. How, then, do leaders accomplish what at times seem to be superhuman demands made of them? First, effective leaders do not "handle" people. They persuade, guide, and organize the tasks of people in order to accomplish certain desired results. Leader-managers have a number of critical functions that are dependent upon their ability to communicate. They develop and maintain a system of communication and through it develop an effective work environment. The leader in a modern organization must plan, control, and delegate duties and responsibilities in a way which will develop the talents and abilities of subordinates to a point of optimization.

Applying these management functions in an organization is an even greater challenge because, as Katz and Kahn point out, "organizational leadership, like other cases of influence in complex social settings, is always a combined function of social structural factors and of the particular characteristics of the individuals making up the structure."[17]

The attempt to apply such management functions is really an attempt to influence behavior. Central to the influence of behavior in an organization is *power, authority,* and *delegation.* Power is the ability, sometimes latent, to influence psychological and behavioral change. Authority is a special kind of power which is vested in certain individuals or organizational positions by an organization. Authority is really a form of official permission to use the resources of the organization. Delegation is thus the conferring of a specified authority by someone in a position of greater authority. These authoritative sources of power, organizational position, and job importance are power sources derived from the organization itself. We may find individual sources of power as well. Individually derived power would include such factors as special expertise, interest and tenure, and any personal characteristics. Power may also come about by the coalition of a group of individuals. Because of its organizational nature, we will be mostly concerned with authoritative type of power.

Management involves the kind of roles which coordinate human and material resources toward the accomplishment of an objective. This sort of coordination is ultimately an effective exercise of authority and other types of power. Management's main generalized role is to convert the disorganized resources of people, machines, time, money, space, and material into an effective and efficient enterprise. Perhaps the managerial role is best summed up by Fremont Kast and James Rosenzweig when they point out that the manager manages "toward objectives, through people, via techniques and in an organization."[18]

Managerial style

It is difficult to generalize about the effectiveness of various managerial styles in carrying out the managerial role. A strict, autocratic style of management may be the most effective style in some situations, while a very loose, easy-going style may work better in others. The appropriate style depends upon such things as organizational objectives and the willingness of the followers to be led in a certain way. The willingness of the followers is especially important, since practical experience has proven over and over again that we actually only manage with the consent of the managed.

The real disparity between managerial styles probably rests in the degree of participation, which in this sense refers to how involved or uninvolved the followers are in organizational planning and decision making. According to Katz and Kahn, "The essential difference between a democratic and an authoritarian system is not whether executive officers issue orders to or consult with those below them but whether the actual power to legislate on policy is vested in the membership or in the top echelons."[19] In other words, participatory management cannot work as long as it is used as a device for getting others to do what management wants them to do. Real, total participation is based on mutual respect.

A strong factor in managerial effectiveness, whatever the style, is flexibility. Managerial flexibility is nothing more than an understanding of, and belief in, the principle of equifinality discussed earlier as a part of the system approach. The effective manager will realize that there is no one right way to manage and lead all followers. Conversely, subordinates can and will be most effectively managed by a managerial style that is tailored as much as possible to their individual personalities and needs as followers. Of course, a complex organization can hardly afford to tailor a different management style for each of its followers; however, failure even to consider individual differences can be disastrous. For example, the author has knowledge of a firm which had a very rigid, authoritarian style of leadership with absolutely no flexibility. The managers were supersalespeople themselves and were so inflexible as not even to allow their subordinates to use different wording in the sales talk or a different method of making out a receipt. Punitive measures such as early morning meetings for failing to meet weekly sales quotas were the rule rather than the exception. In a short time the organization found itself facing an employee vote on whether or not there would be collective bargaining through, of all things, a salesmen's union. Out of slightly more than one hundred salesmen voting, the implementation of collective bargaining lost by only seven votes. After the vote a survey was conducted to determine the nature and levels of employee dissatisfaction. One might easily imagine that the dissatisfaction would most likely lie in the areas of punitive measures or oppressive management, but not so. Almost to a man, the area of real dissatisfaction was the lack of flexibility in the system; the lack of enough elbow room to allow for individual human differences.

There are two general managerial styles cited by Douglas McGregor as Theory X and Theory Y.[20] These two theories are mirror opposites and are really better viewed as extreme ends of a continuum and rarely seen as pure management styles being practiced in any given organization. There is a set of underlying assumptions upon which each of these theories is based.

Theory X assumes that:

1. The average human being has an inherent dislike for work and will avoid it when possible.
2. Because of this human tendency to dislike work, most people must be coerced, controlled, directed, threatened with punishment to get them to put forth adequate effort toward the achievement of organizational objectives.
3. The average human being prefers to be directed, wishes to avoid responsibility, has relatively little ambition, and wants security above all.

Theory Y, on the other hand, assumes that:

1. The expenditure of physical and mental effort in work is as natural as play or rest.
2. External control and the threat of punishment are not the only means for bringing about effort toward organizational objectives.

3. Commitment to objectives is a function of the rewards associated with their achievement.
4. The average human being learns, under proper conditions, not only to accept but to seek responsibility.
5. A relatively high degree of imagination, ingenuity, and creativity is widely distributed in the population.
6. Today the intellectual potentialities of the average human being are only partially utilized.[20]

As stated previously, there are clearly few, if any, examples of a management team practicing either Theory X or Theory Y exclusively. Theory X can offer management a convenient set of excuses for the failure of the organizational subordinates to attain their objectives. Conversely, managing by Theory Y could eventually lay organizational shortcomings directly at the feet of management and imply that management had lost control somewhere along the way.

The real concern should be about the potential disaster that could ensue from practicing either Theory X or Theory Y on people whose attitudes were the opposite. For instance, treat an employee with Theory X attitudes using the Theory Y assumptions and obviously you will get no production and perhaps a lot of dissatisfaction. On the other hand, a Theory Y type employee could be ruined by Theory X treatment. This is especially true when one considers the Timothy Leary notion known as *interpersonal reflex*. Leary says of his concept, "This is a general probability principle. It holds that: interpersonal reflexes tend (with a probability significantly greater than chance) to initiate or invite reciprocal interpersonal responses from the 'other' person in the interaction that lead to a repetition of the original reflex."[21] Interpersonal reflex says simply that, quite unwittingly, our day-to-day actions are really reflexes so that if I shout you will shout back, if I push you will push back, and if I treat you fairly you will probably reciprocate. If this principle is at all accurate, then think for a moment what continued Theory X treatment could do to a dedicated Theory Y person. They might begin to live up or, more appropriately, live down to the label.

There are innumerable examples of dedicated groups of employees who react most peculiarly to continued autocratic Theory X oriented mismanagement. One work unit of competent, well-meaning people known to the author goes absolutely berserk when their Theory X manager leaves the office for anything more than one day. His departure is followed immediately by a cheering, bell-ringing, office-wide, extended coffee break type of celebration. Of course, this bizarre reaction to mismanagement is highly counterproductive. Worse than that, however, is the fact that the manager will never be there to witness this brief rebellion and take advantage of what is really a great opportunity for him to see the fruits of his past errors. If only he could see this scene once and take it to heart he would at least have the opportunity to take preventive action in the future.

Perhaps the best measure of the appropriateness of a management style in a given organizational situation is whether the style promotes the loyalty of the work group. It has been proven over and over again that managers who command the loyalty of a group—that is managers who are liked, accepted, respected—will be most apt to have effective managerial control. Of course, such loyalty from the managed would suggest that an office-wide celebration just because the boss is out of sight and has temporarily lost surveillance over the behavior of employees would be highly unlikely.

Decentralization and the middle to lower-range manager

Our discussion so far has dealt with organizational management in general and top-level management in particular. The focus of the remainder of this book, however, will be directed toward the more pivotal organizational roles, the middle and lower-range managers. We say pivotal roles because managers at these levels are literally the people in the middle; they must be aware of those above and below them and be able to relate effectively in both directions. Most young managers are pretty well aware of the social and psychological needs of their superiors; however, in these lower-range, "firing line" positions where they often find themselves, Katz and Kahn reinforce the obvious fact that:

> In addition to assessing the area in which his superiors will permit movement, the middle manager must face toward the people below him. He must depend upon subordinates for the efficient accomplishment of the subsystem task, and modifications in structure must be acceptable to them.[22]

If problems in middle management do in fact present a challenging situation, the problems seem to be doubled and tripled in field management. Any description of lower and middle-range members of a management team, especially those operating in the field, sounds as if they are each a conglomerate of Superman and Einstein with the hide of a rhinoceros and the endurance of an Olympic miler. Although this seems to be an exaggeration, a field manager can be described as a personal supervisor, the executor of headquarters' plans, a communication link between the market and the home office, and a supersalesperson. Field managers are also literally on their own at times.

How does field management find itself in such a position? Mainly because the manager in the field is usually separated from the immediate personal supervision of the central office. Today one can easily observe the tendency of general management to decentralize and free itself from day-to-day business matters in order better to think about and organize the future of its firms. There is a vigorous effort to force the responsibility for current problems downward, partly because it is evident that those in the field are nearer both the sources of information and the means of treatment.

The typical model of a decentralized organization reveals a central management executive committee which formulates organizational goals and policies. Then, under the principle of decentralization, the operational management located in the various decentralized branches is mainly responsible for implementation of the general goals and policies developed by central management. Operational or field management is usually free to make decisions and set goals provided that they fall within the broad general framework set up by central management. Branches that are truly decentralized appear to be separate organizations rather than parts of a larger whole. Perhaps the greatest example of a truly decentralized operation is General Motors Corporation. Thus, the manager of the Oldsmobile Division of General Motors Corporation is responsible for the inputs, outputs, and profits of Oldsmobile. He comes as close to being the owner of that company as anyone can be without actually owning it. As Rocco Carza and John Yanouzas point out:

> With this type of organization, General Motors is benefiting from both centralization through centralized planning, financing, and staff services, and decentralization through the fast, "on-the-spot" decision making that characterizes small organization. Decentralization also helps to develop managers by giving them experience in making decisions.[23]

Recall that earlier we defined authority as a sort of official permission to use the resources of the organization. Such authority takes on special importance in a decentralized situation. Traditionally, however, authority and freedom to manage must be approximately equal. In other words, when managers are assigned certain organizational duties, they should have the accompanying permission to use and commit organizational resources in order to carry out those duties. This is harder than it sounds for some top-level managers. For many the delegation of duties and responsibilities is simple; however, the other side of the coin, the right to be wrong occasionally, is much harder to delegate to others.

If management of field operations is more difficult than a centralized operation, and if full management authority is difficult to grant, why then do organizations decentralize? According to William G. Scott, businesses have traditionally decentralized for one or more of the following reasons:

> *Cost.* The cost factor is operative when the size of an operation becomes uneconomical. Economists refer to this as diseconomies of scale.
> *Product Line.* This factor is operative when management considers that it is more efficient to manufacture and market a product through autonomous or semi-autonomous product divisions.
> *Market Area.* At times management considers it advisable to manufacture and market through regional divisions geographically decentralized.[24]

Organizational size seems to be the affective factor running ahead of any other need for decentralization. Costs, of course, include such items as transportation of raw materials, finished products, geographical wage differences, etc. When size forces a move to decentralization, the accompanying autonomy often seems to break down better on a product line basis. Geographically separated marketing areas are naturally a big advantage in the area of product development for individualized ethnic and geographical tastes. In the past few years, the advertising business has taken advantage of regional breakdowns in national media. While it has long been possible to buy certain selected network affiliated market areas in radio and TV, it is now possible to advertise regionally oriented products in certain selected circulation areas of national magazines.

Another determinant, which is a growing factor in the decision to decentralize, is communication. Complexity and increasing organizational size are the underlying factors here again; however, they ultimately result in a loss of information flow and the accompanying communication breakdowns. Although these areas will be explored more fully in Chapters 2 and 3, let us point out here that the need for better and more manageable communication systems is fast becoming a major reason for decentralization.

Decentralization is not always welcomed with open arms by those affected by it. Without careful central management and thoughtful planning, decentralization may utilize the intended improved communication, improved marketing, and more efficient cost accounting, and nevertheless produce the completely opposite effect. Whether decentralization is wanted and/or welcome or not, it is still inevitable for many rapidly growing organizations. Accompanying this inevitability is an equally rapidly growing need for management to train itself to handle the previously mentioned difficulties encountered by middle and lower-range managers operating in the field.

SUMMARY

Our exploration of organizations has brought us to the point of defining an *organization* as a human grouping deliberately constructed to achieve certain objectives or goals. The goals, which are a strong key to the identification of an organization, may be either *stated goals* or *real goals*. Stated goals are public goals which are ostensibly the major objectives of an organization. The real goals are hidden agendas and other nonpublic objectives; however, they are at least as central to the total behavioral patterns of an organization as the stated goals.

The foregoing is predominantly a definition of a *formal organization*. Within most complex organizations, however, often the formal organization and many *informal* organizations are operating simultaneously. The formal organization is, again, the public organization depicted by a hierarchically designed organization chart on the office wall. The informal organizations are entities such as the grapevine and clique subgroups which sometimes are more important than the formal organization, because it is in these informal organizations that the really meaningful communication and behavior often takes place.

We have examined briefly three schools of organizational theory. The first is the *classical theory,* or scientific management, which assumes like purposes and goals between management and labor, and pure economics as the main motivation for workers. *Human relations theory,* on the other hand, takes the position that workers are far more strongly motivated by their social needs and capacities. The *structuralists'* approach is a more realistic approach than the first two schools and is basically an attempt to develop the best possible synthesis of the two.

The *systems theory* approach to organizations says that, in order to survive, a system must be open rather than closed to its environment and that such an organization will consist of *inputs,* raw materials and resources, which are put through a *throughput* process and emerge from the system as *output*. The theory further states that it is important for an organization to maintain a steady state by keeping the inputs and outputs in balance. The *principle of optimization* in systems theory is a suggestion of a point of efficiency at which the maximum output is received in return for the minimum input. Ideally, a system that is open should receive and use feedback from its environment so that it is constantly maintaining equilibrium by self-correction.

The roles of the manager in such an organization as we have been describing will be both *task* and *social* roles. That is, in addition to the more obvious task roles a leader must perform, there are many less obvious social roles which must be taken if task accomplishment is ever to be a reality. The managerial style through which these roles are carried out usually varies with each individual. Key questions, however, are how *participative* should the management style be and by what motive patterns will a given group of followers most likely be motivated to produce. Once we have determined the proper degree of follower participation in management, we can determine pretty well at which point on the Theory X to Theory Y continuum our managerial style falls. Theory X characterizes workers as lazy, unimaginative people who must be pushed and prodded, would rather play than work, and enjoy being herded like cattle and having their lives planned for them. Theory Y views the human being as almost a mirror opposite of the one in Theory X.

A special organizational management dilemma we will deal with in the remainder of this book is the plight of the field manager and his semi-autonomous position brought about by decentralization. Perhaps the finest example of decentralization is General Motors Corporation in its member divisions. Within the broadly planned corporate framework, each GM division is so decentralized in its operation that they seem at times to be almost separate firms. For many obvious reasons the manager placed in such a decentralized operation will have much heavier responsibilities than a manager in a centralized organization. Whether centralized or decentralized, an organization must maintain a healthy state to survive. Just as entropy—the tendency of an organism toward disorder and eventual demise—is true of humans biologically, it is also true of organizations. We must therefore manage to slow down or thwart this entropic process in our organizations. It is to this end that the following chapters will be dedicated.

NOTES

1. George Homans, "The Western Electric Researchers," *Bobbs-Merrill Reprint Series,* S-123.
2. Amitai Etzioni, *A Comparative Analysis of Complex Organizations,* New York, Free Press, 1961, p. 19.
3. Jay Hall, "Decisions, Decisions, Decisions," *Psychology Today, 5,* no. 6 (November, 1971), 88.
4. Etzioni, op. cit., p. 3.
5. Edgar Schein, *Organizational Psychology,* Englewood Cliffs, N.J., Prentice-Hall, 1970, p. 9.
6. Etzioni, op. cit., p. 6.
7. Warren G. Bennis, "Leadership Theory and Administrative Behavior: The Problem of Authority," *Administrative Science Quarterly, 4,* no. 3 (December, 1959), 299.
8. Etzioni, op. cit., pp. 31–67.
9. Theodore Caplow, Principles of Organizations, New York, Harcourt Brace Jovanovich, 1964, pp. 26–27.
10. Richard Cyert and James G. March, *A Behavioral Theory of the Firm,* Englewood Cliffs, N.J., Prentice-Hall, 1963, p. 289.
11. Keith Davis, "The Organization That's Not on the Chart," *Supervisory Management* (July, 1961).
12. James D. Thompson, *Organizations in Action,* New York, McGraw-Hill, 1967, p. 162.
13. Daniel Katz and Robert L. Kahn, *The Social Psychology of Organizations,* New York, Wiley, 1966, p. 39.
14. Matthew B. Miles (ed.), *Innovation in Education,* New York, Bureau of Publications, Teachers College, Columbia University, 1964, p. 429.
15. Katz and Kahn, op. cit., p. 388.
16. Warren G. Bennis, *Changing Organizations,* New York, McGraw-Hill, 1966, p. 116.
17. Katz and Kahn, op. cit., p. 308.
18. Fremont Kast and James Rosenzweig, *Organization and Management: A Systems Approach,* New York, McGraw-Hill, 1970, p. 6.
19. Katz and Kahn, op. cit., p. 45.
20. Douglas McGregor, *The Human Side of Enterprise,* New York, McGraw-Hill, 1960, pp. 33–57.
21. Timothy Leary, *Interpersonal Diagnosis of Personality,* New York, Ronald Press, 1957, p. 91.
22. Katz and Kahn, op. cit., p. 320.
23. Rocco Carza and John Yanouzas, *Formal Organizations: A Systems Approach,* Homewood, Ill., Irwin, 1967, p. 59.
24. William G. Scott, "Communication and Centralization of Organizations," *Journal of Communication, 8* (March, 1963), 3–11.

2 the role of communication in management

. . . the most significant factor accounting for the total behavior of the organization is its communication system, and that the dynamics of the organization can be best understood by understanding its system of communication.
Eugene Walton

OBJECTIVES for Chapter 2

After reading the chapter you should be able to:

1. Describe in writing the meaning of the phrase "we cannot not communicate."
2. Define the communication process, both graphically and in writing.
3. Name and describe in writing the six dimensions of communication as detailed in this chapter.
4. Describe in writing the communication variables related to the Berlo model and communication fidelity.
5. Describe in writing the total principle of communication selectivity.
6. Discuss in writing the role played by communication in management.
7. Identify the place of the organizational manager as a trained communication specialist no matter what his management level.
8. Identify in writing the various management communication settings and give organizational examples of each.

It is an obvious, but still overlooked, fact of life that communication is such a vital part of each of us that it contributes heavily to the success or failure of every human activity. It is hard to name a human activity, even the simplest one, in which communication does not play an important role. But such a statement has to be even more true in formal organizations where structured management is the norm, and results, efficiency, and profits are the evaluative measures. According to Ray Killian:

> Large corporations in particular, because of their complex multidivisional setup and the trend toward decentralized operations in recent years, would be helpless without their communications networks for cooperation, coordination, and overall utilization of resources. Such networks may employ computer systems, teletype, telephones, visits, meetings, written messages, and a variety of other means of dispersing information and influence. Efficiency and results, both for individual units and for the organization as a whole, depend on communication.[1]

Since the human communication processes and a knowledge of how they function are so vital to organizational management, we should now examine these processes more closely.

THE SIGNIFICANCE OF COMMUNICATION

The word "human" is used here in connection with communication in order to specify that we are not talking about animal communication, plant communication, or any of the other new and pervasive ways of looking at a communication process. Also, human communication has been studied more extensively and is obviously our immediate concern in organizations. For ease of reading and comprehension when we use the term communication in the remainder of this book, we refer to human communication.

The premise which should be basic to any treatise of communication is the well-worn phrase asserting that we "cannot *not* communicate." The meaning of this phrase, of course, is that in everything we do or say, even do *not* do or say, there may be meaning for some observer. Of course, it is possible to send totally unobserved messages or messages which are understood by no one and thereby are not really communicative. However, a more useful interpretation of the phrase "we cannot not communicate" is that we cannot be noncommunicative, no matter how hard we try, as long as someone observes us and attaches meaning even to our lack of action. For instance, lying passively under a tree and sleeping, totally unaware of our surroundings, we may be communicating to a passerby. They see us, and responses or reactions may be evoked such as, "Look at those lazy bums" or "They must be very tired" or any number of other unintended, but nevertheless perceived, communications. Admittedly, the thought does have an ominous "big brother is watching" aura about it; however, it truly is almost as if we were under constant surveillance. We would not want to become so aware of the fact that we were being constantly perceived that we became boorish or paranoid. But, on the other hand, we will communicate much more effectively if we are aware of the process we call communication and its accompanying inevitability.

The acceptance of the inevitability of the process of communication leads us naturally into an attempt to define communication. Communication appears in so many different forms in its various settings and uses that it is very difficult to find a definitive handle which we might use to get a grip on the concept. Using the foregoing notion of inevitability, however, we might generally define communication as *any transfer of meaning from one person to another*. This extremely general definition indicates the broad, pervasive, and unavoidable nature of communication. On one hand, any definition which is so global as to include everything in the universe really defines nothing. Any concept such as communication which is defined as "everything" is at the same time "nothing." On the other hand, if we define communication more narrowly than the "transfer of meaning from one person to another," we will leave out some of the many uses and settings in which we find communication included.

Dimensions of communication

A satisfactory way to define the process of communication more specifically seems to be through an examination of some of its dimensions. For the moment, we will take a brief look at some dimensions of communication which will be covered in more detail at various appropriate points throughout the book. Some of these dimensions of communication of major concern in an organization are:

    Intentional-Unintentional
    Verbal-Nonverbal
    Oral-Written
    Formal-Informal
    Internal-External

As we just indicated, communication is inevitable, therefore it obviously can be either *intentional* or *unintentional*. Many times we do intend to communicate certain thoughts or ideas to others and it is accomplished effectively. Many other times we may intend nothing in particular and communicate thoughts or ideas to others just the same, with no awareness on our part that a meaning has been attached to our action or inaction. At still other times, we may intend to convey a certain meaning; however, the receiver gets an altogether different and unintended meaning. In these latter two cases we have examples of unintentional communication.

How is it that this unintended communication result can take place in ways over which we seem to have no control? One of the ways it can happen is through another set of communication dimensions. These are *verbal* and *nonverbal* communication. As one might imagine, the verbal aspects are those aspects which employ linguistic symbols such as words and the nonverbal aspects are such things as facial expressions, gestures, posture, moans, screams, and so on. Usually, intentional communication is verbal. Of course, one has only to remember, when misbehaving as a child, the "dirty look" flashed across the room from one's father, to admit readily that nonverbal communication can be both intended and most effective. Normally, however, for intended effect we communicate verbally more often than we do nonverbally.

Since facial expressions and most other similar nonverbal behaviors are almost a reflex action, they are not always under the complete control of the communicator. In other words, nonverbal behaviors are often unintentional communicative acts. When these nonverbal behaviors are unintentional and sometimes uncontrolled they may lack congruity with each other and with the intended communication, as perceived by the receivers. Communication may subsequently break down because of the confusing incongruity between the verbal and nonverbal. An example of such a perceptual confusion would be to assert, through clenched teeth, that you were not angry. Another example is a favorite analogy of the author's grandfather in which he used to allude to the confusion and indecision wrought by "a barking dog with a wagging tail." He observed that it was difficult, if not impossible, to know which end to believe.

Managers can *sound* very interested, and even *be* very interested, in a subordinate's problem but if they are preoccupied with paper shuffling and do not *look* interested they may communicate a feeling to the subordinate quite different from the one intended. In short, what we hear is affected by what we see along with what is heard; they are inseparable.

Another dimension of communication is the *oral* and *written* dimension. The similarities and differences between the oral and written communication style are covered in greater detail in Chapter 9. At this point, it should be sufficient to point out the fact that stylistic dimension is a dimension worthy of consideration and that, while there are similarities between written and oral messages, there are also great differences. These differences are especially important considerations when choosing the most effective communication strategy in an organizational setting.

Another dimension written about in Chapter 1, and one of considerable import to organizational communicators, is the *formal-informal* dimension. Recall that in Chapter 1 we said that in order fully to understand and examine the communication factors in an organization, that organization must be studied as a total milieu. This total milieu or organizational structure has two aspects which must be taken into account, really two organizations in one, from a communication point of view. Recall also that in Chapter 1 we pointed out that one is the *formal* lines of communication that may be found within the organization chart on the executive office wall. The others are the *informal,* emergent lines of communication, sometimes known as grapevines. These informal communication patterns may be ignored by management or attempts may even be made to destroy them; however, the informal communication will continue to exist, regardless. Because of its very nature, informal communication, or grapevine, may tend to flourish all the more if attempts are made to do away with it. Smart managers realize, then, that since the informal organization cannot be uprooted, they would do better to harness it, train it, and make it work for them.

A final dimension of communication worthy of note for the organizational manager is the *internal-external* dimension. The external dimension of organizational communication refers to such communication roles as the public relations business of creating an appropriate public image, and the business of such departments as advertising, customer relations, and sales. Internal communication, on the other hand, is the dimension dealing with the management of the orgaization. This dimension includes such things as personnel matters, the control of the flow of information, motivation of subordinates, and organizational morale, all of which are primary concerns in this book.

Having established the pervasiveness and inevitability of communication and some of the major definitive communication dimensions so necessary to its management in an organization, we can safely say that whether we should communicate or not is no longer a valid question. Communication occurs whether it is intended or not. In many instances, the unintentional communication is more effective than the intentional. The people who hope to manage in a modern organization, then, must realize that communication is much broader than they had probably imagined and extends far beyond the boundaries established by any formal communication program consisting primarily of written memos, talks, bulletin boards, and other structural media.

THE COMMUNICATION PROCESS

To best understand communication and make it work for us in day-to-day situations it is important first to realize that it is a process and then to examine that process.

The word *process* indicates a dynamic phenomenon which is constantly moving and changing; that is to say, never static. Since it is in reality impossible to stop any dynamic process such as communication, even long enough to examine it analytically, the subject of process is difficult to discuss. Such examination and discussion, however, is so vital to our understanding and consequent improvement of the communicative act that we must stop the process long enough to see, at least theoretically, what makes it tick.

Models

One of the best ways to view communication in a sort of stop action, cross-section view is through the use of models. Communication models do have some drawbacks in addition to the unnatural act of stopping a process. For instance, models have a tendency to oversimplify and they can never provide more than a partial view of such a complex process as communication. Additionally, people sometimes confuse the model with the process which it represents and close their investigation of the facts prematurely, accepting a model as the final word.

In spite of such drawbacks related to models, they do provide a definitive method which is clear and easy for most people to use in grasping a set of concepts which are central to an issue. Berlo has supplied us with a simplified descriptive model which shows clearly the major ingredients in the communication process.[2] The model is commonly referred to as the SMCR model. In this case the letters symbolically stand for the *source, message, channel,* and *receiver* in the com-

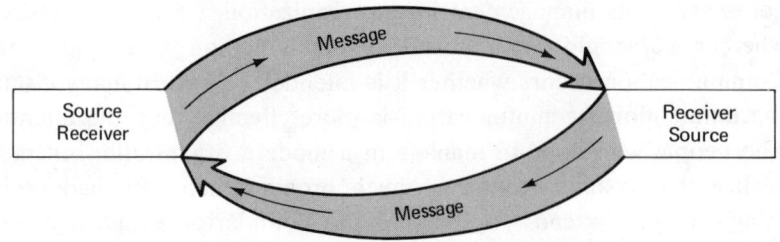

Figure 2-1 A model based upon the Berlo concepts, with a feedback loop added.

munication process. The model simply depicts a source sending a message, over a channel, to a receiver.

The Berlo model is so simplistic in this form that it does not really represent a true picture of the process until *feedback* is added. Recall that in Chapter 1 we found that feedback was an essential component in the effective functioning of an open system. Feedback provides the source with responses, which in turn provide the source with information concerning his success in accomplishing his communication objectives. The result of the perception and interpretation of feedback should be a constantly corrected and perfected set of communication behaviors. Feedback can best be depicted as a message loop from the receiver back to the original source forming a circle. In effect the feedback loop has the original receiver as the new source and vice versa (see Figure 2.1). Now we have a simple representation of communication as a continuous, dynamic process.

Wilbur Schramm has provided us with a useful view of the communication process (see Figure 2.2) in which he has depicted the notion

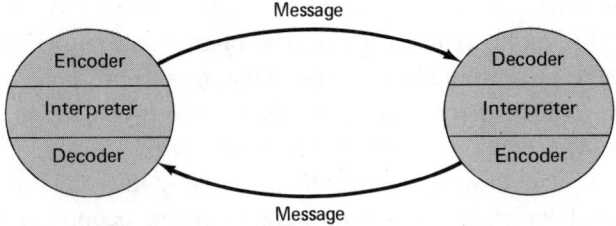

Figure 2-2 Wilbur Schramm's model of the communication process. (Reprinted with permission from: Wilbur Schramm and Donald Roberts (eds.), *The Processes and Effects of Mass Communication,* University of Illinois Press, 1971, p. 24.)

of communication as a continuous, dynamic process much more successfully than have most other models. In so doing, Schramm deals with the communicator as a constant interpreter of messages and both as a source (encoder) and a receiver (decoder) at various times.

In order to be really useful to us, the communication process must possess some ability to predict behavior. This predictive ability enables people to convey intended meanings and establish the desired amount of rapport and understanding. According to Newcomb et al., the ability to predict such a level of understanding is important because "communication is the form of interpersonal exchange through which, figuratively speaking, persons can come in contact with each others' minds."[3] The importance of viewing communication in this way is that the accuracy of the predictions eventually establishes to a great extent the fidelity of the communication which goes on between people. Perhaps this can best be clarified by returning for a look at the variables encompassed by each element of the Berlo model.

Since they contain identical variables, we will postpone our examination of the source and receiver variables until last. The variables involved in channel selection really can be designated simply as the five senses: seeing, hearing, touching, smelling, and tasting. Clearly there are some strategic moments when the selection of one channel over another is advantageous to convey a given message. Equally clear is the value in using as many channels as possible simultaneously in order to solidify meanings between the source and receiver. A prime example is the obvious total advantage to the receiver of a televised or filmed message (the seeing channel is added to the hearing channel) over that of an audio message (the hearing channel only). Incidentally, the foregoing example also points up the value of the use of verbal and nonverbal communication working together.

The message consists of the language chosen to express symbolically the communication purpose of the source. A message is made up of a set of symbols which is selected and arranged by the source (the encoding process) in an effort to convey a desired meaning through the perceptions of the receiver (the decoding process).

The source and receiver variables in the communication process have been placed last in our discussion for two reasons. The first is that it is necessary first to understand the message and channel variables. The second is that, although we often separate the source from the receiver in our communication models, anything we learn about one applies to the other; as we have seen in the Schramm model, the source and receiver are corresponding systems. That is, the factors that shape and affect the behaviors and perceptions of a source also shape and affect the behaviors and perceptions of his receivers.

According to Berlo,[4] these factors which affect both the source and receiver are communication skills, attitudes, knowledge levels, and social and cultural systems.

When we speak of *communication skills* we simply mean the degree of ability on the part of the source to encode messages which, when decoded, will delineate the desired meaning to a given set of receivers. The encoding and decoding of messages involves the use of certain skills. The *encoding skills* are writing and speaking and the corresponding *decoding skills* are reading and listening. The need to take into account the decoding skills of the receivers when a source selects and arranges the symbols in a message cannot be stressed too strongly. Such a consideration is vital if the receivers are to gain anything close to the original meaning of the message without distortion being caused by the encoding-decoding process itself. It is at this point that the predictability notion mentioned earlier has a strong effect on the fidelity of communication. Communication skills for the receiver, then, mean the degree of ability the receiver has to decode the message back into the original idea or purpose of the source so that understanding between the two may prevail.

Attitudes, although difficult to define specifically, refer here to the attitudes of a source and/or receiver toward themselves, toward the subject matter, and toward the other party or parties. The *knowledge level* of the source or receiver is the amount of subjective knowledge concerning the content of the message. It is possible for a source or receiver to have too much knowledge as well as too little. For instance, if one or the other has an extremely high degree of technical knowledge on a given subject, communication between the two is apt to be difficult at best.

Social and cultural systems refer to the background and personal experiences of a source or receiver which affect their expectations from, and perception of, a given situation and/or message. In other words, the cultural and social factors are really a kind of "genetic baggage" a person brings with them to a communication situation which will inevitably limit or broaden what they may perceive from that situation.

We have established that the source and the receiver both possess certain communication skills, attitudes, knowledge levels, and social and cultural backgrounds. It also seems clear that communication is enhanced greatly when there is a high degree of similarity of levels related to each of these factors between the source and receiver. In fact, Wallace Fotheringham defines communication as "A process involving the selection, production, and transmission of signs in such a way as to help a receiver perceive a meaning similar to that in the mind of the communicator."[5]

However, since few, if any, people have identical experiences, the likelihood of a high degree of similarity is doubtful indeed. The best way to solve this dilemma is for both the source and receiver to be aware of the existence of these factors and attempt to take them into account when constructing their messages. As an example, a manager with high-level communication skills, a college degree, a strong company-oriented attitude, and an upper-middle class, establishment-oriented background had better give considerable thought to who the worker on the assembly line *really* is if he expects to have his message understood by that worker. Such a manager-subordinate dilemma has some special implications related to the Theory X and Theory Y concepts discussed in Chapter 1. For instance, a manager who is encoding under the assumption of either Theory X or Y and a subordinate who is decoding under the opposite assumptions are obviously headed for a certain communication breakdown.

In such a situation a great deal of empathy is required in order to construct a message which will take the factors related to the receivers into account. Without this awareness and empathy, successful communication can only be a happy accident. To this point Willard Merrihue says that communication:

> . . . is essentially an interpretive process. This implies that the successful business communicator—like the successful translator of languages—must not only know the languages of both the senders and the receivers, but must also have a sympathetic understanding of the backgrounds, the attitudes, and aspirations of both.[6]

Communication, as we established earlier, involves a prediction of behavior. To make the most accurate predictions, communicators must understand the basic principles of communication and take into account the factors which are apt to affect the perceptions of their receivers when constructing a message. The business of taking the perceptions of the receivers into account is difficult, and sometimes impossible, without feedback. As also mentioned earlier, feedback from receivers provides the sources with information concerning their success in accomplishing the communication objectives. In so doing, the source allows the feedback to exert control over the shaping of future messages that are encoded for that receiver. Just as we cannot *not* communicate, we also cannot *not* give feedback. In other words, even the lack of a response to a message will probably be interpreted in some way by the original source.

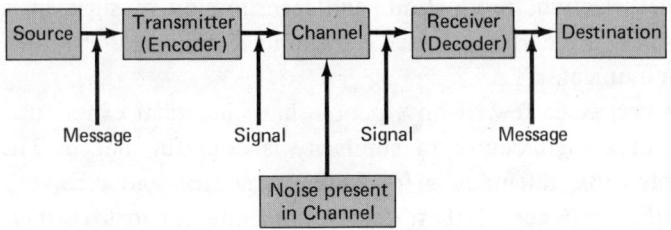

Figure 2-3 The Shannon-Weaver Information Theory model. (Reprinted with permission from: Claude E. Shannon and Warren Weaver, *The Mathematical Theory of Communication,* University of Illinois Press, p. 9.)

There are other popular communication models which are somewhat more complicated than the foregoing models. Such a model is the one developed by Claude Shannon and Warren Weaver (see Figure 2.3) to depict the electronic side of the communication process such as we find taking place in telephone communication. The model has since been used by many to depict a single communicative act in the human communication process.

Perhaps the best way to examine this model is to place it in a real management setting. In such a setting the source might be the top management echelon that wishes to communicate a message to a group of customers which is the *destination*. In order to accomplish this, the *source* will convey the message goals or ideas to the *transmitter,* in this case the field manager. The transmitter will encode the message into a signal which is sent over a channel to the *receiver* who decodes the message. This encoded and decoded message involves the use of a linguistic set of signals. If the message has been encoded in a way that has taken the receivers and destination into account, then the receivers should be able to decode the signal back into the original message for transmission to the destination with as little distortion as possible. The *noise* factor includes such extraneous variables as distractions, conflicting messages, and so on. As can be seen here, the need for predictability and source-receiver understanding is present regardless of the model or viewpoint.

Communication selectivity

One of the principle factors affecting the ability of receivers to perceive and understand communication directed at them is *selectivity*. When we use the term selectivity here we are encompassing receiver choices concerning what information they will give their attention to, how they will perceive that information, and what portions of that information they will retain and remember. Martin and Anderson point out that:

> All communicators are painfully aware that unless listeners and readers give their close attention to messages, those messages are useless. Unless the communication, for however short an instant, occupies a listener's mind at the expense of other stimulation, it will not be perceived (that is, detected or recognized), and if not perceived, will not be understood, and if not understood, can have no effect upon attitudes or behavior.[7]

Considering the extremely high number of different message stimuli to which an individual is exposed in a short period of time, it can be said with certainty that a receiver must, sometimes even involuntarily, select some information into their system and select out other information.

The concept of selectivity states that because of this almost constant bombardment by stimuli, and the desire to keep their world as pleasant and undisturbed as possible, individuals will tend to give their attention only to the information to which they want to attend. The individual accomplishes this by a sort of "tuning in" and "tuning out" process. The concept states further that information to which we have attended, whether by choice or by force, will be selectively perceived according to our own experiences and desires. We will interpret the information the way we want to or are perceptually able to, and our perceptions may have little or nothing to do with reality. Finally, the concept of selectivity states that after we have given our attention to certain information and perceived that information in our own selective way, we will selectively retain only that information which we want to remember or that which is pleasant to us. Selective retention, then, accounts in the main for the common fond recollections known as the "good old days." For the most part, the old days were really not so good, but the portion of the past which we choose to recall, or retain, are in fact very "good."

Thus, when we present a piece of information to a receiver we must consider the abundance of information with which that receiver is bombarded and the principles of selective attention, perception, and retention. It is clear, that there is a great deal of competition between sources to seize and hold the attention and understanding of a receiver. Obviously, this is especially true in the business of organizational management, as the subordinates in an organization are usually buried under a constant blizzard of ideas, orders, memos, rules, and dilemmas crying out for solutions.

THE SIGNIFICANCE OF COMMUNICATION TO MANAGEMENT

Very basically, the business of managing in an organization is a business of human relations. In other words, management is, in part at least, a leadership-followership business. Instances of leadership involve the use of organizational structures to influence others. When people are influenced to engage in organizationally relevant behavior, leadership has occurred. Management is a business of people communicating with other people and a business in which machines are not likely to replace effective people, no matter how automated our society becomes.

It has been said that management and communication are so closely related that they are almost synonymous. Further, it is an established fact that we manage only with the consent of the managed. That is, we cannot really manage anyone who does not want to be managed, so a manager must constantly be persuading the individual subordinates that the goals of the organization are desirable. Communication, therefore, is vitally necessary to an organization, not only to transmit authority, but to achieve cooperation. As such, the organizational communication system should supplement the system of authority.

A sales manager once told those on the first level of management that, when dealing with subordinates, they should only *expect* what they could *inspect*. However, Katz and Kahn state that they consider the essence of organizational leadership to be that influential increment over and above mechanical compliance with the routine directives of the organization.[8] Perhaps this extra influential increment is the same "private commitment" notion referred to in the research of Herbert Kelman.[9] In this influence and opinion change research, Kelman delineates a wide difference in commitment between *public acceptance* and *private commitment*. Public acceptance is characterized by a response to an influence agent which will be performed only when that agent is either present or salient. Private commitment, on the other hand, is a response which is so internalized that it will be performed whether the influence agent is present or not. Such an influential increment derives, at least in part, from the fact that human beings rather than computors are in positions of authority and power. Management, then, is an organizational communication activity which is very human, vital, and is acknowledged by most to be the backbone of any organization.

The title of this book, *Organizational Management Through Communication,* is itself symbolic of this interface between communication and management. Although modern business is simply a part of the total social climate which always demands communication, it also finds itself in the middle of many additional developments which include extra heavy communication demands. A short half decade ago managers knew every individual and every operation in most organizations. These managers could perform most of the tasks themselves if they had to.

Now, however, a different picture exists. The new and more complicated organizational structures of today call for vastly improved communication systems. Some of these new complications are:

* Increased organizational size and complexity
* Increasing organizational specialization
* Decentralization
* Constant and rapid technological progress
* Increasing social consciousness of industry
* Ever-strengthening union power
* Anti-business propaganda
* Enlightened and sophisticated research
* Tougher competition

These factors, coupled with the obvious concern for the best interest of the enterprise, may call for a change in management priorities including an increased interest in communication. The changes in managerial priorities we are describing here are reinforced by Berlo when he states:

> With the development of automation and massive industry, we have witnessed the rise of the professional "manager;" the man who reaches the top of the industrial ladder, not because of what he can do with things, but because of what he can do with people—through communication.[10]

An interesting commentary on this technologically oriented thirst for better communication was made a few years ago by James M. Lufkin[11] of Honeywell, Inc. Mr. Lufkin presented a clever answer to these perplexing problems: a combination of an attempted solution to the real problems confronting today's organizational communicators and a sort of tongue-in-cheek comment on the presently fashionable fetish for formulized solutions. In his "magic formula" for technical communication, Lufkin asserts that formulas that reduce the problems of technical communication to simple measurement of sentence length and word length neglect some important variables. A more useful statement, according to Lufkin, gives proper weight to the factors represented in Figure 2.4.

$$E = \frac{\frac{G}{H} \cdot e^W - (J + C)}{\sum_{i=1}^{n} |\frac{1}{2} [Z_i(b_i) + Z_i(a_i)] (b_i - a_i)|}$$

where

E Effectiveness of communication
G Generalization
H Qualification (the Hedge factor).
W The speaker's will to communicate.
J Jargon.
C Clutter.
i An indexing variable representing the various terms involved in the cross-cultural distance.
n The number of these terms i.
$Z_1(x)$ The complexities of term i at point x.
a_1 The quantity of term i used by the speaker.
b_1 The quantity of term i understood by the listener.

Figure 2-4 James Lutkin's formula. (Copyright 1972 by The Institute of Electrical and Electronics Engineers, Inc. Reprinted with permission from the *IEEE Transactions on Professional Communication,* Vol. PC-15, no. 2, (June 1972), 26–29.)

While this "magic formula" provides a bit of fun, it *does* describe fairly accurately the complexity of organizational communication problems and many of the cultural barriers to effective management communication. Part of Mr. Lufkin's function in his organization is to aid and facilitate the flow of meaningful, understandable communication between the engineers and the rest of the company. At a meeting where he presented this formula, Mr. Lufkin pointed out somewhat grimly, however, that he really had difficulty getting the chemical engineers to use language that had any meaning whatsoever for the mechanical engineers and vice versa. If the engineers had trouble understanding each other, the chance of the rest of the company understanding the engineers and eventually the rest of the world understanding the company seemed slim indeed.

In short, the larger and more technical the organizational structure becomes, the greater the need for a better communication system. In this connection, James S. McCormack says that modern management faces a challenge to achieve results with large and complex organizations, and that in these organizations, complicated by complexity and size, clear and effective communication is a vital necessity to achieve the organization's goals.[12] In his book, *Management By Communication* Willard Merrihue asserts that, "The past decade should be chronicled by historians as the age in which businessmen discovered communication as their principle tool."[13] Now after more than a decade has passed, the need for improved communication is even greater.

THE MANAGER AS A COMMUNICATOR

Why is there still a growing need for better communication in organizations which admitted long ago that communication might well be the keystone of their operations? One reason, of course, is that the complexity of the problem has increased constantly.

Another, and more far-reaching, reason is that many organizations have felt that the primary responsibility for communication should be assigned to a single individual or position, to be held accountable for results and standards of performance. A message center and/or communication consultant type of arrangement is certainly helpful and a definite step in the right direction. The problem with the creation of such a position within an organization is that the communication program often stops right there. In other words, "the communication man" is hired as a panacea, almost in the same manner as one minority person is hired in order for an organization to fulfill its affirmative action needs and to be able to advertise themselves as an "equal opportunity employer." Such a communication specialist quickly becomes the resident expert and a feeling seems to creep over the rest of the management team that they no longer need worry about the problem. The danger is, of course, that it is patently absurd to expect one person, operating out of one position, to solve a problem we have already described as organizationally pervasive. This kind of lip service to the remedy of organizational ills will not relieve anyone in the organization of their own proper communication role, any more than the presence of a training executive relieves individual managers of their responsibility for training.

Because the responsibility for communication stretches across all levels of an organization, it seems logical to concern ourselves first with the problem where it is most prevalent. It is certainly a fact that most of the management force may be found in a hierarchical echelon often referred to as *middle* and *lower*-range management. The interesting plight of the middle and lower ranges of management is that they must face two ways in the organization. They must understand how those above them are likely to act because of their organizational position and how those below them are similarly motivated and limited by their placement in the organizational space. This positional dilemma certainly presents some interesting communcation problems.

The critical task of middle and lower management is to interpret organizational goals, or guide subordinates to do so, in ways which optimize organizational functioning. What is really involved here is setting approprate management goals. Once the goals are determined and the principles understood, the manager must develop and decide upon a more specific set of communication strategies. That is, a manager must survey the means available for communicating these goals to the particular receivers involved, and select the best method, or combination of methods for doing so. The big concern, then, must be how to train management people in the selection of the communication strategies which are potentially the most effective in a given situation.

Motivation, persuasion, influence, or any other management activity which might seek to elicit greater dedication or effort are almost totally dependent on the flow of communication. The job of the manager is, ultimately, communication, regardless of how varied or specialized the activity of the moment might be. Ray Killian cites such examples when he points out that:

> The primary purpose of communication is to motivate a response. It produces the activity which is most appropriate for the achievement of established goals. The communication involved in the newspaper advertisement or the TV commercial is designed to motivate action: a purchase. Safety communication seeks to minimize accidents and injuries through a change in work practices. The sales manager communicates —by means of charts, diagrams, visual aids, and enthusiastic oratory— with the single purpose of motivating the response that will result in increased sales.[14]

So, while it is a pleasant and useful luxury to have a resident communication specialist on the payroll, it is evident that each manager must devote the same careful, systematic, and thorough attention to communication that they would devote to any other phase of the management job. Giving attention to communication is extremely important, since communication provides a link between disjointed organizational activities and interests, binding them into one coordinated whole.

A vast amount of important information, which provides the lifeblood of the organization, is passed from level to level within that organization.

Katz and Kahn point out that communication from superior to subordinate is basically of five types:

1. Specific task directives: *job instructions.*
2. Information designed to produce understanding of the task and its relationship to other organizational tasks: *job rationale.*
3. Information about organizational *procedures* and *practices.*
4. *Feedback* to the subordinate about his performance.
5. Information of an idealogical character to inculcate a sense of mission: *introdoctrination of goals.*[15]

This sort of hierarchical information passing makes accurate communication a major concern at all levels. Such concerns are accented rather vividly when one considers the survey findings which follow. A survey of 100 firms, according to Ray Killian,[16] attempted to determine how much of what top management has to say is actually understood. The results:

* Men at the vice-presidential level understood about two-thirds of what they here from the top.
* Men at the general supervisor level got 56 percent.
* Men at the plant manager level got 40 percent.
* Men at the foreman level got 30 percent.
* Men on the production line got 20 percent.

An attrition rate as high as this one, concerning the information that provides an organization with the nutrition needed to live and ward off the entropy discussed in Chapter 1, is indeed alarming. The lack of understanding between hierarchical levels expressed in this study must be due, in part, to the difference in communication skills, attitudes, knowledge levels, and social-cultural backgrounds discussed earlier in this chapter. Another related cause may revolve around the maxim iterated in the prologue to Part I which states that *you cannot influence a man you do not understand.* Now it appears that the converse is also true, *we cannot be influenced by someone we do not understand.*

The trend away from Theory X and toward Theory Y as described in Chapter 1 is probably a central factor in the development of a better understanding between hierarchical levels and in the significant changes in the method of managing in the modern organization. Basic to these changes is the view that modern managers must think of themselves as working with a team. Of course, managers must still manage individuals, but they must also manage a work group. The new view, then, does not mean that managers should ignore individual differences, but it does mean that managers must also think of their subordinates as a unit or team and supervise them as a group. Perhaps more importantly, the subordinates must think of themselves as a team of employees. Once the team notion is internalized into the behavior of all group members, then the manager obviously becomes the team leader and leadership is extremely dependent upon communication.

Leadership implies interaction between people involving understanding, influence, conviction and—perhaps most important—behavioral responses. Interaction becomes possible only to the extent that communication allows it. The followers respond only insofar as they understand, and leadership does not exist or really function at all until it communicates sufficiently to achieve a satisfactory level of response. For instance, managers get tasks accomplished through subordinates only when those subordinates understand what the manager wants to accomplish, how it is to be accomplished, when it is to be accomplished, and how well it is to be done. This understanding can only be gained through the effectiveness of the manager's communication skill at taking into account the subordinate's ability to understand.

An almost certain ramification of a breakdown in this leader-follower relationship is the potential loss of ability to evaluate work performance and therefore rectify any errors. In their book, *Interpersonal Communication In The Modern Organization,* Bormann et al. point out that: "Poor communication may result in failure to define objectives clearly. When this happens members are unsure as to what they are to do and meaningful review of performance becomes difficult if not impossible"[17]

The need for a communication system that facilitates the controlled flow of information is also vital to the morale of an organization. An example of a very common problem which provides an extreme test of both the communication system and the organizational morale is the implementation of various kinds of automation. The subject of automation continues to be one which causes fear, uneasiness, and over-reaction among employees. The increased growth potential and efficiency achieved through the automatic processing of information and materials is as beneficial as it is inevitable for both the organization and its employees. Nevertheless, unless it is communicated properly, an organizational change such as automation can be very traumatic. Through strategic communication, automation can be explained in ways which will tend to minimize resistance and secure understanding on the part of employees. Communication can explain the value of automation, can create products, can make better use of human resources, and is a necessity for any further growth in many cases.

Without proper communication, a rather different picture is presented. Picture, if you will, a successful small-town manufacturing firm with worldwide holdings. This is a firm liberally sprinkled with employees who have worked there for 25 and 30 years and they still have the family Christmas party every year. When it became necessary to computerize their operation in order to remain progressive and continue to grow, the computer was purchased and installed. There was little more made of it than that; the computer was simply purchased and installed. The days that followed were a very bizarre conglomeration of mistrust, disappointment, and paranoia, followed by job disenchantment and, in some cases, even termination. A consultant was called in by a friend in personnel to look into the possibility of surveying the communication patterns and taking the attitudinal temperature of the firm. The communication research was approved by the management staff and ready to begin when, at the last minute, the general manager made the typically unrealistic statement, "We have no communication problems to investigate." Such a top-level manager either actually did not perceive the problems or, more likely, suffered from a sickness we will call *communicatrophia*. Communicatrophia might be defined as the *hysterical indifference to the communication problems going on around oneself*.

The real irony in this story of the research that did not happen is that at the very moment the manager was claiming that he had no communication problems, plans were being completed to purchase and install a larger computer. All of this at a time when the communicative smoke had not yet cleared from the first abortive attempt to computerize; abortive, that is, from the standpoint of employee understanding and acceptance.

A minimum beginning goal for improving communication in many organizations would be the setting of communication objectives for its managers at all levels. According to William Scholz in his book, *Communication In The Business Organization:*

> At the minimum, effective employee communication should have as its objectives the following:
>
> 1. To assist in the attainment of the operating objectives of the business.
> 2. To help improve performance and job satisfaction of employees at all levels.

3. To enhance the corporate image with the employee and community public.
4. To win understanding, approval, and support of the organization's position on vital economic, political, and social issues.
5. To keep management informed of attitudes, trends, and reactions among employees and other appropriate "publics" as an aid to decision-making and control.[18]

COMMUNICATION SETTINGS FOR THE MANAGER

The communication situations which involve managers span a wide range of settings. Let us think of these situations for the time being as if they were located along a continuum ranging from the most interpersonal settings to the settings which can best be classified as mass communication. General communication levels or settings on such a continuum might look as shown in the diagram below.

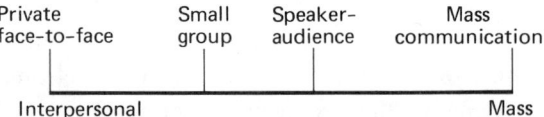

There are really two approaches to an examination of these settings. One is to look at them as descriptive classifications of the kinds of communication activities in which managers might find themselves engaged. The other approach is to think of these settings strategically, as communication methods which may be applied individually or jointly to accomplish particular management tasks. In either event it is important to understand the organizational parameters and functions of each descriptive communication setting and the advantages and shortcomings of each setting from the point of view of communication strategy.

The first of these settings, and the most basically interpersonal one, is *private face-to-face* communication. The basic communication level, sometimes known as the dyad, usually involves one source communicating with one receiver. It is, on one hand, the simplest communication level in an organization and, at the same time, a crucial level. It is crucial because it is at this level that many of the messages that make or break the task functions of an organization are communicated, and simple because private face-to-face is a less complicated source-receiver dilemma than any of the others. This is true, of course, because there is only one receiver with whom the source must be strategically concerned. Specific face-to-face communication settings for managers occur in such areas as interviewing, counseling, leadership, the dissemination of orders and the receiving of feedback.

The real importance of the basic, dyadic communication situation, however, is that it is a central measure of the manager's ability to convey meaning to others. If, for instance, managers cannot communicate their meaning to one receiver, how can they hope to communicate such a meaning to that one receiver multiplied by three, ten, or several hundred in a larger communication setting. If you have difficulty gaining the attention and understanding of an individual, your chances of gaining the attention and understanding of several hundred individuals are certainly far from good.

The opportunity to receive feedback, interpret that feedback, and make the necessary corrections in your communications are obviously much higher in the face-to-face setting than in the other settings.

A communication setting which also offers the opportunity for feedback and is highly interpersonal (although it involves more individuals than the simple source-receiver relationship found in the face-to-face setting) is the *small group* setting. A small group may, for our purposes here, be defined as a collection of individuals who have some common purpose and goal in meeting together. Communication researchers and practitioners have argued long and fruitlessly over how small a collection of individuals constitutes a "small" group and at what magic number does the said group become a large group. Since the answer to this dilemma is a moot point and purely arbitrary, we will set our own parameters for small and large group size. In keeping with our continuum approach to communication settings, we can easily set a lower limit on a small group, such as three. In other words, the small group setting picks up where the face-to-face setting leaves off. Rather than designate an upper limit, we should find it considerably more useful to think of a small group as encompassing any work group or similar organizational unit which would function under the direct supervision of a lower or middle-range manager. Looking at a small group as an organizational work unit is especially appropriate to the concerns of this text and chapter. Specific examples of the small group setting in business beyond the work group relationship might be a fact-finding committee, a board of directors, or a problem-solving committee.

As organizations have made the move mentioned earlier from Theory X to Theory Y, they have naturally felt the need to arrive at their decisions in an increasingly more participative manner. That is, the opinions of the people affected by a given decision are taken into account rather than a more unilateral approach to decision making being used.

The participative approach, with all its long-range advantages, has short-range disadvantages which must be pointed out. Principal among these is the fact that the need for arriving at a group consensus, which is incumbent in a participative format, is almost always highly time consuming. The participative decision is *not* a quick decision making method.

On the other hand, researcher after researcher has found that in the long run the participative decision is far more apt to be the one accepted, adopted, and implemented by subordinates than the more unilateral variety. Much more will be said concerning effective small group management strategies in Chapter 8.

The *speaker-audience* communication setting is usually a far more formal setting than the more interpersonal settings. Due to the formality of the situation and the size of the receiver group, when a source stands up and speaks to these receivers, there is obviously very limited opportunity for feedback. On the other hand, the receivers have the opportunity to become very well acquainted with the source. Specific examples of speaker-audience situations are such situations as external public speaking engagements and formal speeches made internally to the members of an organization.

Mass communication, the last setting on our continuum, utilizes mass media such as radio, television, newspapers, magazines, and—in the case of an organizational establishment—such things as the intercom and written memoranda on the bulletin board. The clearest advantage of the mass setting is that a far greater number of receivers can be reached more quickly and more simultaneously than in any of the other settings. The clearest disadvantage is that there is virtually no way for sources to gain feedback, at least immediate feedback, from their receivers within the mass communication structure.

The strategic uses of these various settings will be discussed in Part II of this book in order to amplify each of them in the most efficient manner.

SUMMARY

We have seen that communication is an inevitability of life and that to manage our personal life as well as our organizational environment properly, we must understand communication principles and use them before they use us. It seems certain that, whatever direction technology may take and no matter how greatly computer techniques modify organizations, the need for managers who can communicate will increase rather than decrease.

The acceptance of the premise that communication is anything and everything that influences a person or group creates a new communication role for managers. Managers soon discover that—formal or informal, intentional or unintentional—communication is going on at all times. If managers do nothing or fail to communicate the desired information, we may assume that some other information, perhaps undesirable information, will be communicated to subordinates. Communication, then, is a broad concept, equally important to business as other accepted practices such as automation, decentralization, or operations research and synthesis.

It is also clear that the success or failure of a communication attempt depends almost totally upon the encoding-decoding process. There is no more accurate way to measure the effectiveness of our communication than to examine how nearly the idea generated in the mind of the receivers after they have decoded the message resembles the idea in the mind of the sources before they encode it.

Managers who hope to be successful really have only one communication choice: to take charge of all communication and influences and guide them toward positive, useful outcomes.

NOTES

1. Ray Killian, *Managing by Design . . . For Executive Effectiveness,* American Management Association, 1968, p. 255.
2. David K. Berlo, *The Process of Communication,* New York, Holt, Rinehart and Winston, 1960, pp. 30–31.
3. Theodore M. Newcomb, Ralph H. Turner, and Phillip E. Converse, *Social Psychology,* New York, Holt, Rinehart and Winston, 1965, p. 219.
4. Berlo, op. cit., p. 41.
5. Wallace Fotheringham, *Perspectives on Persuasion,* Boston, Allyn & Bacon, 1966, p. 254.
6. Willard Merrihue, *Managing by Communication,* New York, McGraw-Hill, 1960, p. 36.
7. Howard H. Martin and Kenneth E. Anderson, *Speech Communication: Analysis and Readings,* Boston, Allyn & Bacon, 1968, p. 126.

8. Daniel Katz and Robert L. Kahn, *The Social Psychology of Organizations,* New York, Wiley, 1966, p. 302.
9. Herbert Kelman, "The Process of Opinion Change, *"Public Opinion Quarterly, 25* (1961), 57–78.
10. Berlo, op. cit., p. 5.
11. James M. Lufkin and Steven C. Krantz, "Cultural Barriers to Interprofessional Communication," *IEEE Transactions on Professional Communication, PC-15,* no. 2 (June 1972), 26–29.
12. James S. McCormack, "Communication and the Organization, *"Advanced Management Journal, 33* (January, 1968), 63–67.
13. Merrihue, op. cit.
14. Killian, op. cit., p. 254.
15. Katz and Kahn, op. cit., p. 239.
16. Killian, op. cit., p. 264.
17. Ernest Bormann, William S. Howell, Ralph G. Nichols, and George L. Shapiro, *Interpersonal Communication in the Modern Organization,* Englewood Cliffs, N.J., Prentice-Hall, 1969, p. 50.
18. William Scholz, *Communication in the Business Organization,* Englewood Cliffs, N.J., Prentice-Hall, 1962, p. 49.

3 the management and control of information flows

> Obstructive barriers are built with blocks of silence that resist penetration and make situations difficult to interpret in their proper perspective.
>
> *Unknown*

OBJECTIVES for Chapter 3

After reading the chapter you should be able to:

1. Describe the basic differences between an open and closed communication system.
2. Understand the conditions under which the grapevine operates best and how to manage it.
3. Display an understanding of the methods of analysis available to us for studying organizational communication networks.
4. Point out the barriers to upward communication and the rewards for organizational systems that keep their upward communication channels open.
5. Describe the causes of information overload.
6. Name, describe, and comment on the functionality of Miller's categories of responses to information overload.
7. Name at least ten kinds of gatekeepers in our society.

THE opening quotation in this chapter speaks of obstructive barriers. These barriers, according to the quotation, are built from "blocks of silence" or conversely, from a lack of information. In Chapters 1 and 2 we have stressed the importance of information and communication to organizational management. Now it is time to go a step further and assert that an organization probably cannot survive for long without a steady flow of information. Information is, in fact, the lifeblood of an organization. When we speak of the flow of information in relation to an organization we mean information coming into and going out of an organization, the accessibility of that information to the organization, and the internal communication networks through which the information must pass.

We have established already that a key dimension for organizational health is effective and efficient management. Management decisions are the vital integration activities which move an organization toward its goals; a system of information acquisition and information processing is vital to that decision making process. Information is vital to the understanding of the feelings of labor. Information is vital to the understanding of the population being managed. Information is vital to the evaluation of alternative courses of action. In short, information makes possible such management functions as planning, organization, and the control of change. Information is also absolutely essential to the important management function of integrating all the subsystems into one healthy system. Finally, information is vital to an equally important management function: the preservation and maintenance of the system itself.

Therefore, an organization and its management team must be viewed as an information processing system. It seems essential, then, that organizations devote a great deal of attention to the establishment, care, and feeding of appropriate systems through which the information may flow. As stated earlier, such a total system implies outside pipelines of information and an organization which can and will remain open to the information coming in through pipelines, as well as carefully designed and administered internal networks through which the information may be passed.

It has been said that management is the process of converting information into action. Seemingly, then, we could expect the organization with the greatest amount of information entering and flowing freely throughout the organization to be the most successful organization. Katz and Kahn tell us that this is not necessarily true, however, when they point out that:

> The importance of information processes to organizational functioning does not imply, however, a simple relationship between amount of communication and organizational effectiveness. The advocacy of communication as a desideratum of organization needs to be qualified with respect to the kind of information required for the solution of given problems, and with respect to the nature of the communication process between individuals, groups, and subsystems or organization. Indeed, social systems can be defined as restricted communication networks; unrestricted communication implies noise and inefficiency.[1]

There has probably never been a time in history when technology has developed as rapidly and steadily as it does now. It has been pointed out that today's technically progressive and successful organizations tend to display similar characteristics as far as the acquisition and utilization of information is concerned. These common characteristics are a readiness to seek a high quality of outside information, effective internal communication networks, and a willingness to share information. Of course, as a technically progressive organization grows, its need for information also increases. Unfortunately, the technology in an organization is apt to grow at a much faster rate than its communication ability, and thus information requirements often grow at a faster rate than does organizational channel capacity.

In view of the prevalence of these informational needs, we will devote Chapter 3 to the management of information. Specifically, we will explore such concerns as the inadequacies and possible improvement of information storage and retrieval, the economic and uneconomic use of communication networks, and the strategic release of information and prevention of communication overloads. Generally, we will concern ourselves with the openness of organizations to information, and with the integration of information into the communication networks of the organization.

COMMUNICATION NETWORKS

The evidence presented thus far concerning open systems shows that, basically:

1. The nature and extent of success and health in an organization depends upon an effective linkage between that organization and the external information environment.

2. It is necessary for an organization to be open to extra-system channels in order successfully to acquire the negentropy necessary for organizational survival.
3. An organization must remain open to extra-system channels if it is to achieve the steady state, which is still partially permeable and viable, called a dynamic equilibrium.

Of course, anything we have said about the exchange of goods and services between the environment and open systems in general can and should be applied to the communication subsystems within the total systems. The energic input, output and internal flow with which we are concerned in communication systems is information. The management and control of information then becomes the paramount concern of any manager. Up until now, however, we have concerned ourselves mostly with the input and output of information in a system. Now let us turn our attention to what happens to the raw energic material of information once it enters the system, and examine the flow of information within a system of communicative networks and the management and control of those networks.

First, we must examine the meaning of the word *network*. In the organizational sense of the word, a network is a structured fabric of the organization, made up of a system of lines, or channels, which are interconnected. Communication networks, then, are these network channels or lines being used to pass information serially from one person to another.

We can safely say that organizational communication is really the flow of information through the networks of interrelated human role relationships. People find themselves placed in certain role functions in an organization and it is the unique juxtaposition of these roles that forms communication networks which in turn are integrated into one large communication network. There is really no difference between the concept of the relationship of the subsystems to their total system discussed in Chapter 1 and the relationship of smaller specific communication networks to the total communication network of an organization. Also, just as is portrayed in systems theory, there is a high degree of interdependence between individual roles in each network and between each network within the total organization.

The interdependent, interconnected nature of these networks naturally calls for some method of connecting the networks to one another. As we have already stated, the individuals in organizations occupy various roles in the network. One such role answering the need for connections in the network and between networks is the linking role. Such a role binds an organization together.

William D. Richards, an expert in the computerized analysis of networks, asserts that: "To understand any system fully it is necessary to know its structure—especially the way in which the various components are linked together."[2] Just as it is vital for an organization to be linked with its outside informational environment, so is it equally important for the organization to provide linkages beween each internal network and eventually between the members of each network. Certainly the middle and lower-range managers we described in Chapter 2 as standing hierarchically between their superiors and subordinates and looking in both directions at once are examples of such linking roles.

Rensis Likert first wrote about the existence of a *linking pin* function in an organization.[3] He pointed out that there were individuals in any organization whose role it is to provide the link that ties, or pins, one network to another.

According to Schreimen and Johnson, network analysis studies have shown that there are two major types of linking roles.[4] One type, *bridges,* do most of their communicating within a particular network but are connected to linking people like themselves in other networks. The other type of linking role brought out by the network research is a *liaison.* Liaisons are members of no particular network but they communicate with more than one network.

Farace and Donowski, in reviewing the network analysis literature, found that the liaisons usually have a higher status in the organization and have normally been with the organization longer.[5] In the structure of communication networks, then, uniquely different information processing demands are made by each role. The network analysis research tells us that information demands are highest for liaisons, next highest for bridges, and least demanding for regular members of the networks.

Formal and informal networks

In Chapter 1 we dealt with the organization primarily in its formal sense and in Chapter 2 we spoke of formal and informal views of the organizational communication systems. Let us now explore these formal and informal information passing systems more closely as networks.

The formal organizational networks may, from time to time, look very much like the informal networks; at other times there may be no resemblance. As Willard Merrihue points out:

A formal organization starts with a broad purpose or plan; this is subdivided into activities, and the activities are assigned to positions. Structural relationships are established between Position A and Position B, not between Mr. Smith and Miss Jones. Since communication is the vehicle for carrying on relationships between positions, we find in any formal organization a phenomenon which can be designated as positional communication. The entire organization, as it appears on an organization chart, can be referred to as a positional communications network.

Positional communication is upset in practice, however, because positions are staffed with beings with total personalities. The relationship between Position A and Position B does not exist apart from the relationship between Joe and Gertrude and the other folks in the office.[6]

Formal communication usually follows a carefully designed network which is really a chain of command or the organization chart on the wall referred to in Chapter 1 and 2. Such a formal communication structure is usually very effective for coordination and control. There is, however, a dilemma here, since organizations obviously require both effective coordination *and* effective problem solving in order to remain in a balanced state. The dilemma is that the very means by which effective coordination is achieved—a restricted and controlled communication network—is detrimental to problem solving. Such restrictions seem to block the communication processes necessary to stimulate effective decision making. The dilemma outlined here tends to make the formal structure dysfunctional at times, which naturally encourages the growth of informal networks.

Let us be more specific. The rules, procedures, and structures which are designed to produce behaviors oriented toward organizational goals may actually produce informal networks instead. We have stressed strongly the inevitability of communication of information and the definite need for it in an organization. The problem solving, decision making functions in an organization require great quantities of information to be flowing freely. The decision maker needs all the information he can get to make the wisest choice from the available alternatives. Also, the decision maker must be able to communicate his decision to those in and out of this decision making role in the network. In coordination, the division of labor and its work-separation function has a tendency to set out certain status roles such as superior and subordinate. The accompanying status relationship may very well be dysfunctional because it inhibits the free flow of information. We will see this when we examine vertical communication in an organization more closely.

When the free flow of information is inhibited within the formal organizational networks, they will almost automatically be supplemented by unofficial, informal networks. Peter Blau reports such behaviors occurring in a small government law enforcement agency,[7] for instance. Although the agents were not allowed to discuss their cases with each other, the need for advice beyond the formal structure caused them to ignore the rule and consult with each other. Hence, inadequacies of the formal networks induced the establishment of supplemental informal networks. It is also interesting that Blau reports that these unofficial networks reduced agent anxieties about the correctness of their decisions, thus improving their task performance. Additionally, the supplemental channels made more information available to the agents when reaching their decisions. A social benefit of these informal channels seems to be that, as they consulted with each other, the interaction caused the group to become more cohesive.

Interaction in this case refers to communication, whether verbal or nonverbal, between two or more people. According to Carzo and Yanouzas:

> Interactions lend themselves to measurement in terms of the direction of interactions, the frequency of interactions, the length of an interaction, the type of interaction, the content of interaction. Interactions need not be confined to oral or written messages. Interactions can occur by any means that involves the passing of a message between people, for instance, a look, a frown, hand and body motions. Note that this concept does not mean that an interaction required understanding between two or more people.[8]

The informal organization has, as its communication arm, the grapevine referred to briefly in Chapters 1 and 2. The term grapevine may be connotatively confusing since it does tend to suggest a disorganized, roundabout and not very well-defined route similar to the vines upon which grapes grow. Evidence obtained from both laboratory and field research, however, reveals that communication grapevines usually operate quickly, selectively, and in a well-defined manner, and can possess high accuracy and low distortion. Often the grapevine may be far more efficient than an inadequate formal network.

As we pointed out in Chapter 2, the grapevine is not necessarily bad for an organization. In fact, most of the research tells us that many organizations would be lost without it. There are some details surrounding the grapevine which bear closer scrutiny. One is the myth that *rumor,* which is information not supported by facts, is a major portion of the grapevine. Researchers estimate that, although it is not always complete information, the information on the grapevine is, in fact, true over 90 percent of the time. Another is that the grapevine is more a product of the situation than of any individual and could not really be uprooted or stamped out even if a manager wanted to. Snuff it out and it will likely spring up again, probably stronger than it was originally. Once managers get over the notion of trying to do away with the grapevine, they can settle down to the more important and productive business of influencing and "training" it.

This author once knew a man in the communication business who had analyzed his grapevine so well that for him it was a major means of disseminating information. He would drop a piece of information into a strategic spot on the grapevine, watch it spread through the organization, and then observe how well it was received by the organizational subordinates. If they accepted it favorably he would say something like, "Oh yes, I put that on the bulletin board, didn't I?" If, on the other hand, he perceived the information to be getting unfavorable reception, he would deny it by simply saying, "Where did you ever get such an idea as that?" Although it sounds a little underhanded, it is a good example of accepting, training, and influencing a grapevine.

Grapevine researchers tell us that the "vine" is most active:
1. When there is high organizational excitement such as policy changes, automation, computerization, or personnel changes.
2. When the information is news rather than stale.
3. When people are physically situated close enough to influence one another.
4. When people cluster in clique-groups along the vine.

Network analysis

How can we understand and make use of the formal and informal communication patterns? First we must analyze the communication networks in the organization. Some methods of investigating these communication patterns have been suggested by researchers such as Keith Davis. They are as follows:

1. *Residential analysis.* In this situation the analyst is a "live in" observer of the existing communication patterns.
2. *Participant analysis.* People are given questionnaires or are interviewed and asked what role they feel they play in the network and certain data about the network.
3. *Duty study.* The analyst sits in a certain spot in the system and observes what passes by like a highway study.
4. *Cross-section analysis.* All of the communications in a process at any particular time are analyzed.

5. *ECCO analysis.* ECCO is an abbreviation for Episodic Communication Channels in Organizations. This analysis method traces a particular unit of information through such dimensions as time and space while it passes through the system.[9]

The ECCO analysis is probably the most widely used method. Perhaps this is true partially because it is relatively easy to execute. But in addition, the ECCO analysis is quite objective because it looks at a system the way it finds it and simply reports the findings.

ECCO analysis has told us that people in an organization communicate interpersonally in chains of clusters. In other words, the total system is made up of a series of small groups or clusters linked together in a chain. This pattern may, of course, be true of an organization's formal networks but will most assuredly be true of the informal networks.

In the *duty study* the "analysts" are normally the workers recording their own communication behaviors. Such a method of studying organizational communication networks is also sometimes called "self-recording technique," "communication log," or a "communication flow sheet." Sometimes, instead of the network members themselves being the respondents, the analysts are trained observers from outside who record the communication behaviors. The advantages of the duty study are that it can provide detailed data on a particular role in the organization and such factors as the amount of communication, the networks used, and the directions communication follows in this organizational role. The major disadvantages connected with the duty study seem to be that it takes time, it collects a large volume of data which may not all be usable, and it depends upon respondent cooperation.

Resident analysis is a useful way to gain a real understanding of how a given organization functions; however, people may be on their best behavior when the analyst is present, which could provide biased data. *Participant analysis* can be very thorough, but a questionnaire may need follow-up or it may never be returned. An interview provides a sure response, but the accuracy of face-to-face answers may be questionable because of such factors as embarassment. The *cross section analysis* is a valuable tool in that it provides a complete picture of the total communication patterns of an organization; however, because it is time and date bound, it must be repeated to gain any real volume of information about the ongoing process of communication.

There are many other methods of studying communication networks which are mostly modifications of the foregoing methods. Modifications are always necessary when studying the communication networks in an organization because of the different structures and needs of various organizations. In fact, the network analysis method used in most organizations is some sort of combination of methods. Such combinations are helpful at covering the disadvantages of each method just stated and are helpful in looking at the organization from as many sides as possible. Organizational analysis methods are usually combined into some kind of organizational audit package. The auditing process will be described in greater detail in Chapter 10.

Communication integration and organizational climate

It becomes apparent that for survival an organization must manage both the formal and informal communication network channels at all times. When properly managed and influenced the channels remain open and we have a very necessary element to the successful operation of an information system, *communication integration*. Communication integration is the interconnectedness of the organizational communication behaviors.

Guimaraes defines communication integration as "the degree to which the subsystems or individuals in a communication system are structurally interlinked."[10] Communication integration, or the lack of it, is a process variable which ranges on a continuum and is measured by the degree to which all members of an organization or system relate to each other through the exchange of symbolic content. It is evident from this definition that the concept of communication integration includes not only the interpersonal relationships between individuals at the dyadic level, but also between individuals and subgroups and between subgroups themselves. These subgroups constitute the total communication network structure of an entire social system.

The job of managers, then, is to influence the system in whatever way they can to maximize the openness of its channels and integration of its communication. Managers must really do this in two ways, through development and control. They must develop not only a corps of personnel who are competent communicators, but a smoothly functioning system of communication networks as well. Managers must control the system, not necessarily overtly or with the proverbial iron hand, but nonetheless they must be in control. This sort of control is more a matter of being in charge and operating from a strategic base in which as little as possible happens accidentally.

Perhaps an umbrella organizational condition which managers would want to strive for is an ideal *organizational climate* in which such development and control of the system can take place. Organizational climate in this sense refers to the organizational environment or, more pragmatically, the working conditions. Educational research tells us that the social climate of the classroom will have a great deal to do with how much learning can take place. For instance, if the climate is an "uptight" situation based on threats and fears, research has shown that little learning is likely. The same can be said of the climate in any organization. For instance, if the organization has a management based on such threats and fears, it is highly unlikely that open, integrated networks of communication can be developed and controlled.

The social work climate of an organization is often an accurate reflection of its cultural history and its present personality. Just as a society has a cultural heritage, so also will an organization reflect the history of its struggles, the type of people it attracts, its internal processes and its communication patterns through its present social climate. Not many years ago a sales manager friend stated that he felt an organization had a personality just as an individual does and much of the discontent experienced by some organizational members is really a personality conflict between the individual and the organization.

INFORMATION FLOW AND DIRECTIONALITY

Since it is clear that the degree of communication integration and the communication patterns within an organization are so integral to the functioning of that organization, let us now turn to the subject of the directionality of informational flows. Basically there are two major directions possible: vertical and horizontal. Horizontal, or lateral, communication is normally communication between peers at any level. Vertical communication can be either downward communication, such as orders disseminated by superiors, or upward communication such as feedback from subordinates. An examination of the direction of communication flows within an organization should tell us a great deal about the communication integration of the systems, since the direction of communication is tied so closely to the total flow of communication within the organization. The direction of the flow may suggest the degree of freedom in the internal communication networks; whether it is possible for information to pass only vertically or if it can move horizontally. That is, we may be sure that communication will flow and communication needs will be met. If this cannot be accomplished through the vertical channels suggested by the hierarchy, then it will be accomplished horizontally among peers; if horizontal communication needs cannot be met people will use other directional networks.

Downward communication

In Chapter 2 we discussed superior to subordinate, or downward, communication. In that discussion we pointed out that such communication involved job instructions, rationale, and evaluation, as well as information about organizational procedures, practices, and goals. Further, we pointed out in Chapter 2 the appalling evidence that only 20 percent of a downward directed message ever reaches the bottom organizational level. In spite of such ineffectiveness, most organizations recognize downward communication as being fundamental to their operation. Perhaps, therefore, it is the choice of communication channels which should assume a large share of the blame for ineffectiveness. Downward communication affords some obvious opportunities for mass communication such as news releases, company memos, company publications, and public statements. This is true because communication of this sort is apt to involve message content of a general nature, which may affect the whole subordinate force of an organization. A contributing factor to the high rate of meaning attrition in downward organizational messages is the lack of ability on the part of management to construct messages with the real meaning for the receivers, as described in Chapter 2.

One of the major difficulties with downward communication, which is really a transmittal of desired action, is that it implies a one-way message from source to receiver. There is often no consideration given to feedback in such situations. This is, of course, more true of written communication than it is of oral communication. Remember, however, without feedback the system has lost its ability to spot error in the system and self-correct; there is not even a way to get an accurate reading of how much of the message was actually interpreted properly and understood. In oral communication, the opportunity is always there to observe the feedback and continually correct until the message is understood. A perceptive manager can never be lulled into the false impression that his downward communication is crystal clear to all receivers if he uses oral communication channels and observes the feedback at all.

Another specialized type of downward communication is evaluative communication from superior to subordinate. A unique feature of this type of downward communication is that it is itself a form of feedback, in this case to the subordinates. We have defined feedback as return communication providing the initial source with information about his success in accomplishing his objective. Such feedback is vital to communication integration within a system because of its loosening effect on organizational morale. Experienced personnel directors and successful managers feel that subordinates are able to function better and will tend to operate more successfully in a free communicative manner when they receive evaluation in the form of frequent and meaningful downward communication from their superiors. This seems to hold true even if the nature of the communication is corrective concerning the performance of subordinates. In short, as long as superiors control the rewards in the system, their subordinates need to know at all times where they stand from an evaluative point of view.

Upward communication

We have seen that, although it is not always successful, downward communication has a definite place in modern organization plans. But what of communication coming up from the other direction on those vertical channels? Even on the surface, it would seem to be an important factor. According to Earl Planty and William Machaver:

> Unfortunately, however, some administrators tend to consider communication to be a one-way street. . . . they fail to see the values obtained from encouraging employees to discuss fully the policies and plans of the company. They do not provide a clear channel for funneling information, opinions, and attitudes up through the organization.[11]

Every time we encourage upward communication we provide the opportunity for feedback, which in turn encourages a free flow of ideas and attitudes between hierarchy levels in an organization. Upward communication can give higher management a great many clues as to which will be the most effective management strategies, if those higher levels will only listen. The majority of effective salesmen will tell you that if they begin by listening, the customer will tell them how they want to be sold. Such a notion seems to be highly applicable to management because the manager is really a seller of ideas, practices, and policies. At the very least, upward communication will provide a reading on how much of a downward message actually reached its destination and how well it was received and understood.

The need for upward communication has never been clearer than during a recent conference with some young executives of a large, well-known automobile manufacturing firm. One of these fellows, who managed about 70 people and is classified at about the 14 level in the company hierarchy, made an interesting observation. He said, "The vice-presidents around here thing they make the decisions." He went on to point out, "They certainly may make the final decisions, but the information necessary to make those decisions comes from about the 6 through 10 level." In other words, if the information coming up through the channels from where the basic knowledge can be found is incomplete, erroneous, or nonexistent, decisions will be seriously affected. The decisions made at the top can be no more effective than the quality and accuracy of the information upon which those decisions are based that is fed up from the lower levels.

Although the important benefits accruing to an organization with highly open channels of upward communication are many, the natural barriers to upward communication are also numerous. One basic overall barrier is the fact that communicating upward to a superior is generally a high-risk type of communication. It is usually risky because we are exposing and revealing ourselves to our receivers whenever we communicate with them. Although such exposure can have positive results from a superior, it also continually increases the risk of negative results. There is a great deal of research pointing to the fact that the greater the risk in a communication situation, the more apt most of us are to avoid communicating as much as possible.

A general barrier to upward communication seems then to be a combination function of the power of the superior as perceived by a subordinate, the subordinate's hierarchical ambitions, and the risk created by this situation. In other words, the simple desire to get ahead will itself cause information, especially negative information, to be highly guarded. It would not do for the person with power to promote to view the subordinate as a negative thinker. Unless a superior cultivates and promotes upward communication very carefully, the subordinate will usually prefer to withhold or dilute such bad news as failures, mistakes, or divergent opinions. This is true in spite of the fact that such information is still the very self-corrective lifeblood which the system needs so desperately.

Specifically, managers can head off a great many superior-caused barriers by exercising some common sense. It is only natural for any of us to be a little defensive about criticism or just simply to be too busy to listen thoroughly or take action on important issues. However, these items are three of the major barriers to upward communication. Perceived defensiveness on the part of a superior will naturally cause a subordinate to avoid communication that might create such defensiveness, or perhaps cause the subordinate to avoid upward communication in general. A superior may often really be too busy to listen to a subordinate's story; however, an effort should be made to make time if it is at all possible. In addition, subordinates are apt to lose all desire to communicate upward if superiors are perceived as being "too busy to bother" because they shuffle papers and give less than full attention to the subordinates. Perhaps the greatest superior-oriented communication barrier is to listen to a problem, promise action, and then do nothing. It takes a great deal of initiative and perhaps courage for subordinates to make up their mind to assume whatever risk is involved and to communicate upward in the first place. If they perceive "no action," it is not likely they will try it again. Since upward communication is—or is at least perceived as—high-risk communication, and if there is no subsequent action, the outcome, or lack of it, may not seem to be worth the risk.

Barriers to upward communication are also centered in the organization itself. The very structure of a complex organization is a barrier because this complexity and the accompanying physical distances between the hierarchical levels can make clear communication difficult if not impossible. When communication upward does occur in such situations it is likely to be distorted and/or diluted as it passes through the many levels. Recall that we pointed this out vividly in Chapter 2 when we cited the research showing what a pitifully small percentage of information ever reached the lower levels of an organization.

The distances between organizational levels may also be power related in that they constitute separation by status, prestige, and position. Another type of organizational distance is really a personality function in that, regardless of how integrated an organization may be, people with similar interests, intelligence, values, etc., will form into clique-type informal networks and limit their outside contacts. The information requirement of superiors and subordinates are not symmetrical. The greater the conflict between the communication needs of these two hierarchically situated senders and recipients of information, the more likely horizontal communication is to increase. Among peers, there is greater complementarity of information needs. When subordinates find their superiors to be unreceptive, they will turn to fellow subordinates to talk about their problems.

Perhaps the most unavoidable barrier to upward communication caused by complexity and social distance is the geographical separation brought about by decentralization. We pointed out the need for, and the advantages of, decentralization in Chapter 1. In many growing organizations decentralization is inevitable if those organizations are to continue to survive and grow. In spite of all the needs and advantages connected with decentralization, the outcome of such action must necessarliy be a spread out, fragmented, and (at least momentarily) damaged system of information networks. Communication is obviously more difficult between a subordinate at the branch office in Buffalo and a superior at the home office in Kansas City than it would be between these same two people if they were a floor apart in the same building. These geographical distances force the use of the telephone, the mails and other non face-to-face communication channels. Actually, where organizations have lately begun to pay special attention to their own communication needs, it has been brought about to a great extent by the obvious communication problems accompanying decentralization.

These barriers to upward communication are far from insurmountable, however, and the benefits to organizational managers who attempt to work around them and keep the information flowing are very important to effective management. The lack of upward communication can result in a loss of contact with subordinates and the public. Conversely, the existence of open, effective, upward communication networks provides several immediate and important rewards. According to Planty and Machaver, these rewards include the following:

1. Management gets an improved picture of the work, accomplishments, problems, plans, attitudes, and feelings of subordinates at all levels.
2. Before becoming deeply involved, management spots individuals, policies, actions, or assignments which are likely to cause trouble.
3. By helping lower echelons of supervision to improve their selection of those things that are to be communicated upward, management gets them to do a more systematic and useful job of reporting.
4. By welcoming upward communication, management strengthens the only device for tapping the ideas and help of its subordinates. This gives management a better answer to its problems and eases its own responsibility.
5. By opening the channels upward, management helps the easy flow and acceptance of communications downward. *Good listening makes good listeners.*[12]

One general bit of advice to managers who are attempting to encourage upward communication is to be constantly aware of the tendency of subordinates to perceive upward communication as risky. Moreover, managers must be aware of the further tendency of subordinates to intensively read, and perhaps even misread, verbal and nonverbal cues from their managers because of this perceived risk. Attention to these factors will certainly enable a manager to react to upward communication from subordinates in ways which will encourage the subordinates to continue the practice.

Horizontal communication

A review of the literature on the directionality of formal organizational communication indicates that vertical communication has been strongly emphasized while horizontal communication has been underemphasized. Ideally, formal horizontal communication channels should supplement and work well in conjunction with vertical channels.

As pointed out earlier, however, when formal vertical communication channels are not open, the informal horizontal channels are almost sure to thrive as a substitute. Often these substitute horizontal channels take the form of the grapevine discussed earlier in this chapter and so are a type of informal channel that is not necessarily bad for the organization even though it may be hard to control. If there is a disadvantage in horizontal communication, it is that it is much easier and more natural to achieve than vertical communication and, therefore, often replaces vertical channels rather than supplementing them. Actually, the horizontal channels that replace weak or nonexistent vertical channels are usually of an informal nature. There are, of course, formal horizontal channels that are procedurally necessary, and should be built into the system. As pointed out earlier, formal horizontal channels must be set up between departments for purposes of planning, internetwork task coordination, and general system maintenance functions such as problem solving, information sharing, and conflict resolution.

We can begin by acknowledging that horizontal communication is essential if the subsystems in an organization are to function in an effective, coordinated manner. Communication horizontally among peers may also tend to furnish the emotional and social bonds which build an *esprit de corps* or team sort of feeling. Psychologically, people seem to need this type of communication and managers would do well to provide for this need, thus allowing peers to solve some of their own work problems. Katz and Kahn point out that:

> if there are no problems of task coordination left to a group of peers, the content of their communication can take forms which are irrelevant to or obstructive to organizational functioning.[13]

In the more formal organization structure suggested by the early classical school of organizational theory, a subordinate in department *A* had great difficulty communicating even about task matters with a fellow subordinate in department *B*. The emphasis on structure and the pyramidal nature of that structure suggested strongly that subordinate *A* would have to go up through the hierarchical complexities of side *A* of the pyramid all the way to the top and then back down the *B* side of the pyramid to subordinate *B* in order to communicate with him (see Figure 3.1). The time being wasted and the level-to-level message distortion going on in the classically managed organization was recognized by Fayol in 1916.[14] Fayol proposed a bridge of horizontal communication between person *A* and person *B* which would enable them to communicate more directly (see Figure 3.2). The only limiting factor to the use of Fayol's bridge is a loss of network control and the subsequent weakening of authority and random scattering of messages throughout the system. Such random communication channels can lead to diagonal lines of communication such as direct communication between a person in department *A* and a person three levels higher or lower in department *B*. Such diagonal lines of communication are not in and of themselves bad; however, they are very difficult to control from the management point of view.

Despite the need for formal horizontal communication in an organization, there may be a tendency among peers not to formally communicate task related information horizontally. For instance, rivalry for recognition and promotion may cause competing subordinates to be reluctant to share information. Subordinates may also find it difficult to communicate with highly specialized people at the same level as themselves but in other technical departments. Horizontal communication

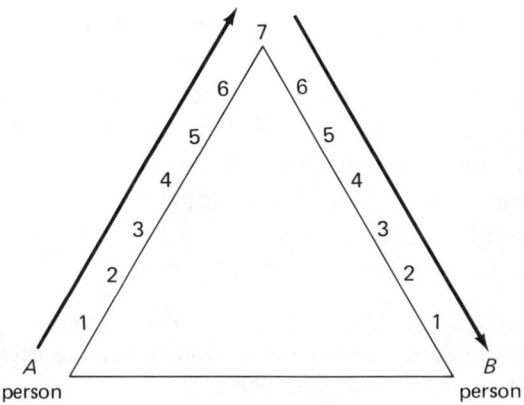

Figure 3-1 Message path from person *A* to person *B* following the classical structured channels.

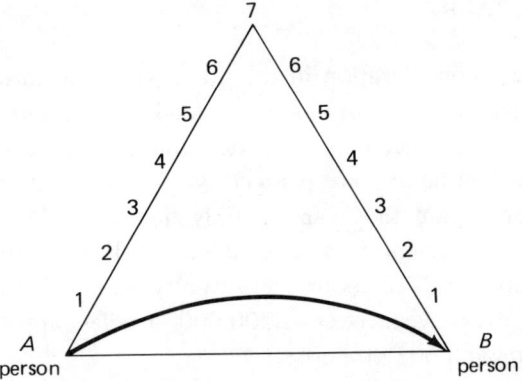

Figure 3-2 Message path from person A to person B following Fayol's bridge.

can, of course, also be thwarted by a lack of motivation. If management does not encourage horizontal communication and reward it, the subordinate is apt to orient himself more toward superiors than peers.

In the main, then, formal horizontal communication channels are a vital necessity as a supplement to the vertical channels in an organization. Conversely, the informal horizontal channels, while needed socially, can be detrimental to the vertical channels. Informal horizontal channels not only may be carrying false or distorted information, but sometimes tend to replace the vertical channels.

Summary

At this point the relationship between upward, downward, and horizontal communication should be clear. Downward communication is essential for the dissemination of managerial decisions, organizational policy, and operating procedure. Upward communication provides the feedback necessary for the maintenance of the system and the making of managerial decisions. Horizontal communication provides for coordination and system maintenance. Perhaps most important of all, each of the three directional communication flows carries in its own way the information necessary to maintain the system, make policy plans, and solve organizational problems.

If the communication networks are effectively managed in all directions, they can be integrated into a smoothly functioning whole which will maximize the work output of an organization.

INFORMATION OVERLOADS

One extremely important consideration in the management of information flows in an organization is information overload. As we hinted in Chapter 2, while discussing selectivity, the individuals as well as the organizations to which they belong are deluged with far more information over a span of time than they can possibly handle. It has been reported, for instance, that scientific and technical publications in the United States have doubled in size about every twenty years since 1800. According to Miller, every year over 1,200,000 articles appear in 100,000 research reports and 60,000 books.[15]

The foregoing statement (and indeed the evidence of our own eyes), indicates that we are constantly experiencing an information explosion. The frustrating part is that, while we have seen that organizations and individuals need information to survive, they may not survive at all if they continue to be overloaded with more information than they can handle. Today's executives are worried that they will be smothered in a blizzard of paper and information from which they will not be able to dig their way out; ironically, many turn around and release the same sort of blizzard upon their subordinates. While being overloaded with information from above, a few years back, an acquaintance of this author complained about it; whereupon the superior said, "Well, you asked for information." The acquaintance replied, "Just because I ask for a drink of water, it doesn't mean I want to be squirted with a fire hose." One fact emerges very clearly: that there are limitations to the capacity of any individual or organization to receive, decode, and effectively deal with bits of information. When that limitation is reached we have information overload.

What causes such instances of overload? It can occur at any level in an organization and for any reason or combination of reasons.

First, let us look at the person, usually an executive, who is really a member of many subsystems. When an organization has many subsystems, the upper levels in the hierarchy are apt to be inundated with information because they are associated with many of these subsystems. What seems like a reasonable flow of information from each subsystem or network can easily become a flood when all of these subsystem networks of information converge at one point to form the too often swollen river of information. Such a prospect of multiplicity of information is frightening indeed but fairly common. In addition, the various subsystems will often create overloads themselves by mercilessly inundating each other with information.

On the other hand, the executive level of an organization, no matter how well meaning, will often overload the subordinates with information to the point where they are unable to process anything. A new department chairman a few years ago found a department ruled by a rather nonparticipative kind of leadership. When he assumed the chair of the department, he began to manage in a more and more participative manner. What started as a drive for an egalitarian administration, reached a point at which the subordinates could not keep their mailboxes empty. Before they could get back to their offices with their mail, the boxes were refilled with a fresh-smelling set of dittoed memos containing items of information and new things on which they should vote. The result for many subordinates was a full wastebasket and very little information actually being processed; a classic example of information overload brought about by originally good intentions. The real irony of this story is that when the successor to this department chairman decided to be a bit more selective about what information he passed along, some of the subordinates interpreted this again well-intended move to be an autocratic, unilateral leadership style. Apparently they had become used to the information overload and now felt relatively uninformed. Others, of course, welcomed the selectivity and eventually the department settled into the new and efficient middle-ground management based upon a controlled information flow.

Another cause of overload is the capacity of the channel. At any given time a channel may reach its natural capacity and, until the situation is alleviated, most of the information which is on the channel may sound like so much "noise." The situation being described here is analogous to what happens to some radio stations at night. The channel capacity of any radio frequency is one station at a time. Sometimes at night we have all received two or more stations on one frequency and the result is that we understand none of it. What we hear is just noise and so it is when an organization communication system is overloaded beyond its capacity. Of course, it is possible to overload one channel and still utilize other channels within the organization.

Whether we are dealing with information or something more tangible such as task completion or production, an overload can be caused by system fluctuations. Organizational equilibrium is naturally disturbed when constancies to which the organization has become accustomed are changed in some way. Fluctuations are apt to overload the system in one or more of the subsystems. Although decreased inputs will create an underload for some in the organization, an overload is still created for those in the upper echelons who must rectify the problem. For example, when the United States was in the early throes of the energy crisis in 1973, automobile sales dropped suddenly on the larger models because of an overload of cars on the market. The layoffs which followed were the result of an underload of jobs, resulting in a tremendous overload on the executives who had to remedy the problem. All of these were caused ultimately by the fluctuations in the system and environment. Information overloads caused by fluctuations generally follow the same pattern. The systems principle of input–throughput–output discussed in Chapter 1 is at work here.

If we are to manage and control the flow of information, the obvious question seems to be: how much information is too much? There does not seem to be a direct answer to this question. It is a decision that must be made situationally, based upon the facts available at the time. It is certain, however, that not all people in an organization need to know all about an issue or change nor do all of the people need the same information. We can only suggest that information be passed along in the clearest, briefest manner, giving the receiver only the information he needs and/or wants to do the job.

It makes good sense, even though it seems to be a bit of an overextension, that information overload can cause mental difficulties if not remedied. According to Kast and Rosenweig:

> Some psychologists have suggested that mental illness results from information overload in individuals. If individuals can remain in equilibrium with the environment, they are healthy. In a sense they are able to cope with environmental conditions and maintain a "normal" role in society. If they are unable to process information—both internal and external flows—efficiently, however, a condition of information overload occurs and there is a breakdown in the individual system. The overload may develop because of the inability to screen out irrelevant data for the individual's decision-making tasks. When a person loses touch with reality, he is described as mentally ill.[16]

Naturally, it is every bit as possible for an organization to become ill from an information overload as it is for the people in it. The notion, then, that the more information flowing in and out of an organization the better it is for that organization is not necessarily true. Often what is needed more is a method for curtailing the input and output of information and restricting its flow.

Restriction and control of information to prevent or remedy overload situations may take a number of forms. Miller[17] categorizes the general types of responses to information overload as follows:

1. *Omission* is failing to process some of the information.
2. *Error* is a response in which information is processed incorrectly.
3. *Approximation* is the cutting of the number of categories of discrimination (a blanket and nonprecise response).
4. *Escaping* from the task is self-explanatory.
5. *Queuing* is delaying information processing during peak periods in the hope of catching up during the lulls.
6. *Multiple channels* refers to parallel channels such as in decentralization.
7. *Filtering* is neglecting to process certain types of information immediately according to some system of priorities.

Some of these responses are dysfunctional, some may be adequate, and still others are apt to be quite functional. It is fairly apparent that omission, error, approximation and escape are probably inherently dysfunctional. Queueing may be functional if not carried to extremes or done so often that the information processing cannot be caught up with during the lulls. We have already examined decentralization and its advantages and disadvantages, so the functionality and effectiveness of the multiple channel response is fairly obvious. Filtering is usually a functional response to information overload. It is the filtering response that makes use of selectivity and introduces the notion of gatekeeping.

The manager as a gatekeeper

If managers are going to control and influence the flow of information in and out of their organizations, they must frequently take on the role of *gatekeeper*. In the communication sense of the word, a gatekeeper is a person who decides what channels will be used for information dissemination and what kind as well as how much information may pass through those channels at any given time.

From this definition we can see that a wide and diverse assortment of people are at least in a position to be gatekeepers. Members of the media, for instance, are in a great position to practice gatekeeping. The newspaper editor, the TV news director on the six o'clock news, and the radio or TV program director all have the power to decide to what information we should or should not be exposed. Certainly a censor of any kind is a first-class gatekeeper. The film rating system is an attempt, albeit a feeble one, at gatekeeping. Have you ever tried, either in person or on the phone, to get an appointment with an executive and been rebuffed by a brisk, businesslike, private secretary? Most of us have experienced this at one time or another. Those superefficient secretaries are gatekeeping and one feels that if one charged the boss's door in frustration, they would even prostrate their bodies across the doorway in an attempt to keep one out physically.

One of our better-known gatekeeping functions these days is that of a political press secretary. Let us look for a moment at the news from the White House. *One* presidential press secretary prepares a news release composed only of what he wants us to hear and passes it on to *two* major news services, who in turn pass it on to *three* major TV network news systems. There is not only a great deal of gatekeeping going on here but the range of opinion on what should and should not pass over the channels is fairly limited in view of the millions of people who will be receiving the information. Conversely, though occasionally it may be misused or of a questionable kind, gatekeeping from the White House is, for the most part, a necessity. There are things that happen or might happen that might upset the economy, cause a panic, or even endanger our national security if they became public. Someone must make these hard decisions.

In any case, the position of gatekeeper is at the same time a vital necessity and a somewhat distasteful role. It is obvious that each of the foregoing gatekeepers, with the possible exception of the censor, is necessary if we are not to be buried almost instantly and smothered in a blizzard of information. On the other hand, to carry out these gatekeeping roles, *especially* the censor role, one must at times play God. A gatekeeper must decide what is best for us and then act on it. Usually, the gatekeeper must make this decision without consulting those affected by it, so gatekeeping is normally a lonesome business.

Looking at gatekeeping from a communication process point of view, we can view it in model form. Bearing in mind the advantages and disadvantages of communication models pointed out in Chapter 2, let us look at yet another different model of the communication process. This model is actually a model by Westley and MacLean depicting mass communication and the "two-step flow" of communication,[18] however, it serves our purpose here very well.

The model deals with objects (x's) and people (A's and B's). In a communication situation (see Figure 3.3) a communicator (A), based upon objects he finds in his environment (x's), selects and sends a message (x^1) to a receiver (B). Person B may or may not perceive some of the same objects in the environment but it is highly unlikely the x's will be completely identical. Nevertheless, upon receiving the message, person B sends a feedback message (f_{BA}) to A.

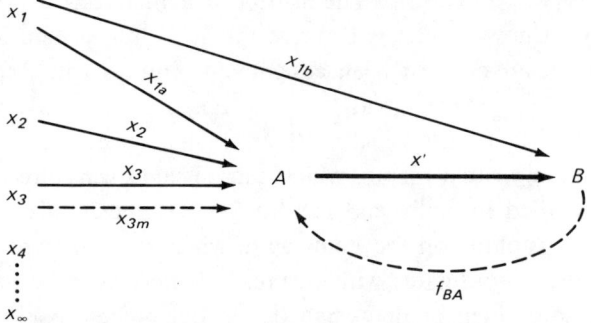

Figure 3-3 The Westley-MacLean model.

The uniqueness of the Westley-MacLean model for our purposes here is seen more clearly in the mass communication version of the model (see Figure 3.4). In this model illustrating the two-step flow, we have added another person (C). This added person is a gatekeeper. The gatekeepers (C's) select information from the sources (A's) and send the selected information along to their own receivers (B's). B receives a message from A, but only after that message has been filtered through the gatekeeper (C).

We have purposely left the gatekeeper with whom we are most concerned until last. That gatekeeper, of course, is often the manager in an organization. During the sales management days, this author experienced many situations similar to the following. The district sales managers are called in for a one-day meeting. The managers are told to tell their subordinates that they must do items one through six and that they must *not* do items seven through twelve. The managers are further told that they must inform their subordinates of these twelve pieces of information within the next 24 hours. Finally, the managers are told,

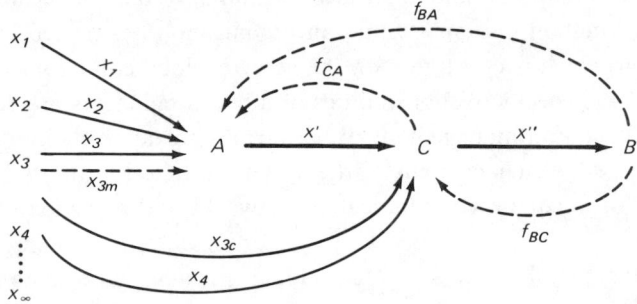

Figure 3-4 The Westley-MacLean model with gatekeeper added.

above all, "don't upset your men." The district sales manager then rides home wrestling with how he can tell twelve things to fifteen men in 24 hours and not upset anyone. Such an assignment requires gatekeeping. The managers may not realize it at the time but that is exactly what they are doing. Managers are selecting their channels; deciding which items might go into a written memo, which can be said over coffee, and which must be handled formally and face to face. Managers also must place some priority ranking on the items as to which is most important to get across to the subordinates with certainty. It may even be necessary to decide if some item or items can be left out or held back until some time beyond the 24-hour period even though those were not among the original options. All of these activities are gatekeeping functions and all of them are designed to provide the necessary information to the rest of the organization without providing too much and causing an overload. This is a business in which all managers find themselves engaging every day.

Because managers get information both from several subordinates and several superiors, which they may or may not pass along in both directions, they become the focal point of a vast amount of information. Much of this information is too confidential to pass along so managers find themselves the possessors and entrusted keepers of a storehouse of information. More will be said in Chapter 8 about being the focal point of information and how it affects leadership. For the moment it is enough to point out the heavy responsibility that managers have as they keep gates on all of this information passing both ways through their hierarchial position.

SUMMARY

Thanks to the computer and increased technology, the much-needed stream of information into and within an organization has turned into a full-sized river which is constantly on the verge of flood conditions.

Many of the specific responsibilities of modern managers are really a form of information management. What any organization really needs is an effective, solid management of the system in question through the development of adequate communication networks and behaviors. This type of management is the process of converting information into action, and managerial success is determined by what information is chosen and how the conversion is executed.

In this chapter we have seen the value of keeping a system open to its outside environment. An open system is self-regulating and will maintain itself in a steady state through its feedback. Because of these features, an open system is able to stave off entropy and achieve a dynamic equilibrium.

An organizational structure will indicate the patterns of the formal communication networks but the informal networks are not so obvious. The informal networks need to be taken into account, however, because that is where a great deal of the organizational action takes place. The grapevine is an informal channel that the smart manager will attempt to harness and influence.

Communication channels in an organization may be either vertical or horizontal and the vertical channel may carry communication flowing either downward from superior to subordinate or upward from subordinate to superior. Although the formal structure usually provides adequately for downward communication, upward communication is not always so open and free. An organization should do all it can to open these upward channels and keep them open. Horizontal channels must also be formally provided for to guarantee adequate organizational planning, coordination, and problem solving.

The greatest danger in the management of information flows is overloading the channels until nothing really gets communicated. As we said earlier in this summary, increased availability of information and ever-increasing technology have caused organizations to be under the constant threat of information overload. Therefore, the manager is constantly cast in the role of gatekeeper.

What is apparently going to happen, with this steadily increasing load on the top management of an organization, is that the managerial structure will have to change. According to *Business Week:*

> The result of the information revolution, then, will be that the top manager is going to be freed to think and plan. And that is all to the good, because in the decade to come he will have to do just that.[19]

The resulting structure, then, will probably be increased decentralization in which the top managers will have to push the decision-making function a step or so away to another group of managers and then coordinate their decisions.

One final problem caused by the information revolution is the inadequacy of information storage and retrieval systems. Computers have done a great deal to help with the problem; however, it is still difficult to keep up with ever-increasing organizational needs. A great deal more will be said about information storage and retrieval in Chapter 5.

NOTES

1. Daniel Katz and Robert L. Kahn, *The Social Psychology of Organizations,* New York, 1966, p. 257.
2. William D. Richards, Jr., "An Improved Conceptually Based Method For Analysis of Communication Network Structures of Large Complex Organizations," Paper presented to the International Communication Association, April, 1971.
3. Rensis Likert, "An Integrating Principle and an Overview," *New Patterns of Management,* New York, McGraw-Hill, 1961.
4. D. Bruce Schreiman and J. David Johnson, "A Model of Cognitive Complexity and Network Role," paper presented to the International Communication Association, April, 1975.
5. R. Vincent Farace and J. A. Danowskley, "Analyzing Human Communication Networks in Organizations: Applications to Management Problems," paper presented to the International Communication Association, April, 1973.
6. Willard Merrihue, *Managing by Communication,* New York, McGraw-Hill, 1960, p. 116.
7. Peter Blau, "Patterns of Interaction Among a Group of Officials in a Government Agency," *Human Relations, 7,* no. 3 (1954), 337–348.
8. Rocco Carzo, Jr. and John N. Yanouzas, *Formal Organizations: A Systems Approach,* Homewood, Ill., Irwin, 1967, p. 144.
9. Keith Davis, from a speech delivered at the ICA convention in Pheonix, Arizona, 1971.
10. Lytton L. Guimaraes, "Network Analysis: An Approach to the Study of Communication Systems," unpublished paper, Technical Report 12, Project on the Diffusion of Innovations in Rural Societies, Michigan State University, 1970.
11. Earl Planty and William Machaver, "Upward Communication: Project in Executive Development," *Personnel, 28* (1952), 304–319.
12. Ibid., p. 142.
13. Katz and Kahn, op. cit., p. 244.
14. Henri Fayol, *General and Industrial Administration,* New York, Pitman, 1949, p. 34.
15. J. G. Miller, "Information Input, Overload and Psychopathology," *American Journal of Psychiatry, 116,* no. 8 (February, 1960), 695–704.
16. Fremont E. Kast and James E. Rosenweig, *Organization and Management: A Systems Approach,* New York, McGraw-Hill, 1970, p. 335.
17. Miller, op. cit., p. 231.
18. Bruce H. Westley and Malcolm S. MacLean, Jr., "A Conceptual Model for Communication Research," *Journalism Quarterly, 34* (1957), 31–38.
19. "A New Breed of Men Will Call the Shots," *Business Week* (December 6, 1969), 144.

4 the changing organization

> Man's fate today, as never before, is to understand this "prevalence of newness" so that we can welcome and even predict the force of change without a guarded frozenness or a heightened susceptibility.
>
> *Warren Bennis*

OBJECTIVES for Chapter 4

After reading Chapter 4 you should be able to:

1. Apply systems theory to the organizational change setting.
2. Identify and discuss the barriers to organizational change.
3. Cite at least six examples of social systems with modern norms and six with traditional norms.
4. Compare the homophily of most communication settings to the hetrophily of the change setting.
5. Give two examples each of optional, collective, and authoritative innovation-decisions.
6. Discuss in detail individual and social system based change resistant forces.
7. Develop a total simulated change plan.

Now, more than ever, the winds of change are blowing in our society. They are blowing away an old order and with it they are blowing away old methods of managing and operating. These same winds carry with them new methods more fitting to the new order. As the quote at the beginning of this chapter suggests, we must welcome and predict change rather than fight it.

We have seen that communication is an inevitability of life. In the same sense, change is just as inevitable. Change in an organization is so inevitable that, over time, an organization and the individuals in that organization must either go ahead or go backward. They cannot stand still for long. As Willard Merrihue points out:

> Paradoxically the only constant in today's dynamic business complex is change. Change, or its highbrow synonym, innovation, is an offspring of the prime mover of our business system which is competition. In our intensely competitive system of working for each other, change is absolutely essential. No business can remain static. It must go forward on the vehicle of change or it will fall backward.[1]

As pointed out in this quote, change and innovation are synonymous. An innovation, according to Rogers and Shoemaker, "is an idea, practice or object perceived as new by an individual."[2] If an idea appears to be new to the members of a social system it is an innovation. The newest miracle drug which will be invented the day after you read this will be an innovation. But indoor plumbing in some remote village is just as much of an innovation to the residents of that village.

In our comparatively modern and advanced society it seems that there is very little that can be totally new to us. An innovation can, however, be a revision or improvement on an existing item. For instance, the nation was inundated with television sets a few years ago but the advent of color television was still an innovation. When a firm computerizes its systems, it is considered an innovation. To be sure, a computer is not new to our society; however, it still can be new to the functioning of a given firm.

An organization usually functions in a changing environment that calls for some sort of organizational and managerial response. If an organization is going to change whether we want it to or not, then our response must be some sort of reliable, appropriate and planned behavior. If change is inevitable, then why not manage that change and, through our influence, control it so that the outcome is favorable. We can either let change occur randomly within our organizations or we can exercise influence and control through our managerial role and make change work for us and our organization.

When an organization undergoes change it is affected in several ways. Since we have looked at an organization as a system, we must understand that when one portion of an organization or one organizational variable is changed, it is very apt to affect other parts of the system. The interrelatedness of the subsystems within a system is most evident when one of the subsystems undergoes some kind of change. Such a change will usually cause structural and social changes in the other subsystems.

Significant changes in an organization can also affect the processes of that organization. For instance, changes in the processes of the technical or social subsystems can affect one another. When the front office of a business firm installs data-processing hardware in order to handle accounting procedure and so on more efficiently, the people in the accounting department and/or the front office are not the only people affected. The production and sales subsystems will also have to change their method of reporting. All departments will have to operate by the one correct method which the computer can interpret and nearly all employees must be able to read and understand the output data processed by the new mechanical system. Still further, customers must get used to reading billings, reports, and so on under the new system. So we can see then when one subsystem changes many other subsystems must adjust their processes and behaviors to accommodate that change.

Significant alterations can also occur in a system because of personnel changes. Changes in supervisory personnel are apt to cause behavioral changes in subordinates. For instance, if a supervisor is an open, flexible leader who believes in participative decision making, then the subordinates will learn to behave in accord with that leadership style. But what if that supervisor is replaced by an autocratic, rigid leader who not only enforces the rule book but seems to have written it? Obviously, at the very least, the subordinates and the entire communication system have some serious and radical behavioral changes to make in order to accommodate these personnel changes.

Since an organization is really a social system made up of individuals, we should look at change on those two levels at least. Change can occur at either the individual or the social-system level although, as we have just seen, the levels are integrated and somewhat interdependent. Although the nature of a given change may be such that the adoption or rejection of that change is an individual choice, the social system is still affected. If enough individuals adopt a certain change, the social system of which these individuals are a part will inevitably be changed as well. On the other hand, if an organization or social system changes, the individuals within that system will have to change or be changed in some way.

THE FORMAL ORGANIZATION AND CHANGE

Let us look again at the structure and characteristics of the formal organization. Although the informal structure is still an important con- ganization are usually made within the formal framework. When we speak of a formal organization we mean such easily identifiable entities as the Red Cross, Ford Motor Company, local hospital and school systems, even the corner grocery. Let us remind ourselves what factors are common among these entities so that we may attempt a broad classification. First, we should point out that a basic distinguishing feature of formal organizations is that they are deliberately established to accomplish some specific and predetermined goal or goals. For example, a university is established to provide the higher education needed by today's human beings. In spite of differences of opinion in what is the appropriate method to achieve these goals, the goals themselves are predetermined, universal, and do not materially change unless someone changes them. For many formal organizations the goal is the largest profit possible; certainly this is one goal often agreed upon.

Rogers and Shoemaker describe several characteristics which they feel set formal organizations apart from other kinds of social systems.[3] These characteristics are *predetermined goals, prescribed roles, authority structure, rules and regulations,* and *informal patterns.*

The *predetermined goals* for which the organization is established will shape, to a great extent, the structure, function and purpose of the organization. For instance, if a consulting firm were established to provide expertise in certain specific areas, then the staff would no doubt be chosen with these specifics in mind.

Prescribed roles are duties and/or responsibilities which are usually distributed along with various hierarchical positions in a formal organization. Positions are the designations graphically described on an organization chart and there is a prescribed role or set of roles for each position. Positions and their accompanying roles are far less likely to change than the individuals who fill them. The positions on the organization chart do not usually have equal authority. The whole purpose of the organization chart is to specify who is responsible to whom and who has authority over whom. Thus, as an organizational chart with positions and their corresponding roles develops, we see the inevitable emergence of an *authority structure*.

Every formal organization must have some kind of *rules and regulations* or at least a set of well-defined guidelines. Although such rules and regulations appear to be the whole organization at times and are often lampooned and caricatured, they are a necessity in the very nature of formalization. For the sake of continuity and fairness to all, a formalized set of rules for practices such as hiring, promotion, discharge procedures, and coordination must be established.

As we have already seen, no matter how formalized an organization becomes, it will always have *informal patterns* such as social norms and socio-emotional relationships among the individuals. Although it never succeeds fully, the formal structure of an organization has a natural tendency to try to subdue these personalized informal patterns. These informal patterns are actually a social necessity in the highly task-oriented formal organization.

Organizational *change* is a noticeable alteration which takes place in the goals, structure, or processes of a system over time. The observer of formal organizations is forced to the conclusion that most organizations are not characterized by rapid change, particularly not formal organizations with the characteristics pointed out by Rogers and Shoemaker above. Indeed, when organizations are reviewed over a long period of time, their outstanding characteristic appears to be stability, rather than change. Because (1) a formal organization is a structural mechanism employed by society to achieve one or more of its commonly accepted goals; (2) the goals do not change noticeably; and (3) each organization's activities are rather clearly demarcated. Any particular organization comes into existence with a great deal of built-in stability. This stability is so great as to constitute a powerful resistance to change.

When a change process occurs, the system can react in one of four ways. These ways are:

1. Ignore the change; pretend things are just as they always have been and will be. Think that the usual is eternal.
2. Resist the change; prefer conditions not as good as they could be for fear they might be worse than they are; a sort of "bird in the hand is worth two in the bush" concept.

3. Adapt and accept with an easy, false enthusiasm under the delusion of action: "We did this." Dedicated to ourselves, our goals are simply adaptation to the past as we knew and loved it.
4. Design and create the future. Mistakes may occur but not by individuals who do nothing. A leader is always exposed to risk. But an effective leader takes the risk in the hope of real gain, where inaction can only court certain disaster.

The first three reactions are forms of resistance to change. A change force has its origin in any aspect of the organization which increases the willingness of the system to make a proposed change. A resistance force has its origin in any aspect of the organization which reduces the willingness of the system to make a change.

One of the most discouraging moments in many a process of change comes when resistance to change suddenly appears in an important subpart of the system. Usually the change-initiating subpart responds by being intensely angry or painfully disheartened. Often it seems incomprehensible to the proponents of change that resistance should occur. "Why are they resisting something that will benefit them as much as it does us?" "Can't they see that this will be an advantage to the whole community, even if they have to give up a little?"

On the other hand, it is clear that organizations *do* change. In many organizations, the increments of change are small, but in others, change is so radical and so rapid as to cause the disappearance of the original organization and the appearance of a new one. As pointed out earlier, when an organization changes, the members of that organization must change also and must acquire an unaccustomed facility for change, if they are to live in a modern world. Such organizational change means that the achievement and maintenance of our mutual wellbeing becomes progressively more important and more difficult to accomplish because change has to affect the stability of an organization and its members. It further means, however, that if we are to maintain our health and a creative relationship with the world around us, we must be actively engaged in change efforts directed toward ourselves and toward our material, social, and spiritual environments.

BARRIERS TO ORGANIZATIONAL CHANGE

There are a great many barriers that tend to inhibit organizational change and encourage resistance. According to Berg and Schuchman, some key factors that inhibit change and the desire to innovate in an organization are as follows:

1. Overcentralization of power and control
2. Lack of planning
3. The building of little empires
4. The spreading of fear and anxiety
5. Limited loyalties
6. Poor communication[4]

Of course, the barrier to change, or factor inhibiting change, that most concerns us here is poor communication. It should be clear that any change effort will most certainly be doomed before it starts without an efficiently functioning communication system through which to convey information about the desired change. Whether we are introducing change into a system for the first time or attempting to persuade a system to adopt an existing change, communication is really the only vehicle through which it can be accomplished. The bulk of the remainder of this book will concentrate on the development of a manager as an all-round communicator and developer of efficient communication systems.

We pointed out earlier that we might as well manage and control communication since it was inevitable in our life. By the same token, if change is also inevitable, we are foolish not to manage change so that we can control the outcome. Such management and controlled change certainly make a great deal more sense than haphazard change which has a favorable outcome only as a "happy accident." If this happens we have lost control of the system and, therefore, also lost the predictive ability necessary to manage a system.

The intent here is not to oversimplify such a management accomplishment. It is, of course, very difficult to gain control and manage organizational change for many reasons, including the ones just pointed out. For instance, if an organization suffers from such ailments as lack of planning or limited subordinate loyalties, management of change in the system is naturally going to be difficult.

Organizational stability

Another basic reason why organizations have difficulty in managing change is that their administrators have been trained instead to manage stability. Perhaps at no time in history have organizations been subjected to more rapid and sudden change than they have since Sputnik; this has not eased the job of management.

Such authors as Katz and Kahn[5] generally point out that the difficulty of experiencing and implementing change in a stable organization should not be minimized. Clearly, successful systems or organizations must be stable if they are to provide the continuity necessary in a formal structure. It is, therefore, unreasonable to expect such organizations to evolve structures which maximize flexibility. A highly flexible organization is poorly adapted to stable conditions, just as a highly inflexible and formal organization is poorly adapted to unstable ones.

The pain and disorganization that arise from finding that our familiar ways of behavior no longer work in a new environment, or in an environment that has been altered, are frequently an unavoidable stimulus toward change. It is not pleasant to feel threatened but that pain can become a force toward change. The system experiencing a threat will try first, and most urgently, to return to old and secure patterns of behavior because members of the system naturally feel more sure of these traditional patterns than of other untried and untested patterns.

What appears to be painfully new to our organizations may not be new because it has never been there before, but simply because it may have changed in quality. One factor that *is* new is the prevalence of newness; the changing scale and scope of change itself, so that the world changes as we walk in it, so that the years of persons' lives measure not some small rearrangement or moderation of what they learned in childhood, but a great upheaval of what has gone before. The Angel Gabriel in *Green Pastures* put it even more succinctly: "Everything nailed down is coming loose."

A smoothly running organization, then, is characterized by stability and yet that same organization cannot survive for long without changing to cope with its constantly changing environment. How do we resolve the problem of the apparently dichotomous organizational needs for stability and change at the same time? The answer lies in the principles of system theory and more specifically among the characteristics of an open system. Recall that we pointed out in Chapter 1 that an important characteristic of an open system is the notion of a dynamic equilibrium. We pointed out that an organization with dynamic equilibrium is flexible enough to allow for growth and change without the loss in the long run of its steady state and the accompanying organizational stability. The self-adjustive, or self-corrective, factor in an open system will allow an organization to accept and assimilate change, live with the momentary disruption to the stability, and move to a new steady state at another level. Once this new level of equilibrium is established, the organization is functioning again and operating just as smoothly, perhaps even more smoothly, than before. But the organization may look and behave differently because it may have new operating procedures.

Social system norms

These operating procedures may be called *norms*. Other important factors that may create a barrier affecting the rate of change adoption in an organization are the social and task norms of the organization. A norm in this sense of the word is any shared expectation of behavior that a social system has for its members. It is a set of behavioral rules, even though they are often not written down or spoken. When they are verbalized, however, they usually appear in the verb forms "ought to," "should," "must," or "had better." To the degree that traditional, more rigid norms represent the status quo, they are more apt to sound like the old familiar phrase, "Oh, but we've always done it that way."

Rogers and Shoemaker define norms as, "established behavior patterns for the members of a given social system."[6] We have already pointed out that when an organization makes certain changes, some sort of behavioral change or changes are expected from the individuals in that organization. Such expectations are nothing more than a new set of norms. Whether they are new norms or old ones, they can still serve as a strong barrier to change, especially when they are enforced by pressure to conform from the social system.

Since norms are the established behavior patterns for the members of a given social system, they can serve as either incentives or restraints for individual decisions about whether to adopt change or not. In other words, a system's norms not only *may* have the tendency to change or not; one of these tendencies is probably present already.

Rogers and Shoemaker describe contrasting, extreme social systems which are characterized by certain sets of norms. They point out that a *modern* social system is typified by:

1. A generally positive attitude toward change.
2. A well-developed technology with a complex division of labor.
3. A high value on education and science.
4. Rational and business-like social relationships rather than emotional and effective.

5. Cosmopolite perspectives, in that members of the system often interact with outsiders, facilitating the entrance of new ideas into the social system.
6. Empathetic ability on the part of the system's members, who are able to see themselves in roles quite different from their own.[7]

It is apparent that the foregoing characteristics would be very apt to lend themselves to the creation and nurturing of a good climate for change.

On the other hand, Rogers and Shoemaker also speak of the more *traditional* social systems which are characterized by:

1. Lack of favorable orientation to change.
2. A less developed or "simpler" technology.
3. A relatively low level of literacy, education, and understanding of the scientific method.
4. A social enforcement of the status quo in the social system, facilitated by effective personal relationships, such as friendliness and hospitality, which are highly valued as ends in themselves.
5. Little communication by members of the social system with outsiders. Lack of transportation facilities and communication with the larger society reinforces the tendency of individuals in a traditional system to remain relatively isolated.
6. Lack of ability to empathize or to see oneself in others' roles, particularly the roles of outsiders to the system. An individual member in a system with traditional norms is not likely to recognize or learn new social relationships involving himself; he ususally plays only one role and never learns others.[8]

It must be realized that the modern and traditional systems as Rogers and Shoemaker describe them are extremes. The norms of most systems fall somewhere between these extremes. Also, it should not be assumed that modern norms are necessarily always desirable or that traditional norms are necessarily always undesirable.

Although it is obvious that the system with strong barriers to change will be the one with traditional norms, these norms do provide a great deal of organization stability in many cases. Conversely, it is equally obvious that the norms found in a modern social system are conducive to change. But the modern social system, with all its progressiveness, has a long list of accompanying social problems. One has but to look around today to see the truth of this statement.

All things considered, however, once we have studied the traditionalism-modernism of an organization's norms, we can make some fairly accurate predictions about the willingness of the organization to accept change. Of course, to make an accurate prediction, we must do more than simply locate the normative position of the organization between the two extremes. The strength of the *commitment* to the norms on the part of the individuals within the organization also is important. The norm is only as important a barrier to change as the strength of the commitment to that norm.

No discussion of social system norms and commitment to those norms would be complete without also examining conformity and deviance from them. The degree to which an individual must conform to, or is able to deviate from, norms has a great deal to do with the degree to which that individual will be able to accept change.

The business of conformity to norms is fairly complicated, but several factors are clear. One of these is that if persons perceive similarity between themselves and their peers, there is likely to be conformity to the norms of the peers. Conversely, if they perceive dissimilarity they are apt to react with nonconformity. Another factor is that such a perceived dissimilarity between the self and peers is an uncomfortable perception. This discomfort can be, and often is, reduced considerably by feeling that we are conforming to a different and more important set of norms rather than feeling we are nonconformists. The individuals, then, who find themselves in this position may be quite susceptible to change.

Momentary violation of norms is usually acceptable; however, the continued violation of norms is usually a more serious and painful situation. Continued violation of norms, according to Shepherd, may exist under one or both of two conditions:

> (1) If the norms in a situation are contrary to more general norms a person holds or contrary to the norms of some other reference group important to a person, he will likely violate them. (2) If a nonconformist finds support from at least one other member of the group, or from the imagined approval of another person or group, he will likely continue to violate the norms.[9]

The foregoing material points out that there are often several different sets of norms that confront one individual. This is a dilemma that a middle and lower-range manager must be aware of and deal with. For instance, recall that we have already pointed out that managers in these ranges serve as the organizational linking systems between the change agency and the client system. This role requires that managers have a continuing and important membership in at least two social systems simultaneously: (a) the social system directed by their superiors in which they and their managerial peers are subordinates and (b) the social system made up of subordinates for which the manager is responsible. Often the norms of these two social systems are widely divergent and at odds with each other. A combination of the level at which membership in a certain group is valued by individuals and the amount of pressure to conform exerted on those individuals, together will cause them to choose the particular set of norms to which they will conform.

A theory researched and written about by Leon Festinger, called *cognitive dissonance theory,* points out that, when people must make a choice, they seek evidence to reinforce their decisions, thereby easing or avoiding the hurtful state produced by the choice.[10] We could predict that, given a situation where we must make a choice between conforming to the status quo or adopting a change, we would follow the behavioral pattern suggested here by Festinger. Further, we could predict that we would behave this way regardless of which choice we made. A choice to adopt change, then, would be likely to make us strong advocates of that change. On the other hand, a decision to follow the norms and stick with the status quo would be likely to make us even harder to change in the future, at least on the same issue.

We have spent some time now exploring social and task norms, conformity, and deviance. In light of this body of information, we can make one or two strategic observations. Because attitudes and behaviors are functions of personality as well as social roles, change processes must be concerned with altering internal individual forces as well as organizational forces. Another observation is that the existing forces for stability in a social system regulate the behavior of individual system members.

ORGANIZATIONAL RESISTANCE TO CHANGE

Resistance to change can occur anywhere in an organization. In Chapter 2 we described a firm that attempted to introduce a computer into their system with little or no planned communication of the change. The results ranged from reluctant acceptance to open rebellion in various corners of the organization. What turned this congenial, compatible work environment into a traumatic combat zone? Resistance to change at both the individual and the organizational level was the problem. But what caused the resistance in that organization? Of course, we can assume that the notions mentioned earlier in this chapter concerning the natural tendency of an organization toward a steady state and the preservation of the status quo will provide some built-in resistance. Change is naturally disruptive to the status quo; such disruption is in itself a painful situation and will usually be avoided when possible.

Understanding the sources of resistance will best equip us as managers to handle that resistance. For instance, the status quo is bound to seem attractive to us when we fear losing something which satisfies us now. Most of us would rather stick with something adequate which we know works rather than try something new which is potentially more than adequate but is accompanied by a perceived risk of losing all. Many of us will go along with the status quo rather than take the plunge.

Another source of resistance to change is a reluctance to attempt something new for fear of failure or a lack of ability to carry out the innovation. This source of resistance, however, is deceptive. It is very unlikely that anyone will admit to a fear, especially fear of failure. It is far more likely that the clients will say they do not like the innovation or that they will not try the change for some reason other than fear. We must often find ways to look at the situation in depth and try to determine the real reason for resistance.

It is further possible that a fear of failure may be well founded, based on previously unsuccessful attempts at change. Picture a person who is by nature reluctant to change. This person finally gets up the courage to try something new after repeated bolstering of their courage. The time draws near and they do it; they try the change in behavior but unfortunately it fails. We are now likely to have a bona fide, confirmed resister of all future change.

A formal organization with its hierarchy and highly centralized power presents a special resistance problem. Most innovations enter the system at the top and if the communication systems are well integrated, the innovations flow downward. The basic assumption here is that when change occurs in a formal organization, it occurs usually from the top down while change coming up from the lower echelons is less frequent. As noted by Miles: "A hierarchical order would enable change to occur from the top down, but the relative independence of the subsystems would tend to slow down the rate of change."[11] Structure makes change from the bottom very difficult; one would expect little, if any, change to be introduced in such a way. Such a statement seems even more true when one considers that in most organizations the organizational power resides at the top.

It seems only natural that the more hierarchically structured an organization is, the more barriers to change will be present. Hierarchical subsystems tend to be segregated further and further from each other until eventually they are highly decentralized and independent. Such segregation and independence makes change difficult to introduce and, of course, even more difficult to communicate from person to person and from subsystem to subsystem.

On the other hand, the amount of dynamic interplay between subsystems will determine how easily changes can be communicated and implemented between those subsystems. When subsystems communicate with each other in an effort to achieve a steady state and organizational harmony they are attempting to minimize conflict. Since change is almost built upon conflict, the subsystems will resist the communication of change just as they resist conflict.

Goodwin Watson points out that:

> All the forces which contribute to stability in personality or in social systems can be perceived as resisting change. From the standpoint of an ambitious and energetic change agent, these energies are seen as obstructions. From a broader and more inclusive perspective the tendencies to achieve, to preserve, and to return to equilibrium are most salutary. They permit the duration of character, intelligent action, institutions, civilization and culture.[12]

Earlier in this chapter we pointed out the somewhat frustrating paradox here. The organizational drive for a steady state will place aggravating barriers in the path of a change attempt. However, once the change is fairly well accepted, such stability can make the new change become a solid part of the system which is apt to be highly resistant to future change.

Goodwin Watson points out that there are some resistance factors built into the individual personality and still other resistance factors within the social system itself;[13] we discuss these below.

Individual resistance factors

As we have already pointed out, the drive for *homeostasis,* a steady state, is a stabilizing force that, initially at least, inhibits change. Another individual change-resistant factor is *habit,* which causes social system members to continue to behave and respond in an accustomed way. In such a case, when change is suggested, the answer comes back, "But we've always done it *this* way."

Primacy is an individual resistance force which is geared to maintaining a behavioral pattern with which we first achieved success. It is not difficult to see why we might avoid the risk of change and stay with a proven pattern. Another individual factor is *selective perception and retention* based upon the same notion as the selectivity discussed in Chapter 2. Once we establish a certain outlook we tend to reinforce the original belief and be less susceptible to change.

We sometimes resist change because we have a *dependence* on someone, such as a parent, and because of that dependency tend to incorporate and hold to the outlook of that valued other. Also, when we are young we learn and internalize a set of moral standards that become a sort of *superego* which may inhibit any desire to change.

Insecurity on the part of social system members may cause them to resist change because of *self-distrust* concerning their own ideas and impulses. *Insecurity and regression* themselves cause people to shrink from social change and seek solace in the security of the past.

Although the foregoing is a rather lengthy "grocery list" of individual change-resistant forces based on personality factors, it does aid us in understanding some common sources of change resistance. There is a proverb that to teach someone a subject, one must know not only the subject, but the person as well. We have to understand the sources of resistance before we can hope to overcome that resistance.

Social system resistance factors

We have already indicated that people tend to cluster around system norms. This *conformity to norms* means that the members of a social system must behave in customary ways rather than with the abnormal, disruptive behavior that often accompanies change. *System and cultural coherence* is Gestalt-like in nature and provides a great deal of system-oriented resistance. The implication of such resistance is that, if one subsystem is changed, other subsystems are apt to be affected because they are interrelated.

One kind of resistance which is very difficult to deal with, even when it is recognized, is whatever in the status quo may be held as *sacrosanct*. "Sacred cows" are so basic to some systems that changing them affects, or seems to affect, almost every facet of the system. Perhaps the most basic single resistance force of all is the natural tendency of a system toward *rejection of "outsiders."* We seem to be naturally hostile and suspicious of an outsider who tries to persuade us to change.

It should be clear after discussing organizational barriers and resistance to change that the communication of change requires very special talent and strategic planning. Let us now turn our attention to the actual communication of organizational change.

THE COMMUNICATION OF CHANGE

One way to examine the problems of organizational change in a formal organization is to place ourselves in the role of communication consultant for a moment. According to Lippitt, et al., "The increased need to modify or invent our patterns of behavior and organization has led naturally to a demand for professional help."[14] Based upon past research, what sort of help or advice could a professional offer an organization?

First, we could state with some authority that resistance to change can be expected if the nature of the change is not made clear to the people who are going to be influenced by the change. Theories of decision making sometimes ignore communication effects. Prima facie, this exclusion seems unjustified. If, for example, organizational decisions are assumed to be based on expectations of needs, costs, and effectiveness of programs, it is difficult to see how we can ignore the process through which such information is communicated in the organization. In spite of these facts, it seems that the dissemination of recommended changes in organizations has not been dealt with adequately, and one of the major problems inhibiting change in our present programs and processes is the lack of sound communication systems between subordinates, administrators, and the public. We might do well in this situation to apply a question and answer posed by Simon when he says:

> The question to be asked of any administrative process is: How does it influence the decisions of the individual? Without communication, the answer must always be: It does not influence them at all.[15]

Of perhaps even greater concern is what happens when there is communication of a change but that communication is either inefficient or inadequate. Let us turn once more to the small-town manufacturing firm which installed the computer and developed more problems than it bargained for, referred to in Chapter 2. Certainly there was communication concerning the computerization in that firm and the firm did not hide the computer in a closet. But the kind of communication that was most needed—such as preparatory communication before the arrival of the computer, or training on how to work with a computer and make it work for them—was sadly lacking. As mentioned earlier in this chapter, when the organization decided to change to a computer system, the individuals working within that organization had to make certain changes in their work behavior. These changes, such as the introduction of a new accounting system and a new method of reporting from the production staff, were sudden changes imposed with little or no help from any adequate communication plan. The plans were carefully made for the change and transition but did not really include a subplan detailing procedures for communicating the change. How, then, does one go about developing such a plan?

More will be said about the manager's role as communicator and manager of change in Chapter 6. For the moment, however, let us examine the communication process and its effect on change.

HETEROPHILY AND COMMUNICATIVE UNIQUENESS

The change situation itself is unique among the various communication situations. It is unique mainly because of the presence of a factor known as *heterophily*. According to Lazarsfeld and Merton *homophily* is the degree to which pairs of individuals, or individuals and groups, who interact are similar in such features as social status, education, values, beliefs, and so on.[16] Heterophily is the mirror opposite of homophily. In other words, heterophily is the degree to which these units are different in certain attributes.

The concept of homophily-heterophily is particularly interesting when we recall the Berlo concepts discussed in Chapter 2. Recall that we said that sources and receivers had communication skills, attitudes, knowledge levels, and social-cultural backgrounds. We further pointed out that the degree of source-receiver similarity on these factors would have a great deal to do with the success of the communication. The Berlo concepts are really close to the homophily-heterophily notions and it is apparent from research that communication is apt to be more effective when the source and receiver are homophilous.

What, then, makes the communication of change unique among communication situations? If we think about it we can see that a person communicating in a group usually has a fairly high degree of homophily with other group members. Likewise, a person asked to speak to an audience is usually speaking to a "friendly" audience, therefore, he probably has a high degree of homophily with that audience. For instance, it is not very likely that a liberal leader would be asked to speak to the John Birch Society or an arch conservative at an impeachment rally. However, the opposite, and more homophilous, speaker-audience match-up is very likely. So we see that in most communication settings homophily is present. We have already seen, however, that there is apt to be a high degree of heterophily between a communicator of change (often an outsider) and his target social system, thus creating a communicative uniqueness.

The social system is functioning happily under the status quo and the communicator of the change comes upon the scene and suggests change. This highly heterophilous situation requires some very well-planned communication strategies and the greater the heterophily, the greater the need for communication strategies. The communication principles brought out in Chapters 2 and 3 must be applied by the manager who really intends seriously to influence the behavior of the people whom he wishes to change. In short, organizational change must be planned change to be effective and that plan must include a definite set of communication strategies. Such managerial communication strategies are the primary focus of Part II of this book, with a particular focus on communication of change strategies in Chapter 6.

TYPES OF ORGANIZATIONAL CHANGE

Perhaps before we examine the various types of change it would be helpful to look at some ways in which change may come about or evolve in an organization. These various change methods may be compared on the basis of the presence or absence of mutual goal setting between the communicator of change and the social system. The comparison may also be based on the relative amount of deliberate intent to change a system or individual and on the distribution of power. Bennis, Benne, and Chin have pointed out such a comparison in their book, *The Planning of Change*.[17] The book lists several ways in which change may occur. The ones which seem applicable to organizations are as follows:

1. *Indoctrination,* which is a deliberate attempt to change both from the point of view of the social system and the communicator of the change, as well as a case of mutual goal setting. The power, however, is not balanced. Organizational examples would be prisons, schools, and many large corporations.
2. *Coercive change* is a method involving the lack of mutual goal setting, imbalanced power and so, of course, deliberateness on one side only. The best examples of coercive change are the well-known brainwashing incidents during recent wars.
3. *Interactional change* involves mutual goal setting, fairly equal power distribution but has little or no deliberate intent. There may

be an unconscious attempt to change the other party such as within married couples.
4. *Socialization change* is a kinship kind of change which is like a parent-child or teacher-pupil relationship.
5. *Emulative change* is most common to formal organizations and is brought about when subordinates attempt to identify with and emulate their superior with goal setting by the subordinate.
6. *Mutual changes* are spontaneous, accidental changes which are not deliberate and have no real goal setting.
7. *Planned change,* as we have already indicated, is usually most effective, involves equal power, mutual goal setting, and deliberateness on the part of all concerned.

Rogers and Shoemaker point out another useful way to view social change which is to focus on the source of the message. These source-oriented viewpoints suggested by Rogers and Shoemaker are known as *imminent change* and *contact change*.[18] *Imminent change* occurs when the members of a social system originate and/or create an innovation and spread that innovation within the system. The innovation is created and implemented within the system, usually with no help from outside the system. *Contact change* occurs when extra-system sources introduce an innovation into the system. Contact is inter-system rather than intra-system and may be either *directed* or *selective*. *Directed contact change* occurs when a person or persons, outside the system to be changed, seeks to implement a planned change within that system in order to achieve predetermined goals established outside the system. In this sense of the word "outside," we usually consider a manager to be outside his social system of subordinates. *Selected contact change,* on the other hand, occurs when the members of a social system are exposed to externally originated change and decide whether to adopt or reject the change based upon their own needs.

Perhaps the best method of all to categorize changes is to look at them from the standpoint of individuals in organizations and see what sort of decision options they have as to whether to adopt or reject a change. Rogers and Shoemaker tell us that there are really three types of innovation-decision positions in which an individual may find himself. These three types are *optional innovation-decisions, collective innovation-decisions* and *authoritative innovation-decisions*.[19]

Optional innovation-decisions are the kind of decisions an individual can make with little concern for the other members of the social system. For instance, an individual's decision to live in a ranch home rather than a Cape Cod home is his own decision and what others choose has little or no effect on it. The decision one family makes to eat only organically grown foods is their business, regardless of what anyone else chooses to eat. Such decisions are usually less common in an organization because the very interrelated nature of such formalized social systems allows far fewer truly optional innovation-decisions as we have defined them.

Collective innovation-decisions, on the other hand, are far more common in organizations. They are decisions which the individuals in a social system agree upon by some sort of consensus. Naturally, such a democratic, participative form of decision making carries with it the accompanying demand for conformity to the change decision from all members of the social system, once the decision is made. For instance, once a school system agrees to a certain curricular plan, the individual in that school system has no choice but to adopt the new curriculum.

A collective innovation-decision is really a sum total of a great many individual decisions as in the case of a formal election or even an informal "straw vote." The participation which goes on in a collective innovation-decision is measured by the degree to which individual social system members are involved in the decision-making process. As we will see in subsequent chapters relating to the small work group, member satisfaction and acceptance of decisions tends to increase as the degree of member participation in decision-making processes increases.

Let us now take an even closer look at *authority innovation-decisions* since a great amount of the change decisions in a formal organization are made in this manner. Authority change decisions are made by a person or group of persons in a superordinate power position and forced upon individual subordinates. The unique factor here is that the decision-making person or group is entirely separate from the group that must ultimately adopt or reject the decision to change. In the other types of innovation-decisions the decision to adopt has been made by the person or persons who will be implementing the change.

There is an *adoption unit* which will put the innovation into practice or refuse to put it into practice as the case may be. Then there is the *decision unit* which is in a position of higher authority and makes the initial decision concerning the adoption of the innovation. For instance, the executive board may make the decision to convert to a data-processing system. However, if the individuals in accounting, sales, production and so on, for some reason are unwilling to accept and implement the change decision, the decision is of little value.

In authority decisions, then, individuals are not free to exercise their personal choice in the innovation-decision process. It must, however, be stated that the very authority structure and top-heavy power distribution in a formal organization tends to influence the individual to conform with the decision.

Let us take one more comparative look at these three types of change decisions. Rogers and Shoemaker point out the following characteristics which distinguish *authority innovation-decisions* from the others:

1. The individuals are not free to exercise their choice in adopting or rejecting an innovation.
2. Decision making and adopting are the activities of two separate individuals or units.
3. The decision unit occupies a higher authority position in the social system than the adoption unit.
4. Because of this hierarchical relationship between the decision unit and the adoption unit, the decision unit can force the adoption unit to conform to its decision.
5. Authority innovation-decisions occur most frequently in formal organizations rather than informal social systems.[20]

It should be clear by now that the manager, especially the manager operating in the field, is a communicator of change and is normally engaged most often in the communication of authority innovations. Since this seems true, let us take a closer look at how the authority-innovation process functions.

The following is a paradigm showing the normal steps in the authority innovation-decision process:

1. *Knowledge* about the need for change and the innovation reach the decision unit.
2. *Persuasion* concerning acceptance or rejection of the innovation by the decision unit.
3. *Decision* concerning acceptance or rejection of the innovation by the decision unit.
4. *Communication* of the decision from the decision units to the adoption units in the organization.
5. *Action* or implementation of the decision: adoption or rejection of the innovation by the adoption unit.

When the decision unit has chosen the innovation alternative it wishes to adopt, messages must be transmitted in a *downward flow* from superiors to subordinates, following the authority pattern of hierarchical positions, to the adoption unit. Key figures in such a vertical communication flow are the liaisons who pass along the information. The decision process may either be *authoritative*, where the subordinates or potential adopters do not participate in the original decision, or *participative*, where they do participate.

Since the decision process in most formal organizations is authoritative rather than participative, many problems are posed for the manager. For instance, while the rate of adoption of authoritative decisions is usually faster than that of participative decisions, authoritative decisions are also more likely to be discontinued.

The foregoing paradigm of the steps in the authority innovation-decision process is a big descriptive help in understanding how the process functions. Rogers and Shoemaker provide us with a comparative paradigm showing the steps in each of the three innovation-decision types. They are in the table below.

Functions in authority innovation-decisions	Functions in optional innovation-decisions	Steps in collective innovation-decisions
Knowledge	Knowledge	Stimulation
		Initiation
Persuasion	Persuasion	Legitimation
Decision	Decision	Decision
Communication	—	—
Action	Action	Action

SOURCE: Everett M. Rogers and F. Floyd Shoemaker, *Communication of Innovation*, New York, Free Press, 1971. Reprinted with permission of Macmillan. Copyright © 1971 by The Free Press, a Division of The Macmillan Company.

The reader will note that the steps in the optional innovation-decision process are really the same as the authority innovation-decision steps except the optional process does not require the communication step.

The collective innovation-decision process requires stimulation of interest in the new idea followed by initiation of the new idea by an individual or individuals within the system. The legitimizers are persons of high power within the system who sanction the change. The decision and action steps are the same basic steps as we find in the other types of decision processes.

PLANNING CHANGE

Once organizational managers have analyzed their social system, determined what course of action seems to be best for the system, and identified the potential sources of resistance, they should develop a plan. In an organizational structure most changes must be implemented through the managerial subsystem even though the change idea may have originated at some lower organizational level. Support for such a notion is provided by Katz and Kahn in the following statement:

> The dynamic for change generated in the adaptive structures must always be implemented through the managerial structure. This is so because change will affect the whole organization and top management cannot delegate the responsibility for modifications in basic policy without transforming the organization itself. When the adaptive substructure develops in an organization, the decision-making power with respect to adaptation remains with management.[21]

Through well-planned management strategies, what appear to be insurmountable resistance forces can be turned around and used as forces for change. Such a reverse use of forces of resistance and their own accompanying impetus is pointed out by Lippitt, et al., when they say:

> It is of interest that many resistance forces can be converted into change forces. Resistance forces come into being originally in response to certain needs of the client system. If the client is saying, in effect, that the stauts quo must be maintained because it is the best way to meet these needs, the change agent may be able to show that the same needs would be met even more satisfactorily in a changed set of conditions. Then the very energy which the client system once used to maintain the status quo may shift direction and become an impetus toward change.[22]

But why form a plan? We have already pointed out the inevitability of change. Change is probably the only constant in today's society. It is, therefore, futile to discuss whether or not we will change. It is a far more profitable use of time and energy to discuss how to control and direct change. Clearly, if we are to control and direct change, we must develop methods of planned change. Of course, a further reason for planned change is that anything done haphazardly loses its predictability. With proper planning we should be able to make changes happen almost on cue and with highly predictable outcomes.

What is planned change? Some writers and researchers prefer to think of planned change as any deliberate change attempt. Considering our stated desire to control, manage, and predict the outcomes of change, we should restrict our definition of "planned" change a bit more. Based upon that premise, planning includes more than simply an overt desire to change something. We will consider the planning of change to include such things as social system analysis, research utilization, and strategic application of existing communication research. Chapter 5 of this book will deal with research in the form of strategies.

If an organization is going to plan its changes, who should do the planning? The question is really where the power to implement change is found within an organization. The placement of such power may range all the way from a totally participative system to a completely authoritative approach.

The *participative approach* involves a great deal of organizational interaction, especially between levels. Decision-making power is shared by all those who are affected by the change. The participative end of this placement of power continuum is characterized by consultation, sharing, and equality. As we have already pointed out, there are some extra advantages accruing to the organization taking a participative approach to decision making.

On the other end of the power placement continuum we find the *authoritative approach* in which those affected have nothing to say about what changes will be made; not how or when they will be made. The authoritative approach may be characterized by one-way communication, heavy power at the top, and very little interaction, with orders being given and obeyed.

With any kind of continuum we find most real entities somewhere along the continuum and not at either extreme. So it is with the foregoing power placement continuum. Very few organizations totally relinquish control to a system of total participation. Just as few organizations in this enlightened age can afford to be totally authoritarian.

If a change plan is developed, then it must follow a definable pattern which would have to include at least some sort of mechanism for a change subplan and a communication subplan. The plan must include provisions for motivating systems to relinquish the status quo, to change, and finally to stabilize the new status quo. Such a plan is suggested by Bennis et al., when they wrote of the process of unfreezing, changing, and refreezing which follows:

STAGE 1 *Unfreezing*: creating motivation to change
Mechanisms: a. Lack of confirmation or disconfirmation
               b. Induction of guilt-anxiety
               c. Creation of psychological safety by reduction of threat or removal of barriers

STAGE 2 *Changing*: developing new responses based on new information
Mechanisms: a. Cognitive redefinition through
  i) Identification: information from a single source
  ii) Scanning: information from multiple sources
STAGE 3 *Refreezing*: stabilizing and integrating the changes
Mechanisms: a. Integrating new responses into personality
  b. Integrating new responses into significant ongoing relationships through reconfirmation[23]

It is interesting to note that once the change is accomplished and implemented, the strategy is to establish the change as a new status quo that probably will eventually become the target of yet another unfreezing and change attempt.

An acquaintance who was a sales representative for a stove company once made the mistake of doing too expert a job of freezing against future change attempts. The firm for which he worked sold only gas ranges and so he constantly told his retail clients that gas cooking was great and electric cooking was tasteless, wasteful, and expensive. He did a very effective job of freezing that attitude in his customers. Suddenly, the firm decided to also manufacture electric ranges and, furthermore, as their newest product, to promote the item very heavily. Embarrassing? Yes, to say the least, it was embarrassing. If it is difficult to unfreeze attitudes and get people who are sold on something to change, it must be even more difficult when you have done the initial freezing yourself. If there is a moral here, it would be that nothing is permanent and part of a good change plan should be to keep as many options open as possible.

As mentioned earlier, the bulk of the remainder of this book deals with communication strategies for managers. For the moment let us look at the elements of a General Electric planned communication program reported by William Scholz. The program is as follows:

a. Preparation of a "source book" outlining the changes to be made, why these changes are necessary, how employees will be affected, and the benefits which will result.
b. Scheduling of one or more meetings with the managers, supervisors, specialists, and others involved, to present to them the full story on the change and answer their questions.
c. Scheduling of one or more meetings with employees, including meetings of the entire group with the manager and meetings of smaller groups with their respective supervisors to give information and answer questions about the planned change.
d. Scheduling of personal interviews between employees and supervisors, or between employees and employee relations people, whenever job changes are involved.

e. A comprehensive program of written and visual communication—including the source book, presentations for managers, presentations for supervisors, discussion guides, manuals, booklets, displays, demonstrations, bulletins, and editorial articles and news items in the employee periodicals.[24]

The process of planned change, then, includes analysis, precise strategies for change and a communication plan through which the change plan can arrive at its destination.

SUMMARY

We have seen in several different ways that the only real constant is change and so change is inevitable. Since it is inevitable, change in an organization should be controlled, managed, and planned or it will be haphazard and unpredictable.

Looking at an organization as a social system and applying what we have already learned about systems theory, it becomes apparent that a change in one subsystem of the system is apt to affect other subsystems. The formal organization is, of course, characterized by stability and the drive toward a steady state. While it would seem that change would be impossible where stability is the goal, the real organizational goal is a dynamic equilibrium. A dynamic equilibrium is a state which allows for change and then is flexible enough to incorporate the new change and readjust to a new steady state at a new level.

There are many barriers to organizational change, such as a lack of planning, the building of private empires, overcentralization of power, and poor communication. These barriers in any organization must be identified and understood in order to successfully communicate and implement a change in that organization. As communicators of change, we must also evaluate the norms of a social system before we can develop and plan a change strategy. We must not only identify the specific norms involved, but we must place the social system norms somewhere on a continuum between the extreme positions of modern norms on one end and traditional norms on the other.

In most communication settings the receivers and the source have a great deal in common, a situation with a high degree of homophily. A communication of change setting, however, is unique in that there is usually a high degree of heterophily present. That is, the source and receivers are apt to be quite dissimilar in attitudes, values, beliefs and so on.

The types of organizational change may be roughly grouped into three categories. Imminent change is change which originates and is handled and implemented within the system. Directed contact change is change in which the members of the social system do not have a free choice of whether to adopt the change or not, while in selective contact change they *do* have a choice. In both types of contact change the change originates outside the social system.

There are also several types of innovation-decisions. Optional innovation-decisions are change decisions which an individual can make without being concerned with the decisions of others in the system. Collective innovation-decisions are decisions reached via participative consensus among the members of the social system. Finally, authoritative innovation-decisions are situations in which one subsystem, the decision unit, makes the decision and another separate subsystem, the adoption unit, must implement the decision.

Every organization is structured to resist change. The resistance may be a function of the individual personalities or a function of the social system itself. Because of this ever-present resistance it is necessary to plan our change strategies. The plan must include system analysis, utilization of research in the form of strategies, and a communication plan.

NOTES

1. Willard V. Merrihue, *Managing By Communication*, Englewood Cliffs, N.J., Prentice-Hall, 1962, p. 141.
2. Everett M. Rogers and F. Floyd Shoemaker, *Communication of Innovations: A Cross-Cultural Approach*, New York, Free Press, 1971, p. 19.
3. Ibid., p. 304.
4. Thomas L. Berg and Abe Shuchman (eds.), *Product Strategy and Management*, New York, Holt, Rinehart and Winston, 1963, p. 49.
5. Daniel Katz and Robert L. Kahn, *The Social Psychology of Organizations*, New York, Wiley, 1966.
6. Rogers and Shoemaker, op. cit., pp. 30–31.
7. Ibid., pp. 32–33.
8. Ibid., p. 32.
9. Clovis R. Shepherd, *Small Groups: Some Sociological Perspectives*, New York, Intext, 1964, p. 70.
10. Leon Festinger, *A Theory of Cognitive Dissonance*, New York, Harper & Row, 1957.
11. Matthew B. Miles (ed.), *Innovation in Education*, Bureau of Publications, Teachers College, Columbia University, New York, 1964, p. 435.
12. Goodwin Watson, "Resistance to Change," in Goodwin Watson (ed), *Concepts for Social Change*, Vol. 1, Cooperative Project for Educational Development Series, Washington, D.C., National Training Laboratories, 1966.
13. Ibid.
14. Ronald Lippitt, Jeanne Watson, and Bruce Westly, *The Dynamics of Planned Change*, New York, Harcourt Brace Jovanovich, 1958, p. 3.

15. H. A. Simon, *Administrative Behavior* (2nd ed.), New York, Macmillan, 1957, p. 108.
16. Paul F. Lazarfeld and Robert K. Merton, "Friendship As Social Process: A Substantive and Methodological Analysis," in Monroe Berger et al. (eds.), *Freedom and Control in Modern Society,* New York, Octagon, 1964, p. 34.
17. Warren G. Bennis, Kenneth D. Benne, and Robert Chin (eds.), *The Planning of Change,* New York, Holt, Rinehart and Winston, 1969, pp. 83–84.
18. Rogers and Shoemaker, op. cit., pp. 8–9.
19. Ibid., p. 36.
20. Ibid., pp. 302–303.
21. Katz and Kahn, op. cit., p. 96.
22. Lippitt, Watson, and Westly, op. cit., p. 86.
23. Warren G. Bennis, Edgar H. Schein, David E. Berlew, and Fred I. Steele (eds.), *Interpersonal Dynamics,* Homewood, Ill., Dorsey Press, 1964, p. 363.
24. William Scholz, *Communication in the Business Organization,* Englewood Cliffs, N.J., Prentice-Hall, 1962, p. 152.

5 communication as a management tool

Communication has loomed so large and has become so vital as a part of business management that it is indeed difficult to ascertain where one commences and the other intermeshes. Management, of course, is the primary director of business enterprise by which the goals of an organization are produced.

Harold Zelko and Frank E. X. Dance

OBJECTIVES for Chapter 5

After reading the chapter you should be able to:

1. Name the reasons for the heavy demand for improved organizational communication and give an example of each.

2. Develop a simulated communication plan including as many factors from Chapter 5 as you can.

3. Discuss the organizational problem areas expressed by supervisors.

4. Describe the need for a linking system and give as many examples of liaisons or links as possible.

5. Give an example of each organizational communication role.

6. Discuss the factors important in settling and adjusting grievances.

7. Compare and contrast the managerial role and change facilitator, motivator, and small group leader.

8. Compare and contrast the three general types of ethical standards.

L ET us now take one final look at the problems that are basically communication problems to be faced by the manager of an organization. The performance of managers is usually measured by the output of their subordinates. The degree of success managers achieve and even their future as managers is highly dependent upon their subordinates and the achievement of those subordinates. Managers cannot be successful unless their subordinates are successful. The subordinates are a mirror of the managerial abilities of the managers and top managers must have the understanding and cooperation of every subordinate.

How do managers gain this understanding and cooperation? There may be management techniques available; however, basically, the success of any technique selected depends upon the quality of the communication. It is communication that provides the transmission vehicle for any technique chosen and controls to a great extent the degree of success attainable. In other words, if the accompanying communication attempt fails, there is no way that the basic management attempt can succeed. As pointed out in the quotation at the beginning of this chapter, management is "primary" to organizational goal achievement and nothing is more vital to management than communication.

In the past few years the effectiveness of communication has been recognized as even more pivotal to organizational success. According to Zelko and Dance, today's organization "finds itself in the middle of more tangible developments which place heavy demands on communication such as growth and size, complexity and technology, competition, unions, and research."[1] These organizational needs will be explored in more detail throughout this chapter. For the moment, however, let us take a brief look at how these factors have caused an ever-increasing demand to be made upon communication.

There has probably never been a time when organizational *growth and size* have been on more of a runaway course than at present. As organizations grow in size and spread out hierarchically as well as geographically, the demands upon organizational communication are naturally increased. The number of additional subordinates, the additional levels of management, and the greater distances between points are all growth and size factors which affect communication. Recall that earlier we cited research stating that as little as approximately 20 percent of the original message reached its destination as it flowed down through only five hierarchical levels. The organizational challenge, then, is really to devise more effective means of communication.

Since the advent of automation and other space age technologies, communication has been challenged particularly by *complexity and technology*. Naturally, the more technical communication gets, the less apt it is to be effective. Meanings are obscure enough from one communicator to another, but technology has multiplied that difficulty many times. The dilemma is further complicated, not only by increasing technology, but by an even faster human growth which causes an even greater tendency toward individuality. Communication effectiveness and the need for innovative communication methods are stretched to their zenith. On one hand, there is a technical society which needs to reduce everyone to a number for the sake of expedience alone. At the same time, the individuals in that society are screaming louder than ever, "Look at me. I'm a living, human individual and not a number." Again, a very taxing communication problem.

Communication is extremely important to an organization in an environment that seems at times to be based almost totally upon *competition*. Competition in business often means that the firm which cannot get its message across to the society will not be very effective and competitive. Communication effectiveness in dealing with competition can be looked at both externally and internally, as we have seen in Chapter 2. Whether we are dealing with external or internal communication, competition does constantly test the ingenuity of our communication strategies.

Probably no single factor in the last several decades has had a greater effect on organizational communication than the advent of *unions*. When unions really began to make their presence felt, the need for communication between hierarchical levels quickly became apparent. Often the unions themselves have had more effective communication internally than the firms. A cooperative organizational relationship is the foundation of a unionized organization, both at the negotiation table and away from it. Such a cooperative relationship is only possible through effective communication.

Improved *research* methods have helped identify and improve upon the solving of organizational communication problems. The conclusions of the communication researcher have provided management with plenty of potential strategies. As we will see later in this chapter, however, the transformation of research findings into useful strategies is not that simple and does not happen nearly often enough.

It is obvious that a organization cannot function without an effective communication system. As managers we must become aware of the communication situations all around us and then develop communication strategies from the available research findings. As we become aware of communication improvement, we must be careful not to be a boor about our awareness. If we carry the awareness to extremes we may be like the cartoon of the psychologists' convention showing the participants singing, "For he's an *adequate* fellow" to the guest of honor.

Before we look into the ways in which communication may be used as a management tool, let us take another look at communication itself. As we discussed in Chapter 2, there are as many different definitions of communication as there are people attempting to define it. Some definitions are fairly elaborate and try to specify as much as possible. Berelson and Steiner, for instance, define communication as follows:

> Communication: The transmission of information, ideas, emotions, skills, etc., by the use of symbols—words, pictures, figures, graphs, etc. It is the *act* or *process* of transmission that is usually called communication.[2]

On the other hand, some communication definitions are very short and general such as Theodore Clevenger's definition which simply states that, "Communication is a term used to refer to any dynamic, information sharing process."[3]

Perhaps the most useful definition of communication for the manager in an organization is, after all, the one that concentrates on the "transfer of meaning." Recall that in Chapter 2, while discussing the Berlo communication concepts, we pointed out how difficult it is for the receiver of a communication to get the same meaning from a message as the original one intended by the source. No matter what type of organizational communication concerns us, the real purpose of that communication is to create a desired meaning in the mind of the receiver. It is really the business of getting information accurately from point A to point B. We should keep in mind that totally identical source-receiver meanings are the "brass rings" we are reaching for and are not very likely to grasp fully. A few years ago a college football coach who is a strong proponent of a grinding ground game said of the forward pass, "There are only three things that can happen when you pass and two of them are bad." Likewise, it can be said that when we communicate, and remember, we *must,* there are only three things which can happen and two of them are bad. When the smoke has cleared from any communication attempt, we will find we have either understanding (good), misunderstanding (bad), or no understanding at all (also bad).

DEVELOPING A COMMUNICATION PLAN

As managers, we must be concerned about the development of an effective communication subsystem plan. This does not necessarily mean a communication director and a formalized message center, although in a large organization these may become necessary. A communication subsystem in this sense means something far more pervasive than a resident expert. The real need is for a subsystem that is actually a part of all other subsystems. Such a plan would train all personnel, especially the managers, to think of themselves as communication experts and practitioners.

First, let us consider the general purposes or uses of organizational communication that can be grouped as being either cooperative or competitive. Cooperative purposes may be simply internal cooperation but also may include such tasks as training, problem solving, and information sharing of any kind. Competitive purposes, on the other hand, may include such things as labor negotiations, the locations of problems, and power position struggles which inevitably seem to develop in organizations.

A communication system and plan must start with a clear statement of both the organizational and the communication subsystem objectives. Further, these objectives should be both long and short range. Short-range goals or objectives might be such things as solving labor problems, communicating various changes, or adjustments in quality standards. Long-range goals might be such factors as public relations programs, training programs, establishment of work standards, or cooperative employee relations plans.

The organizational structure will have some natural hazards of its own built in. Any plan must take these into account and include some methods of overcoming the existing structurally oriented communication problems. Any new communication, plans and/or structural alterations in the total plan, must be prioritied according to importance. The most immediate and pressing needs of the organization will have to come first, with other projects taking lower priorities. If too much is attempted at once, all projects are probably doomed to certain failure. An important consideration in the setting of priorities is timing. Not only can the organization not stand too much all at once, but it is more susceptible to certain programatic changes at one time than it is at another.

The plan of the communication subsystem must also include motivational considerations. If we are to expect a plan to affect the attitudes and performance of subordinates we must motivate them in terms of *their* needs and in terms of what is good for *them.*

Finally, the plan must include a method of selling ideas and evaluating the results. We can develop the best communication plan ever devised but if we have neglected the selling of the plan, it is all for naught. In other words, we must develop a way of communicating our communication plan. There must also be a follow-up method through which we can evaluate the results and make any corrections necessary in the plan.

Communication planning and development is not so different from other kinds of planning. According to Scholz it requires:

1. The setting of specific goals.
2. Analysis of factors which may facilitate or hinder the attainment of the goals.
3. Weighing of alternative courses of action.
4. Choosing the most appropriate course.
5. Setting down in black and white the specific steps to be taken to reach the goals.
6. Providing for a definite sequence and timetable of activities, pinpointing of responsibilities and measurement of results.[4]

Although such a plan does not seem too difficult to devise, in practice the improvement of organizational communication is not always so easy. According to A. W. Lindh, a management consultant, there are several clues to what may be wrong with today's efforts to improve communication. They are:

1. A failure to grasp what good communication is in the first place.
2. The "canned" approach to communication inherent in many "how-to" programs, often ignores the fact that communicating is a changing, highly personal activity with roots deep in each individual's personality—and not just a mechanical process of "words in and words out."
3. Many current efforts to achieve better communication imply that the process can be learned in a classroom or from books.
4. Much of management's present effort to improve communications assumes that people are willing to admit that they lack communication skills, and they are eager to overcome their shortcomings.
5. Most important of all, much of the effort to achieve "good communications" seemed to be focused on the paperwork and mechanisms of communicating—thus, the emphasis on house-organs, employee bulletins, memos, and other paraphernalia.[5]

Given the organizational needs for communication improvement and the foregoing barriers to that improvement, what approach would work? Apparently, according to research, what is needed is an approach based on voluntary participation, an honest "leveling" between hierarchical levels, and a real effort to diagnose organizational communication problems.

DIAGNOSING ORGANIZATIONAL COMMUNICATION PROBLEMS

It is often very difficult to identify organizational communication problems and determine their origins. This is especially difficult if we are to attempt to identify and head off these problems in any kind of preventive manner. A great deal more is required than just a scientific guess method in order to diagnose organizational problems. Borman et al., in their book *Interpersonal Communication in the Organization*,[6] report the results of a pilot study which rather clearly points out the potential inaccuracy of such a guess. They report that when they asked a group of managers to rank ten already identified morale factors in order of probable importance to their subordinates, the managers ranked the following as the last three:

 8. Full appreciation of work done.
 9. Feeling "in on things."
10. Sympathetic help on personal problems.

The researchers then asked the employees to rank these same ten morale factors in order of importance to them. They ranked these same three factors as follows:

1. Full appreciation of work done.
2. Feeling "in on things."
3. Sympathetic help on personal problems.

It is hardly reasonable that a group of managers could be so wrong about the attitudes and the needs of their subordinates; the fact remains, they were, and the discrepancy may not be all that uncommon. Most important, however, is the obvious need for improved communication and for research entailing considerably more than just guesswork if we are to make any meaningful diagnosis of organizational problems and needs. A sensitivity must be developed between management and its subordinates if we are to get accurate information.

By the same token, the middle and lower-range manager or supervisor also has unanswered problems and too little understanding coming his way. As we pointed out in Chapter 2, the manager at this level has the unusual problem of facing both directions in the organizational hierarchy, sometimes simultaneously. The problem seems to be the same from level to level regardless of what position on the hierarchy we isolate, except that those on either the extreme top or bottom only have one way to look when communicating.

A general question, which seems to be highly pervasive at all levels in all organizations, is how to be a more effective manager. Haiman and Hilgert note that:

> The common question which all supervisors ask is, "What can I do to be a more effective manager of people?" This question has been at the core of supervisory management for all recorded history. It is the key supervisory management question today, and it will continue to be the key question in the future.[7]

Perhaps there is no better way to get to the heart of the organization than to open up the lines of communication by asking the subordinates what we want to know. At a recent seminar for first-line supervisors we asked the participants to brainstorm for the sort of questions that troubled them most. The list was as follows:

> What information should be passed upward and what should be handled at that level?
> Upgrading worker self-image and tying to self-image.
> Working smarter and not necessarily harder.
> Hiring screening—knowing Mr. Right for your operation.
> How to improve management-labor relationships?
> How can you effectively supervise so that the work is done well and not create ill feeling?
> How do you control rumors?
> How do you communicate ideas clearly?
> Can problems be effectively handled with individuals privately without causing problems with other members of the department?
> How can you fire someone gracefully?
> How can you hire someone effectively?
> How can you handle grievance problems?
> How to maintain effective discipline among subordinates?

Interestingly, the organizations and the people may change but the questions stay pretty much the same. One of the major faults with diagnostic methods is that they have remedies for unknown problems, answers where there are no questions, if you will. Actually the fault is caused by making definitive statements instead of asking questions. For instance, after asking the participants of that seminar what their problems were and accumulating the list above, the areas for discussion were clear.

Through open communication between levels, we can develop the ability to forecast and predict organizational needs and problems. We should be able to forecast in a way that increases management's lead time in recognizing problems. The lead time would enable an earlier diagnosis of problems and early remedial action. How, then, do we measure the communication practices and their effectiveness in an organization?

In Chapter 3 we examined briefly several methods of organizational analysis. They were resident analysis, participation analysis, duty study, cross-section analysis, and ECCO analysis. Whatever method, or methods, are employed, the analysis must answer questions about the formal flow of written and oral information, the informal flow of oral information, the role relationships between superior and subordinate, and any existing barriers or factors contributing to communication breakdowns. The method of analysis used to examine organizational communication must be devised from existing research and be based upon the organizational needs and structure at a given time. In other words, there is no method of analysis that will be generally right or wrong, but, if we follow these precepts, we will probably end up with a tailor-made measuring device.

RESEARCH UTILIZATION

The validity of any measurement, diagnosis, or research depends, or should depend, upon its usefulness to others as a foundation for strategic planning. Knowledge is of no value whatever if it cannot be imparted to, and used by, someone. The paucity of research and knowledge utilization is one of the great wastes of our time. It is really more of a problem of understanding and implementation. According to Warren Bennis, the problem poses the following questions:

1. How does the organization get its information? from its staff? outside consultants? specialized sources? other firms?
2. How does the organization store and retrieve information?
3. What social processes inhibit implementation of valid ideas and what social processes facilitate implementation? For example, the *relationship* between staff and line is probably significant in understanding the process of knowledge utilization within the firm. Similarly, the relationships between external consultants and members of the firm are equally crucial. Can we identify and understand the

qualities of an effective "helping relationship"? What modes of collaboration have been developed which lead to achievement of goals?
4. I am particularly interested in understanding how ideas are transmitted across political and academic frontiers, another variant of the knowledge-utilization process.[8]

This author is in the somewhat unusual position of having been a practitioner—a district sales manager—and now is a teacher, researcher and author. There is knowledge and communication research available now and within the span of awareness of the author that would have been a great help during the sales-management days. But, typically, few managers know where to look for the results of helpful research. Even if the research results can be found, the managers do not really have time to read them and, even if they take the time to read them, can't understand the jargon in which they are written. This very real communication problem is pointed up vividly by Revans, when he says:

> And what papers describing original research do appear in management literature are not usually about the real time activities of management as such: They are generally about economics, or mathematics, or psychology, or other established disciplines. And even if they are then of some relevance to industry or commerce, it is not always easy to see this relevance in terms of management action or management education.[9]

So the practitioner-managers look at the research and say, "So what? What do we care about that stuff." They see a piece of source credibility research and say, "We don't have the time for that. What we need to do is improve our image with our subordinates." Imagine that! They are standing right in the middle of a valid, well-researched answer to their problem and are looking all around for remedies.

The problem here is a crying need to get the man of knowledge and the man of action together. The man of knowledge seems to feel that once he has created a body of knowledge through his research, it is up to the man of action to find it and use it. On the other hand, the man of action may look upon the man of knowledge as some sort of effete snob who works in an ivory tower and might live under a rock. There is a tremendous communication problem here and, unless that communication is improved, knowledge utilization will naturally suffer.

Researchers are wasting their time if they run off in all directions at once doing first this piece of research and then that without ever asking the practitioners what they need to know or can put to use. No wonder they cannot use the research when it does not deal directly, or perhaps at all, with their real needs. Of course, the practitioners must also share any blame, since they also have communication responsibilities. It should be the practitioners' responsibility to make their problems, wishes, and needs known to the researcher.

In 1972, Clarence Smith and some other members of the organizational communication division of the International Communication Association conducted a survey entitled "Closing the Gap Between Communication Researchers and Practitioners." Of the 105 respondents to the survey instrument, 31 were practitioners, 26 were researchers, and 4 described themselves as both.

The survey first asked a question concerning the needs of the organizations and then asked a question related to the perceived differences between organizational researchers and practitioners. The survey results were as follows:

QUESTION 1. *What are the two greatest communication research needs in your organization?*

29 responses—How to find out who's supposed to do what to whom in this organization
13 responses—How to find out what the boss wants
12 responses—How to evaluate methods and media
 4 responses—How to implement what we know
             How to measure communication effectiveness
             Credibility of communication
             Interpersonal networks
             How to apply systems approach to communication
 3 responses—How to find out how well the organization is performing
             How to plan and implement communication efforts
 2 responses—How to interview better
             Feedback
             What should be taught to whom
             Communication as a change agent
             Effects of goal setting on values
             How to measure communication needs
             Cross-cultural communication
             How to identify communication problems
 1 response—Socio-psychological aspects of communication
             Making a skills inventory
             Effects of attitude on behavior
             Effects of communiction on personal and organizational health
             Group process
             Organizational structure
             How to change people
             Compressed speech
             Handling complex data

QUESTION 2. *Define and discuss the differences you perceive between organizational researchers and practitioners.*

[Responses to this second question were essays written on the backs of the questionnaires. The researchers felt that an attempt to abstract a valid statistical report from responses would have little merit but perhaps something can be learned from impressions gained in reading them:]

1. There is general agreement on the specific activities engaged in by practitioners and by researchers.
2. Many make the point that to be effective, the researcher and practitioner each need some of the skills of the other.
3. Comments made by researchers and practitioners about each other frequently gave off a somewhat supercilious air; perhaps bad news for "closing the gap." Practitioners seem to sometimes feel that researchers are not sufficiently scientific.
4. In some cases, both practitioners and researchers appeared to see surprisingly little relationship between the concerns of research and practice. That is, some practitioners seem to assume that research has little to do with their work; some researchers reciprocate the feeling.[10]

Actually the worlds of the person from the knowledge system and the person from the action system are so far apart that the answer to the problem may lie in the area of a third party mentioned in Chapter 3. We may very well need some kind of *linking system* to bridge the gap between the research system and the client system. For instance, in the agricultural area it is a long communication distance between the agricultural researchers and the farmer client. The link that is provided in this case is embodied in the cooperative extension agents who have access to, and understanding of, each system. They can, therefore, communicate information both ways from their position. The linker referred to here is really what we have called a liaison in Chapter 3.

The term *liaison* denotes a connector, a linker, a coordinator. Within the social sciences there have been a number of terms which have some degree of overlap with the concept of the liaison communication role. Managers of organizations have realized, for quite a long period of time, the importance of a component such as this, which serves to coordinate the activities of some larger set of components in the system. Some of the earliest formal organizations in history—military and religious organizations—have employed liaisons in their formal structure to coordinate the operation of various units.

We must also develop the skills of retrieving and organizing knowledge that can link up to the needs of the practitioners. It is equally important that we develop a method of clarifying practitioner needs. This needed development undoubtedly means we must set out in a very overt way to train linking agents.

One big linking system which already exists is our library system. One interesting variation of the library system has been the Diffusion Document Center gathered by Everett Rogers which has on file several thousand research documents, many of them unpublished, one-of-a-kind materials. The linking function and facilitation of research utilization brought about by such a knowledge center is immeasurable.

In summary, Warren Bennis provides us with several issues in research utilization:

1. Organizations are microcosms.
2. Behavioral scientists are becoming more committed to the problem of application of their knowledge.
3. The utilization of knowledge and its implementation is a key problem for behavioral scientists.
4. The key to the knowledge utilization problem is collaboration between the producers and the users of knowledge.
5. The value systems of the scientists and the practitioners must be enriched and revitalized.[11]

As Bennis further points out concerning the need for linking, "And while the French moralist may be right when he says that there are no delightful marriages, just good ones, it is possible that if practitioners and students of organizations get their heads together, they will develop delightful organizations—just possibly."[12]

THE DESIGNATION OF COMMUNICATION ROLES

One way to examine communication as a management tool is to look at the organizational roles a manager may assume at one time or another. As we pointed out in Chapter 2, some organizations hire their token "communication man" and feel that they are being super progressive. While it is sometimes helpful to have a resident communication specialist for consulting or special communication problems, the rest of the management staff must not take this as a cue to think of themselves as something other than communication strategists.

We also pointed out in Chapter 2 that the communication situations for a manager may range all the way from face-to-face communication, through small-group and speaker-audience communication, and into mass communication.

Earlier in this book we spoke of the role of communication in management. The role we speak of here is a list of functions that go with a certain position in an organization. A definition of role in this case might be *a shared expectation of behavior which accompanies a position in the organizational hierarchy.*

There are, of course, formal and informal role designations. For a manager, the formal role designations would be such functions as might be made clear in a management-training program or even spelled out in writing in the form of a job description. There are, however, a set of functions with which a manager must deal classifiable as informal role designations. These informal roles are every bit as important to the successful manager and every bit as much of a shared expectation. The difference is that they are more subtle and not written down anywhere. For this reason, the effective manager must be even more aware of them.

According to Haiman and Hilgert, there are several basic management functions: planning, organization, staffing, directing and controlling.[13] All of these are obviously dependent upon some form of communication in order to achieve any amount of success.

Planning, as we have seen earlier in this chapter, involves the setting of predetermined goals, policies and procedures. Planning not only requires a well-developed communication system but serves as a primary function to the rest of these functions. *Organizing* involves such things as assigning and allocating jobs. It may be necessary to design a workable structural framework in the system before one can even consider any kind of division of labor. *Staffing* involves recruiting, hiring and firing. Although a personnel department often gets involved in these activities in larger organizations, the manager is still the primary selector and trainer of the staff.

The *directing* function includes such supervisory activities as guiding and motivating subordinates. The communication skills necessary to give orders and instructions and to carry out the coaching activities for which a manager is responsible are extremely important. Finally, *controlling* involves goal achievement and is really the essence of management. It includes the evaluation results of any corrective action deemed necessary. All five of these managerial functions are closely related and cannot really be separated.

More specifically, Zelko and Dance tell us that there are certain management practices which require communication to make them go. They are:

    Leadership
    Recognition and participation
    Consultation
    Delegation

Teamwork
Counseling
Decision making
Climate developing[14]

These practices are in a very real sense managerial roles, or subroles, as we have defined managerial roles. *Leadership* is basically self-explanatory and will also be covered in detail in Chapter 8. *Recognition* and *participation* and *decision making,* as well as *consultation* and *teamwork* have to do with human relations, face-to-face communication and the degree to which subordinates are involved in decision making and such things as the setting of work objectives. Again, these matters will be covered in greater detail in Chapter 8.

Delegation requires skillful and well-planned communication. Delegation is partially the giving of directives and orders which need to be communicated accurately. Delegation is further, however, the dissemination of portions of administrative power and authority. Many managers fail because it is said that they cannot, or will not, delegate responsibility but are really unable or unwilling to relinquish the other half of delegation which is the right to be wrong occasionally.

Counseling has become an important management function in recent years, particularly as a morale factor. A highly emotional level of communication is often required for counseling since it frequently takes the form of sitting down with great empathy and talking through a problem with a subordinate. Many organizations train their managers specifically in this skill because of its special importance.

Climate development is perhaps the most important management function simply because it is so basic to all the others. The manager of a work group, just as the teacher in a classroom, must develop a social and work climate in which inputs can be maximized and optimization will occur. There is an abundance of research pointing to the notion that little productivity is apt to occur in a climate that makes people so tense, for instance, that even concentration is not possible. In many work environments all that is really needed is to develop the proper climate, tell the people what needs to be done, and then get out of their way and let them do the job.

Conflict reduction

We have pointed out that an organizational role is a "shared expectation." The term shared in this case means generally agreed upon, since there will always probably be some degree of *conflict*. Conflict refers to such things as antagonisms, tensions, and frustrations and is, of course, always present to some extent in organizations or any relationships. It is safe to state there never has been, and never will be, an absolutely conflict-free organization. Therefore it becomes another key function of management to reduce conflict. We say "reduce" because it is already clear that conflict will never be eliminated as long as people are involved.

Before discussing the manager's conflict-reduction function it might be helpful to examine the causes of conflict. Richard C. Huseman points out that there are three major causes of conflict: *organizational structure, inadequate performance measures,* and *ambiguity.*[15]

The *organizational structure* itself is a conflict-causing factor because of its formalized hierarchy and division of tasks. Without setting out to do so, the formal structure can pit one substructure against another. The accounting department feels that the sales department is receiving "favored nation" treatment of some kind. An attempt to appease the accounting department then will frustrate the sales department. And so it goes, on and on. The whole business of structure-oriented conflict resolution requires all of the communication strategy and other management techniques that a manager can muster.

Performance measurement can also cause serious conflict in an organization. The measurement of success in a sales department, for instance, is usually sales volume. In an insurance company a tremendous sales volume may be good for the sales department but indiscriminate customer selection can cause the underwriting department—and, in the longer run, the claims department—a great deal of trouble. Many insurance companies have resolved such conflicts by making "accepted" business the criteria for their sales contests, thereby making it a futile waste of time to sell to unacceptable customers. At any rate, a reward for a performance which is not in the interest of the entire organization is bound to cause conflict.

Communication enters most strongly into the scene of organizational conflict when we consider *ambiguity.* The complexity and uncertainty common to large organizations are bound to result in a certain amount of ambiguity. We have already seen that communication, at its best, is ambiguous. Directives, for instance, which are given ambiguously have conflict built right into them. Each subordinate who hears the directive perceives it as something different. Naturally, then, this added ambiguity presents additional communication problems which must be managed through improved communication strategies.

There are a number of methods through which the manager may

reduce conflict. We may, in fact, refer to this entire managerial communication function as *conflict management*. What is really involved in such a management function is the simultaneous filtering, selecting, and training of subordinates who can perform well under normal conflict conditions. In other words, people must be able to function well in an environment that contains some conflict, because it will never be abolished completely. Further, they function best in this environment if they know that management is doing all it can to minimize conflict and keep the conflicts limited to areas and levels that they can tolerate.

The place of communication in conflict reduction cannot be overstated. Such conflict-reducing techniques as participative decision making require a great deal of communication expertise. Decentralized decision making, open channels for information flow, and training (especially communication training) are all methods of conflict reduction involving communication as their principal tool. It is apparent, then, that conflict can either be functional or dysfunctional and, when it is dysfunctional, communication can play a significant role in reducing such conflict.

Labor and grievance settlement

Another management function requiring a full complement of communication skills is any form of arbitration—from the settlement of minor grievances to the signing of major labor contracts. It is interesting to note that minor grievances not handled quickly and properly often result in major labor problems. Communication is the key to the proper handling of these grievances.

According to Haiman and Hilgert, a manager attempting to develop a sound interpersonal communication strategy in order to satisfactorily adjust grievances should observe the following checklist:

1. Be available
2. Learn how to listen
3. Do not become angry
4. Define the real problem
5. Get the facts
6. Check the contract
7. Avoid delay
8. Consider the consequences
9. Be consistent
10. Give a clear answer
11. Adjust grievances early
12. Keep records[16]

In any case, the grievance not handled properly in its early stages may develop into a major labor problem. Labor unions are most certainly a permanent part of today's society. Whether in the midst of contract negotiations or between contracts, it is most essential for organizations to keep constructive channels of communication open with their labor unions. There can be no doubt that supervisory problems are multiplied many times by the very presence of a labor union which is really another organization superimposed on the original organization. If a labor union has approximately the same goals as does the organization from which it springs, the effect of a congruently operating organization with the contracted right to challenge management decisions and actions is quite a threat. On the other hand, if the labor union has different goals and is at cross purposes with that organization, the communication problems automatically increase greatly. Basically, the problems, or the lack of them, may be a direct result of the interpersonal relations and communication openness between first-line supervisors and their union counterpart, the shop stewards.

Communication and labor relations must take into account, not only the internal communication between the union and management, but also the internal communication patterns in both the management group and the labor union. As mentioned above, the tone of the relationship between management and the union is set at the supervisory-steward level. Certainly the job of collective bargaining requires special skills and is itself a difficult facet of management-union relations. Our concern here, however, is that the manager's day-to-day relations with the union are such that bargaining difficulties are minimized. The management team that feels that open communication with unions and a genuine concern for an informed worker group is only important at contract time has made a serious error. If the day-to-day supervisor-steward relations are not a constant and paramount concern, any negotiations are apt to be an impossible nightmare.

Self-appraisal of performance

Looking back at the many communication roles involved in management, we can see once again that a manager has to be many things to many people; often all at the same time. Obviously, it is important for managers to have a thorough understanding of the various aspects of the managerial role. It is also just as important for managers to be able to evaluate their managerial success at any given time. No manager is likely to be able to handle all functions equally well. Managers must, therefore, maximize their strengths and minimize their weaknesses by understanding what the weaknesses are and working constantly to improve them.

Perhaps managers who intend to be students of their own abilities should create a checklist for themselves like the one shown in the table.

	I do it poorly	I don't like to do it	I find it very tiring	I find it very time-consuming	I find it satisfying	I do it very well
Dealing with people						
Dealing with paper or forms						
Making small decisions						
Working with numbers or data						
Formulating plans or ideas						

Figure 5-1 Chart for appraising one's work in several areas of managerial performance.

Any functions appropriate to the specific manager's job could be used on such a chart. No matter what the criteria, such a chart is a graphic way to categorize the strong and weak points possessed by a manager.

We have already described many of the roles a manager must carry out in an organization. We will now examine briefly three areas, to be covered in greater detail in future chapters, that view managers as communication strategists. The three views look at managers as change agents (Chapter 6), motivators of subordinates (Chapter 7), and as leaders of small task-oriented groups (Chapter 8).

COMMUNICATION OF CHANGE AS A MANAGEMENT TOOL

In Chapter 4 we discovered the inevitability of change, especially in organizations. It was equally obvious that this change must be managed and controlled. One of the most important communication functions of a manager, then, is that of a change agent. More basic, however, is the fact that to exist and lead in a constantly changing environment, managers must be open to change themselves. In order to be open to change a person must have some curiosity. Curiosity is also an essential ingredient in the make-up of effective managers. Managers cannot say that they know their business until they know themselves, their subordinates, and the personality of any group for which they are responsible. All these people look to their managers for help in producing to the limit of their capabilities.

With this thought in mind, perhaps it would be helpful for each of us to examine our own flexibility toward change. To check this flexibility the following questions must be answered "yes" or "no":

	Yes	No
1. Do you dislike getting new/additional assignments?		
2. Do you feel that experience is a poor teacher?		
3. Do you find yourself making the same mistakes over and over?		
4. Are you always up to your neck in today's work when tomorrow's work hits your desk?		
5. Are you usually the last to give up on a cause?		
6. Are people around you always doing the unexpected?		
7. Do you usually come up with one answer for a problem rather than many possible solutions?		
8. Do you find a routine more congenial than doing a constant variety of things?		
9. Do situations often arise which surprise you?		
10. Do you mistrust situations which involve risk?		
Total		
	Yes	No

The ten responses made on the foregoing chart provide a rough indication of a bias toward flexibility or inflexibility. Seven or more "yes" responses indicate a preference for familiar people, tasks, and situations. Seven or more "no" responses indicate that the opposite is true; variety is preferred in work and working colleagues. It does matter whether managers are relatively flexible or inflexible, but it matters even more that they should become aware of their degree of flexibility.

Managers must use their flexibility to influence change in the system and changes in system members. Communication of change strategies take on a great deal of importance for managers as they attempt to influence the organization. Managers must account strategically for resistance to change whether it occurs in the social subsystem, technical subsystem, or both.

Communication is an irreplaceable tool in the successful accomplishment of change. As we unfold the intricacies of the management of change in Chapter 6, we shall see that an equally intricate set of communication strategies is the only answer.

MOTIVATION AS A MANAGEMENT TOOL

Man is an extremely complex being and must be understood in order to be managed. Managerial ability to induce people to work productively and efficiently depends a great deal on how well the manager knows those people as individuals. Managers cannot expect superior results from subordinates unless they know exactly what every subordinate is contributing at the time, and what they are capable of contributing in the near future. As we said before, a manager needs curiosity to uncover this information and a memory, or a filing system, to keep track of it. As managers get to know each of their subordinates over the years, and as each of them changes and develops, the managers will need to make a conscious effort to keep their knowledge up to date. When managers deal in any way with a co-worker or subordinate, knowledge is power. The quality of the results that a work group achieves depends basically upon the knowledge a manager has of the subordinates.

Knowing the subordinates is really the only way a manager can hope to plan a communication strategy for motivating them. This knowledge will help a manager understand which specific needs or wants motivate the subordinates. Most people, however, are generally concerned about:

1. The necessities of life
2. Fair treatment
3. Firm leadership
4. Recognition as an individual
5. A chance to succeed

If we were to make an exhaustive list of the motivation underlying people's behavior it would be very long and very different for each person. However, the general list above does cover the subject pretty well. It goes almost without saying that communication is an ever-present need for most of us. A few people will tell you they do not "need" anyone. Fortunately, an even fewer number actually mean it and for nearly everyone it is true that "people *do* need people" as the song goes. The rare persons who feel no social pressure and *really* do not need to communicate with anyone bear watching, since they have very little to "keep them honest."

Interpersonal trust

It is unlikely that much motivation can take place where there is interpersonal suspicion instead of interpersonal trust. If managers expect to influence their subordinates, the managers must earn their trust. Open communication has to be a key to developing a high level of interpersonal trust. Dean Barnland, in his book *Interpersonal Communication: Survey and Studies,* provides a set of research questions designed to reflect subordinates' trust in their superior. These questions are as follows:

1. Does your superior take advantage of opportunities that come up to further your interests by his actions and decisions?
2. How free do you feel to discuss with your superior the problems and difficulties you have in your job without jeopardizing your position or having it "held against" you later on?
3. How confident do you feel that your superior keeps you fully and frankly informed about things that might concern you?
4. Superiors at times must make decisions which seem to be against the interests of their subordinates. When this happens to you as a subordinate, how much trust do you have that your superior's decision is justified by other considerations?[17]

It becomes apparent from the tone of these questions that trust may be defined as "confidence" or "assured behavior," such as an expectation or predictability. In order to be really effective, interpersonal trust must be a mutual thing. A great deal more can be discovered about trust and its effect upon motivational communication when we examine the findings of source credibility research in Chapter 7.

Morale

An important morale factor in an organization is a trusting relationship. If managers are willing to open up and share things like information and decision making then they are apt to build trust and, in the long run, increase organizational morale. Most subordinates expect to be treated with respect. Even though respecting individual dignity is often time consuming, the time invested can pay large dividends.

A subordinate who is genuinely trusted and whose dignity and point of view is respected will normally be a satisfied subordinate. If a subordinate is dissatisfied with his organizational relationship, probably several things will happen. First, subordinates will suffer morale problems which unfortunately are contagious in an organization. Dissatisfaction also will cause subordinates to search elsewhere for the satisfaction they need. Subordinate needs will be satisfied eventually, whether in or out of the organization. Managers and organizations that can build morale through the satisfaction communicated in a trusting relationship make the managerial role much easier. Such managers are certainly in a position to motivate their subordinates through effective communication.

GROUP LEADERSHIP AS A MANAGEMENT TOOL

Organizational tasks are accomplished most often in small groups. Most managers in the middle and lower ranges of management are really leaders of small task-oriented groups. The research available on small groups and their leadership is highly applicable to management strategy in small organizational work groups. This strategic application will be made more thoroughly in Chapter 8.

We have seen that individuals in organizations have personalities all their own, which must be understood in order to communicate effectively. However, a manager's understanding and knowledge must not be limited to the individuals themselves. Groups are collections of individuals and are therefore also collections of the individual personalities. The result is a group personality.

Managers need to know the personality of each group within their area of responsibility. Each small group has work habits of its own, its own characteristic spirit, and its own pace. One work group will thrive on competition among its members, while another unit will produce more while banding together to out-perform a rival unit. If managers, then, are to help a group realize its potential more fully, they must take into account the distinct personality of that group.

The participative style of management mentioned earlier in this book is based upon small-group research and techniques. The subject of people interacting communicatively in an organization is what participative management is all about. It follows naturally that a manager as a leader of the small work group is responsible for the degree of participation within that group. Managers can be any kind of leader they want within reason. But successful managers will fit their leadership style to the needs of each work group.

Certainly, if the organization is going to have a high degree of participation and the managers are really going to manage, then managers must be skilled in small-group leadership techniques.

THE ETHICAL SIDE OF COMMUNICATION

The subject of ethics is always a difficult one. It is difficult enough for each of us to reach an ethical standard definitely acceptable for ourselves. But to prescribe what is ethical and what is not ethical for someone else is virtually impossible. There is usually, therefore, as little said as possible about ethics in books such as this one. However, if we are to motivate others by persuasive communication, we must be guided by some sort of ethical standards. Warren Bennis points out that:

> Man, before Darwin, was elevated as the "darling of the gods." This Victorian fiction has been dissolved by too many wars, too much poverty, and too many diseased. But we remain a moral and ethical animal; our survival and security depend on the exploitation of moral and ethical systems.[18]

The persuasive motivational techniques available to managers are neither ethical nor unethical; they are simply available techniques. The basic persuasive techniques used by Adolph Hitler, Fidel Castro, and Al Capone are the same as those used by Albert Schweitzer, Billy Graham, and Martin Luther King. The difference is that some of these people "persuaded" from certain ethical standpoints and some from others.

There are no doubt a great many types of ethical standards; however, we can cite three general approaches to ethics. These three types of ethics are *absolute, situational,* and *machiavellian.* An *absolute* ethical standard is one that says "A lie is always a lie." Such a standard is rigid, unalterable, and supports the point of view that "right is right" and "wrong is wrong."

Situational ethics are far more flexible and may be altered to fit the circumstances. In other words, a certain behavior may be unethical in one situation and ethical in another depending upon the circumstances. A *machiavellian* ethic means simply that the "end justifies the means." This type of ethical standard says that any behavior is justifiable and ethical if the final goal is noble enough. Of course, wars have always been justified from a machiavellian point of view by extolling the notion that God was on the side in question, and that it was fighting to preserve freedom in the world.

Each of these ethical standards has drawbacks. The absolute ethic is usually too rigid and, in a free country, is not enforceable, depending rather on individual taste. The situational and machiavellian ethics are, on the other hand, quite flexible and unfortunately quite easily misused. Instead of standards by which we may live, these two ethical styles *can* become post facto shields behind which we may hide. Perhaps the biggest ethical pitfall of all is the fact that so many people live by a situational or machiavellian standard themselves, and at the same time expect everyone else to behave from an absolute standard.

SUMMARY

We have seen that organizations are human groupings which are constructed to attain certain specified goals. We have further seen that the attainment of these goals is far more dependent upon management and communication than we would ever normally imagine. Communication is not only the most important single management tool, some knowledgeable people say that management *is* communication.

If we are to improve organizational management, then we must first improve communication by setting clear organizational communication objectives. As we pointed out in Chapter 2, William Scholz[19] asserts that minimum effective employee communication should assist in the attainment of organizational objectives and the desired organizational image, improve work performance and job satisfaction, and keep managerial decision makers informed relative to employee and public attitudes.

One of the greatest sources of communication improvement could be the existing research. But as we have seen, there is a paucity of research utilization and an urgent need for linking systems to act as two-way intermediaries between the research systems and the client systems.

Although the manager is a communication strategist in everything he does, most particularly he is a facilitator of change, a motivator, and the leader of a task-oriented small group. With this thought in mind, in Part II of this book we will explore these communication strategies. We will also expand on the ethical considerations brought out in this chapter since, without ethics, these strategies can be dangerous weapons.

And now let us move into Part II and the examination of the practical, strategic applications of communication research so vital to effective organizational management.

NOTES

1. Harold Zelko and Frank E. X. Dance, *Business and Professional Speech Communication,* New York, Holt, Rinehart and Winston, 1965, p. 17.
2. Bernard Berelson and Gary A. Steiner, *Human Behavior,* New York, Harcourt Brace Jovanovich, 1964, p. 527.

3. Theodore Clevenger, Jr., "What Is Communication," Taskgroup Letter No. 2, NSSC Committee on Extant Theory, *Journal of Communication 9,* (March, 1959) 5.
4. William Scholz, *Communication in the Business Organization,* Englewood Cliffs, N.J., Prentice-Hall, 1962, p. 49.
5. A. W. Lindh, "Plain Talk About Communicating in Business," *Business Management, 26* (April, 1964) 91–95.
6. Ernest G. Bormann, William S. Howell, Ralph G. Nichols, George L. Shapiro, *Interpersonal Communication in the Organization,* Englewood Cliffs, N.J., Prentice-Hall, 1969, p. 190.
7. Theo Haiman and Raymond L. Hilgert, *Supervision Concepts and Practices of Management,* Cincinnati, Ohio, South-Western Publishing, 1972, p. 1.
8. Warren Bennis, *Changing Organizations,* New York, McGraw-Hill, 1969, p. 204.
9. Reginald W. Revans, *Developing Effective Managers,* New York, Praeger, 1971, p. ix.
10. Clarence Smith, "Closing the Gap Between Communication Researchers and Practitioners," research conducted on behalf of Division IV of ICA, 1972.
11. Bennis, op. cit., pp. 207–208.
12. Ibid., p. viii.
13. Haiman and Hilgert, op. cit., p. 30.
14. Zelko and Dance, op. cit., p. 30.
15. Richard C. Huseman, in Huseman, Logue, and Freshley, *Readings in Interpersonal and Organizational Communication* (2nd ed.), Boston, Holbrook Press, 1973, pp. 192–193.
16. Haiman and Hilgert, op. cit., pp. 403–408.
17. Dean Barnlund, *Interpersonal Communication: Survey and Studies,* Boston, Houghton Mifflin, 1968, p. 460.
18. Bennis, op. cit., p. 2.
19. Scholz, op. cit., p. 49.

THE MANAGER AS A COMMUNICATION STRATEGIST

A single success proves it can be done. Therefore it is necessary to learn what made it work.

R. K. Merton

In Part I we learned that organizations consist of individuals and groups whose work is related in many different ways. The problem of getting all of these interrelated work routines to function smoothly calls for high ability in decision making, programming, controlling, and evaluation. All of these functions depend upon the effective management of communication systems.

While such qualities as determination, independence, originality, self-confidence, and aggressiveness are the personal characteristics of most successful workers, they are also the ones that may make such workers rather difficult to control and manage. This is particularly perplexing when one considers the widely acknowledged management fact that we are really able to manage only with the consent of the managed.

Because a manager must constantly face this dilemma of acceptance or nonacceptance, the above quote from Robert K. Merton has considerable relevance for us. The quote, of course, points out that the only thing worse than a failure which cannot be isolated and prevented in the future is an accidental success which cannot be strategically repeated on cue. Any future success in such a case would have to be just another happy accident.

Probably the best guarantee for planned success is a knowledge of human behavior, particularly communication behavior, and the development of strategies from the mountain of existing behavioral research.

The term strategy may have a connotation of devious, scheming action to many people. This connotation is, of course, an invalid generalization and for our purposes, strategy simply means a planned or designed sequence of events leading to a predesignated goal. Martin and Anderson provide a particularly apt definition of the word strategy when they state:

Strategy, in the original military sense of the word, meant a grand design framed to accomplish stated objectives by means of intelligent deployment of a host of resources. Strategic decisions involved knowledge of available alternatives and the judgement and "art" to bring all of one's available resources to bear in the most advantageous and economic way.[1]

Since it has already been established that communication is both an inevitability and a necessity for individuals in an organization, a successful manager must learn to control strategically the communication systems. For example, the manager must control communication at the interpersonal level, the small work group level, and the communication of organizational change must also be controlled.

One certainty is that an organization has problems and it expects solutions, not additional problems, from its managers. The organization does not, in fact, usually care how the problems are solved, only that they *are* solved and solved as rapidly and inexpensively as possible by the managers they pay to manage. There is an old parable about the grasshopper who decided to consult the wise owl about a personal problem. The problem was that the grasshopper suffered each winter from the bitter temperature. After a number of these winters he presented his case to the owl. The owl, after

---

[1] Howard H. Martin and Kenneth E. Anderson, *Speech Communication: Analysis and Readings,* Boston, Allyn & Bacon, 1968, p. 126.

patiently listening to the grasshopper's story, said, "Simply turn yourself into a cricket and hibernate during the winter." The grasshopper jumped happily away, however, after discovering that this important knowledge could not be transformed into action, the grasshopper returned to the owl and asked him how he could perform such a metamorphosis. The owl replied, "Look, I gave you the principle. It's up to you to work out the details!" So through improved communication strategies the manager must find better ways to "work out the details" and implement the principles.

Part II, then, is designed to help students of organizational management see themselves as communication strategists. Part II should assist managers in managing more effectively, and with greater understanding, support, and approval from the people they are managing. The purpose of Part II is also to show managers how strategically planned communication can be applied both inside and outside the organization in the attainment of optimum long-range profit, growth, and survival objectives.

6 the change agent

Change is implicit in the term enterprise. It makes an enterprise out of a business.

Willard V. Merrihue

OBJECTIVES for Chapter 6

After reading the chapter you should be able to:

1. Discuss in writing the role of the manager as a communicator of change.

2. Discuss in writing the skills and abilities necessary for a manager to act as a change agent.

3. Describe in writing the effect of social and cultural norms upon the implementation of organizational change.

4. Develop in writing a general strategic plan for the communication of change, using as many different approaches as necessary and appropriate.

5. Demonstrate an understanding of the relationship between a change agent and his opinion leaders, and the spread of change information through the organization.

6. Recognize existing organizational forces for and against change and demonstrate the ability to utilize this information in the planning of a change strategy.

7. Demonstrate an understanding of the importance of effects or consequences as a consideration in attempting change.

As indicated in the quote above, an organization must change to survive and ward off the entropic state discussed in Chapter 1. We also pointed out in Chapter 4 that no organization can stand still and "tread water" for very long. It must eventually go forward or backward. It has been said that change is the only constant in life. Since organizational change seems to be every bit as inevitable as communication itself, it should be the business of management to see to it that they manage this change or they will be managed by it.

While countless research projects point out that the major source of technical change in an organization comes from outside that organization, there are few human traits as predictable as suspicion toward outsiders and the changes they bring. As long as people are involved in organizations, it will be impossible to have the necessary amount of technical change without an accompanying social change. Organizational management, then, is faced with a basic problem. That problem is, how can the extrasystem changes and ideas so necessary for the survival of an organization be accomplished by that organization and still accommodate the needs of the members of the organization for internal stability?

The materials presented in this chapter will concern themselves mainly with communication strategies designed to accomplish these seemingly dichotomous organizational needs. As pointed out in Bennis et al., good management and good agents of change operate from the same set of assumptions and so are, in many ways, synonymous. These assumptions are that:

1. Change is an alteration of an existing field of forces.
2. Effective change is bringing about an alteration of these forces so as to reduce tension and gain commitment to ("ownership" of) change.
3. The effective change agent and manager accomplish this by understanding the total array of forces operating on a particular equilibrium and reach consensus on a change strategy.
4. Consensus is built by obtaining as much participation and commitment as possible in the diagnosis and manipulation of the revelant forces.
5. Organizational cultures must be changed to reinforce and maintain changes achieved by individuals.[1]

MANAGERS AS COMMUNICATORS OF CHANGE

As we pointed out in Chapter 4, the authority innovation-decision process calls for change which is initiated at the top of the management hierarchy and, in order to be considered successful, must be adopted by workers near the bottom of the hierarchy. Bennis et al. point out that, "If thoroughgoing changes in a hierarchical structure are desirable or necessary, change should ordinarily start with the policy-making body."[2] When the adaptive substructure develops in an organization, the decision-making power with respect to adaptation remains with management. This is so because change will effect the whole organization, and management cannot delegate the responsibility for modifications in basic policy without transforming the organization itself.

Most innovations, then, enter the system at the top and, if the system is well integrated, they flow downward. The basic assumption here is that when change occurs in an organization, it occurs from the top down while change coming up from the lower echelons is less frequent. As it is noted by Miles, "A hierarchical order would enable change to occur from the top down, but the relative independence of the subsystems would tend to slow down the rate of change."[3] The structure makes change from the bottom up very difficult; one would expect little, if any, change to be introduced in such a way. Such a statement seems even more true when one considers that in most organizations, the organizational power resides at the top. However, no matter where the power resides, the dynamic for change generated in the adaptive structures must always be implemented through the managerial structure.

Of particular interest to us in this chapter are those observations which point to the fact that a manager is an executor and communicator of plans from headquarters and often is a communication link between the market and the home office. These observations lead us to a categorical label, or pair of labels, for a manager. A manager could normally be described in communication parlance as a *gatekeeper* or *change agent*. As described in Chapter 3, the term gatekeeper refers to a person who filters messages as they come over the channel, controls which messages are passed along the channel, and determines the most effective method of presenting them. According to Rogers and Shoemaker, in this context the term change agent is defined as "a professional person who influences innovation-decisions in a direction deemed desirable by a change agency."[4]

The middle and lower-range managers are most particularly change agents because their daily activities might be most accurately described by the foregoing change agent definition. This description fits because the main function at this level of management is certainly to spread new ideas from the original source to the ultimate users and to influence them to adopt these new ideas. For instance, every waking, working hour a manager is attempting to gain maximum support, acceptance, and eventually commitment from the subordinates, whether the manager is introducing a new product or communicating a change in company policy. Introducing and implementing a change so that the desired innovation-decisions are achieved from the subordinates and the organizational benefits are fully realized, is one of the most complicated and difficult aspects of the manager's job.

Managers play a variety of roles as change agents: researchers, trainers, consultants, counselors, teachers, and, as we have just pointed out, line managers. Some specialize in one role, but mostly the managers shift and switch from one role to another. In some cases the change agent is not an actual member of the organization. There are some who maintain that significant change gains its impetus from external change forces. On the other hand, the insider is said to possess the intimate knowledge of the client system and the managerial power to legitimize decisions that the external change agent lacks. Additionally, the internal change agent does not generate the suspicion and mistrust that the outsider often does. The manager acting as an internal change agent has some degree of guaranteed acceptance and credibility due to his organizational status.

To approach institutional change solely in individual terms involves an impressive and discouraging series of assumptions—assumptions which are too often left implicit. According to Katz and Kahn they include:

> . . . the assumption that the individual can be provided with new insight and knowledge; that these will produce some significant alteration in his motivational pattern; that these insights and motivations will be retained even when the individual leaves the protected situation in which they were learned and returns to his accustomed role in the organization; that he will be able to persuade his co-workers to accept the changes in his behavior which he now desires; and that he will also be able to persuade them to make complementary changes in their own expectations and behavior.[5]

One general assumption underlying all of these, and an erroneous one at that, is that a communication plan will take care of itself. Since communication is often taken for granted, a communication plan is often neglected in a change process. As an example, one business communication text, which shall remain nameless, blithely states that the communication of organization change is routine, and that supervisors consider it a part of their day-to-day managerial role.

While some managers may *treat* the matter routinely, there are innumerable examples from the business world that deny that the development of a strategic plan for the communication of change *is* a routine managerial role. One such example is the one presented earlier in Chapter 2 and Chapter 4 concerning the diffusion of a computer system into an existing firm. The change to a computerized operation unquestionably was technically vital to the future of the firm. The individual social changes which inevitably followed, however, were almost a social "disaster." Why? One main reason has to be because the computer was suddenly wheeled-in and plugged-in one day with virtually no attempt to communicate the need for the change or even that the change was forthcoming.

Another instance of the importance of communication to the change process is one in which the author was involved several years ago. In this case, the company came out with a new line for its salesmen. While this new line provided the salesmen with business they had never been able to handle before, which was a definite plus, it paid less commission than the percentages which the salesmen ordinarily were paid. The additional income to be provided by this new line was communicated in an ill-conceived, evasive, almost negative manner and the result was low acceptance, low sales, and even insubordination resulting ultimately in the termination of one salesman's job.

In both cases attempts were made to redefine goals and develop a communication plan after the change was presented, but to little avail. Adding the communication plan after the change is often quite like adding seasoning to a dish as a substitute for seasoning which was not originally cooked into it. It is rarely as effective. In any case such incidents are prime examples of an ineffective job of managing the communication of change.

SKILLS NECESSARY FOR THE CHANGE AGENT ROLE

We have already seen that the effective realization of a change is a stringent test of any manager's total abilities. And the success with which the anticipated benefits are achieved is dependent, in large measure, on the extent of that manager's abilities.

According to Judson,[6] those periods when changes are being carried out in an organization can be the times when the most effective development of managerial talent and abilities is taking place. The process of introducing and implementing changes can be regarded as a crucible for management development and genuine development will occur only when managers are helped by their immediate superiors to learn the most fruitful lessons both from their successes and their failures. Without such guidance and coaching, the full benefit from these experiences might not be realized, and the antithesis of the Merton quote at the beginning of the Part II prologue would occur and we would never "learn what made it work."

Judson further points out that how much any management actually achieves compared to the full benefits that could be derived from a change is determined by three independent variables:

1. Their skill in identifying and analyzing the objectives of that change, and those problems requiring solutions.
2. Their skill in devising successful methods to accomplish these objectives and solve these problems.
3. Their skill in gaining acceptance and support for both the objectives and the methods of their achievement from the people affected by and involved in the change.[7]

But can we expect managers to be skilled in all three of these respects? Can managers improve their skills in introducing and implementing changes? To do these things well, a manager would need a keen, logical, and imaginative mind, together with sufficiently reliable abilities obtained through an appropriate, well-designed training program. This training program becomes all important because the backgrounds, training, and values of most managers have tended to stress task aspects and ignore the more human socio-emotional factors. When these human factors are ignored, task competency tends to be reduced. Managers brought up and trained under this system are not very well cast to play an effective change agent role in a modern participative system.

Remember, we have said that we will define a change agent as a professional who influences innovation-decisions in a direction deemed desirable by a change agency. According to Rogers and Shoemaker, the change agent generally fills seven roles in the change process:

(1) he develops a need for change on the part of his clients, (2) establishes a change relationship with them, (3) diagnoses their problems, (4) creates intent to change in his clients, (5) translates this intent into action, (6) stabilizes change and prevents discontinuances, and (7) achieves a terminal relationship with his clients.[8]

More specifically, many of the duties and necessary abilities of a change agent are built into the job. A change agent, simply by virtue of being one, must pass judgment on unproductive or maladjusted problem-solving processes; he must determine standards of efficiency; he must propose ways to improve interpersonal relationships. Still more specifically, a manager acting as a change agent must possess skills of conceptualization, evaluation, and appraisal. These cognitive skills must in turn be integrated with another body of knowledge known as *action skills*.

These action skills involve relating well to a client system in a particular change agent role such as counselor, trainer, consultant, or whatever. As a minimum, a manager acting in a change agent role should be able to:

1. observe and detect the situational climate;
2. organize and control the factors operating in a given situation;
3. implement whatever strategy decisions have been made; and
4. evaluate outcomes and make corrections as he goes.

Abilities related to *observation* actually are such skills as the ability to perceive accurately and diagnose the attitudes, values, and needs of a social system. In his book, *People and Productivity,* Sutermeister states that:

> This is especially true when the new data are seen as objective and at variance with common perceptions and expectations. Change processes organized around objectives, new social facts and one's own organizational situation have more force for change than those organized around general principles about human behavior.[9]

Another set of important abilities are the *organizational* ones which involve the ability to plan thoroughly based upon the aforementioned observations and muster all forces to be included in that plan, in the most effective order. Neither of these abilities is of much value, however, if the change agent cannot *implement* the plan after it is designed. The change agent must be able to seek and gain the support of as many people in the organization as possible. Gaining such support is bound to require the ability to persuade, influence, and motivate others in a direction deemed desirable. In order to make full corrective use of available feedback, the manager change agent must be able to *evaluate* the results of the change effort through an accurate assessment of the effects and outcomes. The term corrective refers to the valuable process of examining both the successes and the failures in the hope that the

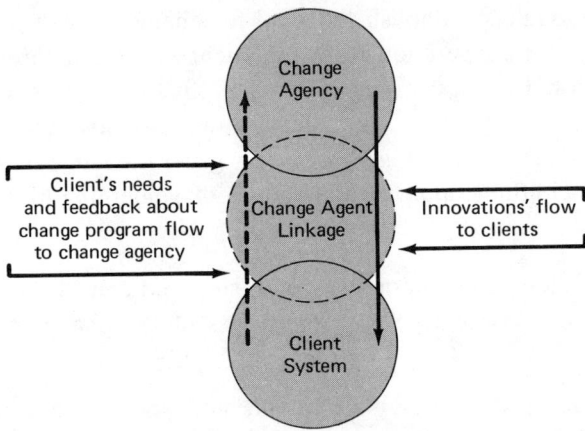

Figure 6-1 Change agent as linkage between change agency and client system. (Reprinted with permission of Macmillan. Copyright © 1971 by The Free Press, a division of The Macmillan Company.)

successes can be purposely repeated and the failures definitely avoided in the future change efforts.

Further advantageous change agent abilities that apply equally to all four of the foregoing specific abilities are communication skills and the ability to "read" and understand people. Communication in this case is used in its broadest sense, which includes keenly honed abilities in both the sending and the receiving of messages. The ability to understand and read people simply means that the manager change agent must be able to perceive people as they really are through their behavior and be able to make full use of these perceptions.

The position in which a change agent usually finds himself is perhaps best described graphically by Rogers and Shoemaker (see Figure 6.1) as they show the change agent as a linking pin system between the change agency (i.e. the top echelon of a firm) and the client system (i.e. the workers in that firm).[10]

MANAGEMENT STRATEGIES AND THE DECISION TO CHANGE

A manager communicating change to the members of an organization must simultaneously consider the communication of the technical change itself, planning for the personnel involved in the change, and the development of a flexible communication plan. The communication plan must be flexible enough to establish the need for change and then gain the maximum level of cooperation from the client system. In order to manage organizational change strategically, it is obviously necessary to move slowly and be certain that communication lines are open and clear before, during, and after the change process. A general change plan, as the social system is initially approached, might look something like this:

1. Are change goals appropriate to social system? — If not, stop and consider appropriateness of the change at all.

If yes, then:

2. Is the state of system norms open to change? — If not, stop and examine areas where change is possible or needed.

If yes, then:

3. Are people involved and committed? — If not, stop and examine ways to develop more commitment to program.

If yes, then:

4. Are members of the target system properly prepared to begin to accept the need for change? — If not, stop and examine ways to develop more commitment to and understanding of the need.

If yes, then:

5. Is voluntarism (regarding participation) reasonably well assured? — If not, stop and examine attitudes toward the change and why people do or don't accept the change. After diagnosis, attempt to communicate the change accurately.

Recall that according to Rogers and Shoemaker, when a change is communicated to a social system, that system and the individuals in it go through a process known as the innovation-decision process (see Figure 6.2).[11] In Chapter 4 we stated that this process includes four phases: the knowledge, persuasion, decision, and action phases. The knowledge phase is the one in which the members of a client system first become aware of the desired change. The persuasion step is the phase in which the members of the target system are directly persuaded as to the desirability of adopting the change. The phase which follows is the one involving a choice in which the decision is made either to adopt or reject the change and then the action step is taken. We might also include the action as a part of the decision step and add one final step. That final step, the confirmation phase, is where a second decision is made. This time, reinforcement is sought for the original decision and the client decides whether to continue or discontinue the initial decision.

It seems important to our overall change strategy that we understand the process through which members of the client system usually go to determine whether they will ultimately adopt or reject the change. According to Rogers and Shoemaker, when individuals are making such a decision they consider the innovation or change from several points of view. These points of view are relative advantage, compatibility, complexity, trialability, and observability.[12] Let us examine closer these considerations, which seem to be a part of any decision, whether they are utilized subconsciously or in a very conscious way.

Relative advantage refers to the degree to which the change is perceived to be advantageous as compared to the status quo. *Compatibility* deals with the degree to which a change or innovation is seen as being consistent with the norms, values, and experiences of the receivers. *Complexity* is the degree to which the change is difficult to understand and implement. *Trialability* is the degree to which a change may be

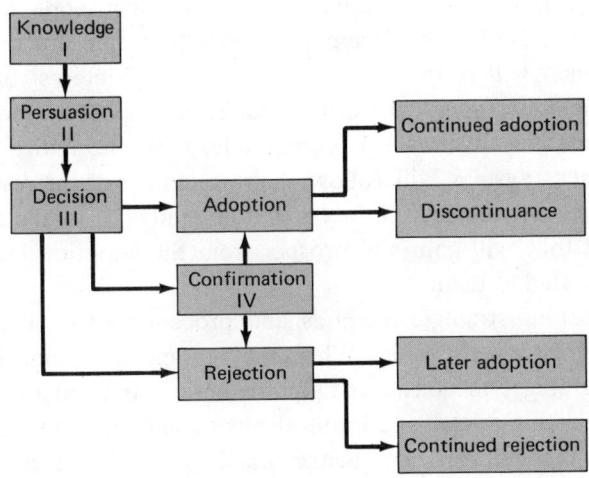

Figure 6-2 Diagram of the innovation-decision process. (Reprinted with permission of Macmillan. Copyright © 1971 by The Free Press, a division of The Macmillan Company.)

tried on a limited basis, or in other words, the degree to which an individual may try the innovation or change with little risk economically or in any other way—a free trial or a money-back guarantee are examples of high trialability. *Observability* is the degree to which the outcomes of adopting the innovation or change are visible to others in the social system. In short, the degree to which a change or innovation is highly advantageous, compatible, trialable, and observable coupled with how low it is in complexity will determine the degree of ease or difficulty with which a change attempt can be accomplished. These factors obviously must be taken into account in the development of a set of management strategies.

Similarly, change agents who deal with large systems recognize the importance of establishing realistic expectations for change and of attempting to insure an early experience of success for the participants. It is true that all agents face the problem of keeping the client's motivation toward change alive and vigorous. But a linkage between the decision to change and the actual motion toward change may be more tenuous in large authority innovation-decisions, where the two functions may lie in separate subparts. When it comes to the problem of assuring the effectiveness of the contemplated change action, agents who work with large groups concentrate on "methods" and "procedures."

Of the several strategies and change procedures available, according to Chin and Benne,[13] one seems to be the most popular: the *empirical-rational* strategy. This strategy assumes that men are rational and that these men will follow their own rational self-interest once it is revealed to them. In other words, if a change is proposed which has an observable relative advantage, is compatible, trialable, and not too complex, the client system will follow their rational self-interest and adopt the change. Of course, the fact that the change is in their self-interest and that they will gain and prosper from the adoption must be clearly communicated to them.

A second set of strategic methods and procedures for change is known as *normative re-education*. While the rationality of man is not denied in this strategy, the basic assumption here is that client action is based upon existing social and cultural norms and the commitment of the clients to these norms. To change practices in the client system, then, the change agent must first change the orientation of the clients from the old normative patterns to new ones.

A third group of strategies is based on the application of *power*. Whether the power is political or some other kind, the assumption is that change will occur through an influence process which involves the compliance of those with less power and the leadership of those with greater power.

In a study in 1965 Greiner identified the most commonly used change approaches. They are:

1. *The decree approach.* A unilateral authoritative announcement issued by a powerful person with formal authority.
2. *The replacement approach.* Key organizational personnel are replaced with new people who believe in the desired change.
3. *The structural approach.* A change in the organization chart and the subsequent relationship of who is working for whom.
4. *The group decision approach.* Emphasizes group participation and agreement on a predetermined course.
5. *The data discussion approach.* Change data is presented as a catalyst and clients are urged to discuss them.
6. *The group problem-solving approach.* Problem identification and problem solving is accomplished through group discussion.
7. *The T-group approach.* Clients are trained in sensitivity methods since it is assumed that changes in work patterns follow from changes in interpersonal relationships.[14]

None of these strategic methods is necessarily better than another. Rather, the knowledge of the existence of each method and facility in implementing each can provide the manager change agent with a variety of approaches. Such a variety of approaches should enable managers to harness the existing social forces in a system and make these forces work for them, as pointed out earlier.

CHANGE AGENTS, OPINION LEADERS, AND THE TWO-STEP FLOW

Obviously, in organizations, the manager change agent faces the problem of insuring a spread of information throughout the entire client system. Change agents working with client systems of all sizes are aware of the problem of locating a leverage point as an early step in the actual process of change. Agents working with organizations typically look for structural leverage points—that is, subparts or individuals that are especially accessible or that possess a particular strategic value by virtue of their location in the total system.

Now the change agent may be either from within the organization or he may be what we may generally term an "outsider." It is a moot point which is the most effective. On one hand, the internal change agent knows the social system and the individuals in it better than an external agent could possibly know them. However, that familiarity can turn to contempt when either the change agent or the clients operate on too personal a level. The external change agent, on the other hand, is not apt to have any such personal problems. This is a problem of a different nature. We have already seen in Chapter 4 that the outsider has difficulty in gaining acceptance, particularly from a more traditional system.

Another potential problem for external change agents is that they may be specialists and be concerned about the change itself, while taking a pretty cold attitude toward the social system because they have little or no vested interest in that system. This set of circumstances may lead to some blind spots. As an example, a president of a furniture firm told this author during a recent airplane trip about a computer specialist with his firm whose blind spots worked him right out the door. It seems that this computer man was hired from the outside because he knew the computer intimately; however, he had little patience with resistant traditionalists in the firm or even with those who, though willing to learn, did not understand immediately. The president said regretfully, "That bright young man could have written his own ticket with us but we couldn't tolerate his impatient attitude and his blind spots toward the firm."

Another major concern is the source of the change agent's power. Manager change agents are dependent upon their sources of power to legitimize their behavior, especially where the communication of change is involved. Internal change agents normally derive power from their hierarchical position within the organization. External change agents normally derive power from the outside expertise which they bring to the situation, like the aforementioned computer specialist. In either case, effective change agents attempt to legitimize what they are doing by gaining the support of key organizational people through the use of their power.

Whether a specific manager change agent is labeled as an insider or an outsider is open to question and highly dependent upon who is doing the labeling. On one hand district sales managers could be considered to be insiders or internal change agents because they work for the same sales division in the same firm as the subordinate salesmen. On the other hand, these district sales managers are in the management group and the salesmen are not, which probably gives each of them a different set of goals and surely puts each of them in touch with information to which the other is not priveleged. These factors tend to make managers seem sort of outsiders or external change agents to the people they are trying to influence.

Regardless of whether manager change agents are considered internal or external, their main concern is the spread of change information and the ultimate adoption of that change. The most common method of spreading such information through a large organization today is the multistep information flow in which the receivers are a variable number of times removed from the message origin. The receivers in the client system are a variable number of times removed from the origin because some clients are relatively quicker than others to adopt the change. Among the earlier adopters, some will be highly respected by peers who are further removed from the change agent. Therefore, these earlier adopters may be able to influence the decisions of their peers. These respected early adopters are known as *opinion leaders*. Opinion leadership is the degree to which an individual is able to influence informally other individuals' attitudes or overt behavior in a desired way with relative frequency. The concept of opinion leadership was originally so labeled as part of the two-step flow model, which hypothesizes that communication messages flow from a source, via mass media channels, to opinion leaders, who in turn pass them on to followers. The multistep flow method is similar to the two-step flow except that the multistep flow takes into account the size of a large organization and the obvious fact that the size and many accompanying hierarchical levels will necessitate many steps in the complete spread of information.

In using a multistep flow method it is most important that opinion leaders be properly sold on the change idea. If they do not fully comprehend your message, they will certainly not be apt to spread the information accurately or very enthusiastically. In Chapter 1 we discussed the story of the research project that did not happen because the general manager would not go along with it. The firm in question was obviously in need of communication consultation and advice. The middle-range managers on the firing line were very much in favor of the project. They decided to carry the project message in the form of an enthusiastic request to the general manager who, as already mentioned, said no, flatly. The general manager appeared to be a bit afraid of such close scrutiny. However, the point here is that, had the middle-range managers been as sold on the idea as they seemed to be, they might have been more persuasive and persistent.

In short, change agents, whether they are highly familiar with the client system or not, will do well if they get the message even to a large segment of the client system by seeking out persons of influence within the system and letting them do the further bidding with their peers. In other words, A (change agent) tells B (opinion leaders), who in turn tell C (the other members of the system). In a very large system it may be necessary for the information to spread on from C to D, from D to E, etc.

STRATEGIES TO OVERCOME CHANGE RESISTANCE

As we pointed out in Chapter 4, the natural tendency for any organization is to cling to a state of equilibrium or a steady state. In most cases, this tendency alone provides considerable resistance to change. Additionally, as we pointed out in Chapter 4, in organizations we encounter the criterion of productivity as a main factor in motivations toward or away from change. The principal resistance force in any organization may be a fear that change will effect the organizational productivity negatively.

Creating change is equivalent to solving problems, and the good manager and good change agent are interchangeable. Managing change requires the ability to identify forces of change, forces of resistance, and to develop consensus about the relevant forces as well as a strategy for manipulating these forces.

If changes in a hierarchical structure are desirable, change should ordinarily start with the top policy-making body of the organization, at least from an approval point of view.

In diagnosing the potential for change in a given institution, it is always advisable to assess the degree of stress and strain at points where change is sought. A good place to begin change may be at one of those points in the system where some stress already exists. Stress is apt to give rise to dissatisfaction with the status quo and its norms, thus becoming a motivating factor for change in that system toward the new set of norms being communicated. But one should ordinarily avoid beginning change at the points of greatest stress simply because there is probably too much dissidence and turmoil at such points.

Both the formal and the informal organizational structure must be considered in planning any process of change. As pointed out by Benne and Birnbaum, "To change behavior on any one level of a hierarchical organization, it is necessary to achieve complementary and reinforcing change in organizational levels above and below that level."[15]

Often employees are not actually resisting technical change as much as they are resisting the changes in their human relationships that generally accompany technical change. This may still be true even though employee objections to change seem to be manifesting themselves as resistance to the technical change itself. The human relationships are changed because in order to change a system technically, certain relevant aspects of the environment must also change.

As a change is attempted in an organization, it naturally moves through a cycle of phases. In the first phase, the few people willing to adopt the change are usually dismissed as "crackpots" by the rest of the social system. In fact, the other members of the social system usually find solace in each other as they conform to the status quo and oppose the change. In the next phase, the pro and con sides of the change issue are more clearly defined. This phase develops into the crucial state in which the change and resistance forces occasionally enter into direct conflict and the change forces either grow or weaken. Power struggles are sometimes very evident at this point in the cycle. In the final phase, if the change is succeeding, change forces will begin to be in power and eventually, as the change takes effect, the final resisters will be seen as the "crackpot" minority.

It can be demonstrated that people often like change and even do not mind changes in their human relationships provided that they play a part in making the change. It may not be change that is really resisted, then, but authoritarianism and pedantic experts making unilateral decisions. If this is true, we might say, in keeping with the notions expressed in Theory Y:

1. Employees want to improve and succeed just as much as the supervisors do.
2. Everyone likes to "join" and run together. Most of us need to be a part of the group and take part in its activities and decisions.
3. Everyone likes to feel that they are a worthwhile contributor.

The effectiveness of a change attempt, then, is often related to the degree to which members at all levels of an organization are able to take part in the diagnosis of needed changes and in the formulation of goals and change plans. Taking all of this into account, managers must seek the aid and counsel, the ideas, and the support of those around them at all levels. The alternative is a "boss" who already has all of the answers. The form of participation being discussed here is one based upon mutual respect.

Another form of participation often encountered is one in which people are used unfairly to legitimize decisions already made by someone else. When managers ask for assistance on a decision they must be sincerely asking for a real decision and not simply a phony rubber stamp. This author recalls a management situation in which the district sales managers were called together each year to set "their own" sales goals for each of their salesmen and ultimately for their entire unit. Top management, however, would give these district men the total expected production figures, which had bounced down from the top of the hierarchy, and some very strong hints as to what goals would be acceptable from each of them. And so the district managers proceeded to make the "decision" which suited top management and take part in some sort of highly ritualized lip-service participation. The irony was that six months later, if sales were running below quota, the district managers would be reminded by the managers that these were *their* sales predictions and that *they* had set them. Top management was making an attempt to apply a common piece of small-group participation research which says people will be willing to implement decisions more readily when they have taken part in the decisions. Of course, when the participation was not real, the commitment was probably not very real either. Most important, however, is that such a sham can be destructive later if a firm ever wants real participation from these same managers. It becomes a little like the proverbial boy who cried "wolf," in that the response to a call for participation becomes negative, nonexistent, or, at best, passive.

In the form of "mental wages" and the subsequent overcoming of resistance to change, perhaps nothing can equal the feeling of *really* being taken into the confidence of a hierarchical superior concerning important decisions. There is, in fact, a considerable body of research which points up the fact already alluded to: that individual participation in decisions will induce a stronger commitment on the part of the participants to the implementation of those decisions.

As a result of considerable research in overcoming change resistance, Goodwin Watson lists some generalizations dealing with overcoming resistance to change. He deals with who brings the change, what kind of change succeeds, and how it is best accomplished. The generalizations are as follows:

A. Who brings the change?
  1. Resistance will be less if administrators and managers feel that the project is their own—not one devised and operated by outsiders.
  2. Resistance will be less if the project clearly has wholehearted support from top officials of the system.
B. What kind of change?
  3. Resistance will be less if the participants see the change as reducing rather than increasing their present burdens (relative advantage).
  4. Resistance will be less if the project accords with values already acknowledged by participants (compatibility).

5. Resistance will be less if the program offers the kind of *new* experience which interests participants.
6. Resistance will be less if participants feel that their autonomy and their security is not threatened (trialability).

C. Procedures in instituting change
7. Resistance will be less if participants have joined in diagnostic efforts leading them to agree on what the basic problem is and to feel its importance.
8. Resistance will be less if the project is adopted by consensual group decision.
9. Resistance will be reduced if proponents are able to empathize with opponents; to recognize valid objections; and to take steps to relieve unnecessary fears.
10. Resistance will be reduced if it is recognized that innovations are likely to be misunderstood and misinterpreted, and if provision is made for feedback of perceptions of the project and for further clarification as needed.
11. Resistance will be reduced if participants experience acceptance, support, trust, and confidence in their relations with one another.
12. Resistance will be reduced if the project is kept open to revision and reconsideration if experience indicates that changes would be desirable.[16]

In summary, a communication plan for overcoming resistance to change should take into consideration the following points:

1. The need for change must be established in the minds of the clients.
2. The need for change should be reiterated when making the announcement of the change decision to the clients. They must see how favorably it will affect their lives.
3. Head off resistance problems before they become serious by anticipating them. The easiest time to answer an objection is before it actually becomes one.
4. Reinforce and amplify the need for change while it is being implemented.
5. All during the change period continuous feedback must occur in the form of progress reports. Secrecy can be very detrimental and can contribute to resistance.

CONSEQUENCES: THE ETHICAL SIDE

When considering an organizational need for change and the appropriate change-agent strategies for a manager, one must also consider a subject which is normally far more difficult, the ethical side of change. Recalling the discussion of ethics in Chapter 5, we find that in the case of the communication of change, ethical considerations are usually talked about in terms of change consequences or effects upon the social system. In change situations of all kinds, the consideration of the consequences of adopting a certain change and the effect on those involved are too seldom a major part of the diagnosis and plan. There are stories to numerous to detail here concerning foreign policy of the United States being based upon intervention in the business of other cultures and societies, with little regard for the future consequences to that culture. Then there are the ribbons of superhighway cutting through once fertile farmlands and forests in the name of progress. Or, closer to our topic here, there are progressive firms and organizations who mechanize and computerize their operations with little or no warning, training, or even communication to those whose lives will ultimately be affected.

According to Rogers and Shoemaker, consequences are "changes that occur within a social system as a result of the adoption or rejection of an innovation."[17] They refer to consequences as *functional,* desirable effects, or *dysfunctional,* undesirable effects; *direct,* immediate consequences, or *indirect,* resulting from direct consequences; *manifest,* intended and recognized in advance, or *latent,* neither intended nor recognized. Let us say, for example, that a change effort results in dysfunctional, indirect, latent consequences. This means that we have undesirable effects which came about as an indirect result of the actual change and were not intended or recognized initially. Those things do happen and there is little we can do to head them off. This is, of course, not a reason never to attempt change and certainly is no excuse for not attempting to account for the manifest and more direct dysfunctions before we even consider beginning to implement the communication of a change.

In an organizational setting, once the decision is made that change is needed, the change plan must be developed. It is at this early stage that the consequences must be considered even if the result of the consideration is sometimes the bitterly disappointing decision that such a change is not right at that time. Some typical considerations which organizations might want to consider in relation to contemplated change would be:

1. What machines and/or people would be displaced, if any?
2. Would the change rate allow for necessary retraining?

3. Is the change apparently going to produce functional effects for most of those affected?
4. What latent effects might occur with regard to social subgroups, particularly informal groups?
5. What effects will the change have on the community or larger social system in which the organization literally *lives*?

A strategic case in point

The story which follows in an actual communication of change incident complete with the consequences to this date. The setting is a middle-sized midwestern community of 35,176 people which we will call Changeville. The community probably has more amenities than any town its size in the United States. They have beautiful schools and churches, a thriving business district, several public swimming pools, golf courses, and a beautiful fine arts complex, most of which are due mainly to the success of a single industry. Changeville is the headquarters and main plant of a well-known industrial firm. So on one hand we have a firm that has been a bit of a local pollutant and at times gives off some unpleasant odors in the area. On the other hand, the firm has either directly or indirectly provided the community with more outstanding incomes and facilities than any town of its size could hope for.

In 1966 some local businessmen and the owners of industry foresaw that there would ultimately be a power and energy shortage which could have a serious effect on local operations. With this in mind, and in cooperation with the power company, a feasibility study concerning new sources of power was undertaken. The results of the study indicated that nuclear power might be a workable answer. The power company already had built a smaller pilot type nuclear power plant in another community in the state.

The federal Atomic Energy Commission also figures heavily in this drama. Although their role is becoming clearer, the original charge to the AEC was a confusing one at best. They were at one and the same time charged with promoting peaceful uses of atomic energy and also with controlling the use of atomic energy and the issuance of licenses. These sorts of conflicting, even antithetical, roles naturally caused a great deal of internal and external role confusion for the AEC.

The findings of the feasibility study in Changeville recommended the further exploration of atomic power by the power company and the local industry. At this particular point in time, approximately early

1969, the ecology movement was reaching a fever pitch around the country. The movement was reaching almost fetish proportions for some zealots in some situations. So the stage was set in 1969 for a very drawn out and involved battle between some men in a power company and a manufacturing firm, and the protests of a very vocal group of interveners. On one hand, there were these two firms with an urgent need and few alternatives at their disposal. On the other hand, there was a superheated group of people with a different set of priorities. If they understood industrial needs and what the fulfillment of these needs, or the lack of it, might mean to the area, they gave all of this much lower priority than the condition of the local ecological systems.

Chronology of Events

**Key steps in the diffusion process

  October, 1966 Feasibility study began. Approximately 27 months passed before anything really happened.

  January, 1969 Ecological opposition was raised concerning the planning process by the Valley Nuclear Study Committee. They were guided by a sharp, young attorney as their legal counsel.

  July, 1969 Clearing of designated land and other preliminary site work was begun.

  August, 1970 Government Committee on Environmental Quality asked for more study on thermal pollutants and considered additional cooling towers over and above the planned cooling.

  ***October, 1970* The Changeville Nuclear Power Committee was formed (a pronuclear power group).

  October 30, 1970 AEC hearing dates in Changeville were set.

  November, 1970 Official intervention during the upcoming hearings was announced by the Valley Nuclear Study Commit-

	tee (sometimes known as the Interveners).
**November 9, 1970*	The Changeville Nuclear Power Committee chartered a plane and flew 48 carefully selected citizens to the Atomic Energy headquarters and laboratories. The citizens were exposed to the facts about nuclear power and met the scientists who had been with peaceful atomic uses since their inception.
**November 12–24, 1970*	The atomic energy scientists were brought to Changeville for a series of nuclear power workshops open to the public. During these 17 workshops, 450 people heard lectures, became familiar with the language, built nuclear power plant models, handled geiger counters and so on.
December, 1970	AEC hearings began in Changeville. Citizens who went to the atomic energy labs filed a position paper with the hearing committee. The committee, which was to be constantly plagued by procedural difficulties, met for two days and then suspended the hearings for six months.
March, 1971	Data concerning radioactive releases were checked.
June 17, 1971	Cooling towers were added to the plans.
June 24, 1971	Preliminary emergency plans were challenged by the interveners.
July 7, 1971	Emergency evacuation became a part of the master plan. Now a small group of interveners from a nearby town with about 20 families registered a complaint about potential icing and fogging in their area

	from the cooling ponds. Also, a court decision elsewhere made the AEC responsible for the environment as well as health and safety.
**October 12, 1971*	The big, pronuclear power rally planned by the Changeville Nuclear Power Committee was held at the county fairground, attracted 22,000–25,000 citizens, and was a huge success.
October 23, 1971	The plan was refiled with all of the revisions and new facts.
**October 25-28, 1971*	Changeville group went to the nation's capitol for meetings with the AEC staff and the Environmental Protection Agency, the Council of Environmental Quality, the State's legislators, and the Joint Committee on Atomic Energy.
**February, 1972*	Changeville group went to the capitol again, this time with a giant 8 × 20-foot billboard full of signatures.
**April, 1972*	AEC report favored the plans for the construction of the nuclear plant in Changeville.
May, 1972	Some more intervention hearings were held but the attorney for the Interveners was not present. Many felt that this weakened the Interveners case.
**December, 1972*	The construction permit for the plant was issued and Interveners filed against the issuance of the permit.
**June, 1973*	Construction began on the plant.

Description of the communication of change process

As one can see from the foregoing chronology, the early days of the attempt to get a nuclear power plant built in Changeville were fraught with all sorts of vicissitudes. Interventions, indecisions on the part of the AEC, and some rather haphazard planning were running rampant.

The actual diffusion campaign involved here really began with the formation of the Changeville Nuclear Power Committee in October 1970. The committee was formed by the local Chamber of Commerce director but without any actual overt involvement on the part of the chamber. A committee chairman was selected and the committee represented the broadest possible community participation. The committee chairman was a Presbyterian minister who had sought his own training in the peaceful use of nuclear power before the committee was even formed, simply because he wanted to be informed.

After raising the necessary funds, the committee chartered an airplane and flew 48 carefully selected citizens for a quick training session at the federal atomic energy headquarters on November 9. At this point there were at least 48 believers. Then from November 12–24, 1970, there were 17 nuclear energy public workshops held in Changeville. The director of the atomic lab operation, and others from the labs came to Changeville for these workshops, which deeply involved the participants. They were allowed to ask questions, build nuclear power plant models, handle geiger counters, and most of the 450 people attending the workshops came away as quasi-experts who could speak the technical language.

With the supporters of nuclear power steadily increasing, plans were started by the committee for a huge pronuclear power rally. Buttons stating "We Need Nuclear Power Now," and bumper stickers with the same message were distributed. There was a public plea for money for the rally and trips to the capitol. The money literally poured in, basically in small $1.00 and $5.00 amounts, until $30,000 had been raised.

During the rally planning stages there were, however, storm clouds brewing on the other fronts. Intervention and all sorts of "picky" stalling tactics on the part of opposition forces were making the hearings and the quest for nuclear power a nightmare of confusion. During this period, the local industry quietly pulled a few of its smaller units out of the Changeville operation and transferred them to other locations where power was cheaper and more readily available. Finally, when the confusion and opposition reached a peak, the executives of the firm came to the director of the Chamber of Commerce asking that they drop the plans for the rally. The reason given was that there seemed to be an increasing opposition to the power plant. The industrial people said they were giving up on nuclear power, would not renew their contract with the power company, and would simply have to make other plans. It is possible that these "other plans" might not have included the city of Changeville so the Chamber people swung into full action on the rally.

It was felt by the Changeville Nuclear Power Committee that there was support for the power plant and the rally now began to take shape as an effort to prove a point simultaneously to the local industry, the power company, and the Atomic Energy Commission. The date—October 12, 1971—was set for the rally and plans were finalized with the leadership coming from every part of the community.

On October 12 this community of 31,176 people was alive with excitement as some 22,000–25,000 of these people swarmed into the county fairgrounds. As the citizens entered through the four entrances they signed their names on 5 × 8-foot panels stationed at each of these entrances. The rally consisted of bands and speeches by civic leaders, state officials, as well as industry and power company officials. There was a personal appearance by a TV star, union officials, atomic energy experts, and state and federal legislators. As the rally reached a definite high, the band played the Battle Hymn joined by the crowd singing parodied words from a song sheet. During the song, a truck pulled a giant 8 × 20-foot replica of an AEC license by the grandstand. The license replica was actually the four panels with the 22,000–25,000 signatures pieced together. A big finish to an exciting rally which said loud and clear to all concerned: "Changeville wants nuclear power and wants it now."

All three target groups of this rally were duly impressed; however, those most impressed, for the moment, seemed to be the local industry. They said that they had no idea that Changeville wanted them and nuclear power that much and that they would stay with the project all the way from that point on.

Following the rally, the committee made two trips to the national capitol on October 25, 1971, and February 1972, for further hearings. For the February visit they took the giant billboard with them and set it up in the hearing room as a petition.

An AEC report in April 1972, favored plant construction. Despite more late interventions, the construction permit for the plant was issued by the AEC in December 1972, almost six years to the day from when it all began.

Construction began in June 1973, and a series of reactors will be completed over approximately the next four years. In the meantime, the power company has and will continue to come in about three times a year to update the citizens and provide progress reports.

Analysis

The campaign was unique in at least two major ways. It provided a textbook example of a successful communication of change campaign and it was also unique in that it represented mass communication from the many to the few.

Mass communication is usually thought of as a comparative handful of people sending a message to a great mass of people simultaneously. It was in this campaign that we saw the slow, steady spread of information, with all of the accompanying attitude changes from one person, to a committee, to 48 people, to 450 people, until the work eventually reached 22,000–25,000 people. At this point that mass of 22,000–25,000 people communicated a single message to a few hierarchical decision makers. Under the circumstances, there would really have been no other credible source to transmit this message effectively. It would have had little impact on executives trying to decide whether or not the citizens of the area wanted nuclear power in their area if they had heard it from the director of the Chamber of Commerce and a few businessmen. The word, to be really credible, had to come from the people themselves.

If we examine the credibility research of Berlo, Lemert, and Mertz,[18] for instance, we find that the factors encompassed in source credibility are safety, qualification, and dynamism. In the situation described here, the massed citizens at the rally were the source. Applying the source credibility factors outlined by Berlo et al., we would have to say that the source was a credible one. Due to the educational programs conducted during the campaign, many of these people actually were qualified concerning nuclear power. Further, there can be little doubt they were highly qualified concerning what they wanted and what was best for them. The opinion of the citizens was certainly more trustworthy, and therefore safer, than the opinion of the bankers and Chamber of Commerce. Most important here perhaps is the dynamism factor. Dynamism may be defined as participation or activity, both of which were present in abundance throughout the campaign.

We can label the campaign a textbook example, not only because it was so successful, but because so much of what a textbook dealing with change strategies would recommend actually took place. For instance, the plan was really an operational definition of the conceptual term *diffusion*. Rogers and Shoemaker define the concept of diffusion as "the process by which innovations spread to the members of a social system."[19] The campaign for nuclear power in Changeville was certainly a slow, well-planned spread of information.

Recall that, according to Rogers and Shoemaker, the steps an individual goes through in the innovation-decision process are knowledge, persuasion, decision and confirmation.[20] There can be little doubt that the members of this social system went through these steps. Even the confirmation step is still being repeated from time to time. As mentioned earlier, confirmation continues in Changeville as the power company periodically reinforces the beliefs of the citizenry in nuclear power.

Placing the Changeville cast of characters into the diffusion paradigm, the director of the Chamber of Commerce would certainly be the change agent. The opinion leaders, whose function it was to spread the information, were first of all the highly credible chairman of the nuclear power commmittee, and then the 48 citizens who were taken to the atomic energy labs.

There is, of course, a constant ethical concern about the form of consequences of any diffusion campaign. There can be even less doubt that there was, and still is, considerable concern that the consequences of a nuclear power plant must be functional. A great many safety precautions have been taken to insure functional outcomes, because the potential dysfunctional outcomes are unpleasant, to say the least. At this point it would seem that both the consequences stemming directly from the power plant as well as the indirect ones will be functional. The manifest consequences have all been scrutinized carefully in the master plan; however, latent consequences will always be a problem in that they are not really controllable.

The foregoing true story points out many of the strategic points we have been discussing in this chapter. It should be clear that the strategic application of the communication of change principles discussed in this chapter are a fact of everyday life in the real world.

SUMMARY

Rogers and Shoemaker defines a change agent as a "professional person who influences innovation-decision in a direction deemed desirable by a change agency."[21] We have seen that managers, especially the lower and middle-range managers on the firing line, are operational examples of such a change agent. Since managers are change agents, whether voluntarily or involuntarily, they must develop an ability to construct appropriate strategies for change situations. Strategies in this case may be looked upon as a general set of policies underlying a specifically planned set of action steps or tactics designed to gain maximum adoption of the change.

The most desirable plan is one that takes into account both the technical and social sides of change, the attributes of the change as perceived by the client system, the existing forces for change, and resistant to change, and the potential positive and negative effects upon those adopting the change. Most importantly, the plan must incorporate a communication subplan which should permeate the entire plan.

NOTES

1. Warren G. Bennis, Kenneth D. Benne, and Robert Chin (eds.), *The Planning of Change,* New York, Holt, Rinehart and Winston, 1969, p. 317.
2. Ibid., p. 333.
3. Matthew B. Miles (ed.), *Innovation in Education,* New York Bureau of Publications, Teachers College, Columbia University, 1964, p. 435.
4. Everett M. Rogers and F. Floyd Shoemaker, *Communication of Innovation: A Cross-Cultural Approach,* New York, Free Press, 1971, p. 227.
5. Daniel Katz and Robert L. Kahn, *The Social Psychology of Organizations,* New York, Wiley, 1966, p. 391.
6. Arnold S. Judson, *A Manager's Guide to Making Decisions,* New York, Wiley, 1966, p. 177.
7. Ibid., p. viii.
8. Rogers and Shoemaker, op. cit., p. 248.
9. Robert A. Sutermeister, *People and Productivity,* New York, McGraw-Hill, 1969, p. 277.
10. Rogers and Shoemaker, op. cit., p. 228.
11. Rogers and Shoemaker, op. cit., p. 25.
12. Ibid., pp. 167–168.
13. Robert Chin and Kenneth D. Benne, "General Strategies for Efforting Changes in Human Systems" in Warren G. Bennis, Kenneth D. Benne, and Robert Chin (eds.), *The Planning of Change,* New York, Holt, Rinehart and Winston, 1969, p. 34.
14. L. E. Greiner, "Organizational Change and Development," unpublished Ph.D. dissertation, Harvard University, 1965.
15. Kenneth D. Benne and Max Birnbaum, "Change Does Not Have to Be Haphazard," *The School Review,* University of Chicago, 68, no. 3 (1960), 283–293.
16. Goodwin Watson, "Resistance to Change" in Goodwin Watson (ed.), *Concepts for Social Change,* Washington, D.C., National Training Laboratories, 1966.
17. Rogers and Shoemaker, op. cit., p. 342.
18. David Berlo, James B. Lemert, and Robert J. Mertz, "Dimensions For Evaluating the Acceptability of Message Sources," *Public Opinion Quarterly, 33,* (Winter, 1969–1970), 562–576.
19. Rogers and Shoemaker, op. cit., p. 32.
20. Ibid., p. 103.
21. Ibid., p. 227.

7 the interpersonal motivator

It is generally accepted that the ability to persuade others to your point of view and to have this acceptance translated into a satisfactory response is the real test of leadership. *Ray Killian*

OBJECTIVES for Chapter 7

After reading the chapter you should be able to:

1. Create your own definition of persuasion.
2. Describe the levels in a belief system and give examples of each.
3. Describe and give examples of Katz and Kahn's four motivational patterns.
4. Discuss the factors involved in source credibility and how it affects the persuasiveness of a manager.
5. Describe and give examples of each kind of nonverbal language.
6. Discuss the use of the various message appeals and when they will be most effective.
7. Describe the various defense-training methods available to prevent effective counterpersuasion.
8. Discuss the factors of persuasibility.
9. Describe and give management examples of the concept of self-persuasion.

THE opening quote seems to indicate that leadership can be measured best by the degree to which it serves as a catalyst for progressive and effective forward movement of an organization. The implied message here is that a continued existence at the same level of effectiveness, or the simple understanding and acceptance of a message without any actual change in behavior, is not effective, persuasive leadership. In order to accomplish the desired results from a motivational attempt, a manager must secure both the attention and the understanding of the subordinates. The effectiveness of such motivational attempts can be further measured by the subordinates' willingness to yield to what they have understood, their retention of the persuasive message they have accepted, and their willingness to behave in keeping with that which they have accepted. There is obviously a vast difference between persuasion and a persuasive attempt, at least from the point of view of results.

The same statement can be made concerning any type of communication. A communication attempt is not the same as successful communication. If persuasion or any type of communication is judged by its effectiveness or success, then there are naturally a great many more communicative attempts than there are incidents of communication. One important reason for this disparity is that we often lack a plan with a predictable outcome in our communication attempts. Instead, we communicate from habit, and anything we do habitually rather than with some thought is apt to be poorly done and haphazard.

Clearly, what is needed is a system of strategic communication plans to replace the haphazard, hit-and-miss programs often found in today's organization and, probably more important, tomorrow's organization. Willard Merrihue points out that:

> the future will involve strategic considerations of the highest order: it will start with being sure that actions are sound and in the public interest; it will involve surveys of the ideological market, planning short and long-range goals, planning of the ideological product, and merchandising the needed understanding and information product through modern marketing techniques and the development of much more precise methods of evaluation and feedback.[1]

In order adequately to develop a set of strategies of any kind, we must first be familiar with the sources of the material from which the strategies are formed. This is at least as true in the development of communication strategies as it is in any other type of strategy. But the major obstacle confronting most modern business organizations is their inability to perceive that the communication, as a process, can be studied, analyzed, and strategically applied. If we would *really* make use of these realizations, we would be well on the way to vastly improved communication systems.

Individuals within organizations are all separate, discrete personalities which must be dealt with in small groups, and, at times, individually. For instance, people who are high in intelligence are apt to be better able to attend to and comprehend messages, yet they are often less prone to yield to persuasion and controlled management. On the other hand, people who are low in intelligence are open to persuasion; however, they may very well have difficulty in attending to and comprehending the messages themselves. These individual disparities are not only frustrating but make individualized motivation in management extremely important. In order to insure any kind of predictable success in human motivation, the motivation must be tailored to individual needs.

All of these factors add up to one important piece of management advice. *You must manage the individual and not the job.* The way to get desired results from managerial motivation attempts is to deal individually with each subordinate whenever possible.

PERSUASION, BELIEF, AND ATTITUDE

In this chapter we have already used the terms motivation and persuasion interchangeably. The study of persuasion and persuasive techniques will provide us with the tools we need to appeal to and influence our subordinates, with the object of motivating them.

Persuasion

Before we attempt to define persuasion perhaps we should examine what persuasion is *not*.

Persuasion is not necessarily logical. Although it may contain elements of logic, persuasion is more likely to be effective if it concentrates on psychological appeals for its impact. Persuasion is not just a science but also an art. Persuasion is not necessarily lasting and usually needs to be reinforced and restated from time to time for prolonged influence. Persuasion is not an end in itself but a means to some other behavioral end. Persuasion is not determined by the sender but by the receiver. The receivers will decide whether they are persuaded or whether there has just been another persuasion attempt.

Many communication scholars feel that persuasion is not a special type of communication but rather that all opinion, and even knowledge, has a persuasive bias in it. These scholars, in fact, feel that no communication can be characterized as totally nonpersuasive. David Berlo points out that "there is reason to believe that all use of language has a persuasive dimension, that one cannot communicate at all without some attempt to persuade in one way or another."[2]

Put a little differently, but still reinforcing to the Berlo statements, is the following point of view from Martin and Anderson:

> But almost all of the talking or gesturing we do in the presence of other people, all of the writing we willfully expose to others' view, is directed toward the accomplishment of some goal, in short, is motivated. Therefore, "communication" and "persuasion" are nearly synonymous terms.[3]

Now that we have looked at what persuasion is *not* and examined its pervasiveness, let us define what persuasion *is*. There are many varied definitions of persuasion. The definition seeming to serve our needs here as well as any is one offered by Erwin Bettinghaus even though, in our terms, it is really a definition of a persuasive attempt. Bettinghaus tells us that persuasion is "a conscious attempt by one individual to change the behavior of another individual or group of individuals through the transmission of some message."[4]

The term "conscious attempt" indicates the need for the presence of an intent to influence in order to call a communicative act a persuasive attempt. It is further evident in the Bettinghaus definition that all communication is not considered to be persuasive. This definition seems appropriate to organizational application because of the overt intentional aspect. Rather than feeling that we must define persuasion as always being present in communication or only being present some of the time, it is more beneficial to examine a particular communicative act to see whether or not its main thrust is persuasive. In other words, a piece of communication may have persuasion as its main goal, however, it will still have elements of informative and entertaining communication. By the same token, a communicative act whose main thrust is to inform will still contain persuasive elements.

In the organization, however, communication takes the form of one individual, the manager, expecting to elicit some specific response from another group of individuals, the subordinates. Such a communicative form obviously has a basic persuasive thrust and fits the Bettinghaus definition pretty well.

Our basic concern, of course, is how persuasively managers conduct their day-to-day leadership functions. The basis of the leadership function is the psychological relationship between superiors and subordinates. To manage psychological relationships adequately, managers do not "handle" people. Instead they motivate by persuasion, influence, and the shaping of individual attitudes.

Attitudes and beliefs

Some scholars tell us that a belief is made up of a set of attitudes, others that an attitude is made up of a set of beliefs. Any real separation between the two terms is obscure, for our purposes, as we look at the management of individual personalities within organizations.

Attitudes are blueprints for behavior; let us recall that we have already established that effective persuasion is the influencing of behavior. Persuasion, then, must also be the influencing of attitudes. Although it is difficult to define what an attitude is, the following are some apparent properties or components of attitudes:

1. An attitude is emotional in nature.
2. An attitude involves feelings (not necessarily logical).
3. An attitude is shaped by experience.
4. An attitude spreads from person to person.
5. An attitude is influenced by individual perceptions.

The attitudes which subordinates hold concerning themselves in relation to the organization should be especially important to the manager. These attitudes are almost the same as behavioral needs or motives. Some well-documented empirical research points to the following basic pattern of subordinate attitudes:

1. Organizational programs must make sense.
2. Most people want to improve (mostly because they do not want to fail).
3. Most people want to be known as a pro.
4. Most people want to be part of a top-notch group.
5. Most people want rewards; personal and/or economic.
6. Most people want personal integrity (respect and confidence).

The attitudes people bring with them to a communication situation will to a great extent control what they hear and how they behave. Through past experiences and learned responses each individual develops a system of attitudes and beliefs. Individuals develop their beliefs from a full range of life experiences, therefore a manager must take into account a great deal more than the personality seen on the job when dealing with subordinate attitudes. Subordinates usually have a family, hobbies, friends, and so on, which affect the attitudes they bring with them to the job. The behavior of a person is a product of all their experiences, both organizational and nonorganizational.

Belief systems

Each individual has a system of beliefs that is made up of many single beliefs. It is through this belief system that the individual perceives, reacts, behaves and is either persuaded or not persuaded by the manager. As with any other management function, we must understand beliefs and belief systems before we can manage the individuals that hold them. This is really the only way to motivate and persuade people, because they do things for their own reasons and not for the reasons of their managers. When we persuasively manage, therefore, we are connecting our persuasive message to the motives and needs of the subordinates.

The existence of an interconnected, often complex, system of beliefs makes the job of managing the subordinate's needs and motives very difficult. What it does makes crystal clear, however, is the need to manage individuals, and manage them individually. As we grow and gain new experiences, we develop new beliefs to add to our total system. During our lifetime we add these new beliefs to the system, drop others from the system, while still other beliefs are with us all the way and are never changed or dropped.

The belief system notion is described in great detail by Milton Rokeach in his book *The Open and Closed Mind*.[5] Rokeach points out that some beliefs are more central to the system than others. These central beliefs, which Rokeach calls primitive beliefs, are not usually subject to much change and are key beliefs found right at the core or foundation of the total system.

Rokeach points out that there are also intermediate beliefs which are subject to change but are resistant toward it. These intermediate beliefs consist of beliefs derived from friends, books, and the more important ones derived from authorities such as the teacher, minister, or the Bible.

Finally, Rokeach notes that there are peripheral beliefs which are relatively inconsequential when compared to the foregoing beliefs. These beliefs are so lightly held that they are fairly easy to dislodge from the system and change.

The main point concerning the interconnectedness of these belief systems is that attempts to change one belief or attitude, even a peripheral one, is likely to have unplanned and unpredictable effects upon other beliefs within the system. For example, it might be a waste of time to attempt to change a derived belief without directing any change effort toward the authority from which such a belief is derived. On the other hand, if someone's belief in an authority is shaken in some way, it might be relatively simple to change a belief derived from that authority. Another example might be what would happen if, for instance, a person believed wholeheartedly and steadfastly in the merits of Christianity. If such a belief were so strongly held that Rokeach would call it a primitive belief, then the chances are very good that any change in that belief would tend to send out shock waves throughout the entire belief system. Due to the centrality of the belief and the interconnectedness of the system, many other related beliefs would probably be affected.

INTERPERSONAL TRUST AND MORALE

Interpersonal trust and morale were touched on briefly in Chapter 5. Let us now examine more closely what effects they may have upon interpersonal motivation. Most successful managers know that they must develop a high level of interpersonal trust and that morale must be kept high if communication systems are to be effective. Managers must treat their subordinates as individuals and enhance the subordinates' self-esteem by developing a trusting relationship. The trusting relationship can be demonstrated by participative management, which allows the subordinates to be involved in setting goals, standards, and policies.

Morale is really a business of individual satisfaction. If the subordinates are satisfied with the organization, its management, and their role within the organization, they are likely to have high morale. A satisfied subordinate with high morale is very persuadable and manageable. Managers must manage, then, with the notion that their communication strategies must be geared persuasively toward the development of attitudes that enhance morale and build trust.

How is a trusting relationship developed? Although we do not wish to oversimplify the matter, a trusting relationship is really developed by a manager doing everything possible to fulfill the needs of the subordinates. It is a certainty that people are apt to direct their communication toward those who can give them security and satisfaction for their needs. Conversely, subordinates are at least as apt to direct their communication away from those who threaten them and provide discomforting and unrewarding experiences. This is important to the manager who is developing a trusting relationship because the flow of communication is so vital.

The type of management, participative or nonparticipative, Theory X or Y, etc., has a great deal to do with the organizational attitudes of subordinates and the degree of interpersonal trust that has been developed. Researched estimates of the percentage of performance improvement obtained through various public and private modes of communication tell us what sort of management is most likely to pay dividends. The communication methods studied were reprimand, ridicule, sarcasm and praise. These methods were then compared when done publicly and privately. As we might expect, the two most productive methods of communication were public praise and then private praise. Just as predictably, public ridicule and sarcasm came last as productive methods for subordinate improvement.

As we can well imagine, then, more subordinate improvement can be expected if the manager-to-subordinate communication method is positive rather than negative. Further, it is interesting to note that, with the exception of praise, the private communication situations—even the negative ones—were far more effective than the public ones. Naturally, public praise ranked higher than private praise because of the ego factor alone. However, the point is that the more negative methods did induce some subordinate improvement if handled privately and that the reprimand was, in fact, very effective when handled privately. There is a great amount of personnel psychology research that reinforces this by pointing out that most subordinates abhor uncertainty and want feedback, even if it is negative feedback. Perhaps the most frustrating thing for subordinates who know they are doing poor work is for their manager to fail to zero-in on this poor quality and help them correct the problem. Subordinates in such a case *want* to be reprimanded, but on their own terms. "Their terms" almost always include privacy. So it is not so much *what* is communicated as *how* and *where* it is communicated that will determine the persuasive positiveness or negativeness of the results.

Only recently a case occurred where a superior reacted somewhat violently and negatively to a subordinate's request for permissions to miss an important meeting. The request and reaction happened in the office of another person. The reaction, however justified and reasonable, was seen by the subordinate as unjustified and unreasonable and he was livid. The main reason the subordinate saw the reaction in this light was, as he put it, "He made a fool of me in front of the supervisor and a secretary I didn't even know." When the subordinate later confronted the superior with what he had done, the superior said, "You mean I should have stepped out in the hallway with you to give you my negative reaction?" The subordinate's reply was clearly and simply, "Yes, that is exactly what I mean." Being rebuked and turned down on his request was not nearly so troublesome to the subordinate as was the serious dent that the public reprimand put in his dignity.

The real danger in such a management strategy, or the lack of it, is the sort of reactionary manager-subordinate trust relationship it can develop and the detrimental effect that relationship can have on things such as the job performance, morale, and attitudes of the subordinate. Often the uncooperative attitudes and decreasing productivity we, as managers, receive from subordinates is highly deserved and quite predictable. In that regard we should recall that the Timothy Leary notion of interpersonal reflex discussed in Chapter 1 may explain such reactionary, reflexive behavior.[6] Such behavior as hitting back, shouting back, or being a childish subordinate in reaction to being managed like a child are simply unplanned. There is no better example of interpersonal reflex than the poem *Pershing at the Front* by Arthur Guiterman.[7]

In the poem, Guiterman describes a visit to the front by General Pershing and his aide. The two were being escorted from third to second to first-line trench by a captain and a top sergeant. As the sergeant passed along information *in a whisper,* they each repeated the information *in a whisper* until the general discovered the enemy was three miles away. Upon finding this out, he roared, "What in hell are we whispering for?" and the seargeant answered, "I have a cold." In the poem, all were whispering like unthinking robots because the sergeant had lost his voice due to a cold.

The poem reiterates very well the point that, whatever concept you choose to explain the action-reaction phenomenon taking place when people attempt to communicate, it is clear that the behavior of the person "in charge" has an effect upon the behavior of the others.

In view of the foregoing statements, we could expect well-organized managers with a definite management plan to get quite different results from each different persuasive management style. Suppose, for instance, that a manager uses direct hierarchical pressure for results, including the competitive, results-oriented sort of practices traditionally used in sales organizations. Such a manager will probably begin to notice less group loyalty, more conflict and less cooperation, less favorable attitudes toward management, and less motivation to be productive from the subordinates. These symptoms are likely to lead to lower productivity, higher costs, and infinitely lower morale.

On the other hand, if the same manager with the same organized plan implements and communicates that plan from the principle of supportive relationships and participative management, quite different results may be expected. These are likely to be increased group loyalty, more cooperation, improved attitudes toward management, and a much greater loyalty, more cooperation, and a much greater motivation to produce. Generally, there will be a far more positive attitude set toward the organization and its goals, leading to a greater productivity at reduced costs (an application of the principle of optimization from systems theory), and a much improved subordinate satisfaction and morale.

There is a small "job shop" type manfacturing firm which has in the past two decades experimented with a Theory Y-oriented, participative style of management. They have been treating their workers like people instead of machines, children, chislers, and/or slaves. The results have been profit increased two and one-half times; absenteeism is under 1.5 percent, and productivity has more than doubled. In addition, the return on the investment has tripled, products sell for less than they did in the fifties and, most important of all perhaps, the workers are happy with the company. There is no union and turnover is about 0.5 percent per month. In a recent survey, 97 percent of the workers were satisfied with the company.

What the employees of this small firm like is the feeling that *the* company is partly *their* company rather than the property of the owners and bosses. Under participative management, the subordinates help make the important decisions—the setting of production standards, for instance, or the purchase of equipment—and they are encouraged to redesign their own jobs for greater efficiency. They even set their own raises.

Logically, subordinates who are treated like automatons are not going to be imaginative in finding and creating new ways to improve. They must be motivated to think independently, to take the initiative, and to believe in the value of their own ideas. To do these things they must be allowed to discover their own human value. The credo of the owner of the small industrial firm just described is ridiculously simple. He says, "If you treat people properly, they respond well. If you want to be fair to people, you can expect good results from it. And, on the other hand, if you want good results you ought to be fair to people." This credo is really another way to restate Leary's concept of interpersonal reflex. Remember, shove and they shove back.

ATTITUDE MANAGEMENT

These are, then, some of the methods by which we can persuasively manage and motivate for results. Choosing the proper methods for ourselves, the subordinates, and the long-range goals of the organization is up to us as managers. We must discover what motive pattern causes each of our people to behave in the desired manner. Katz and Kahn in their book, *The Social Psychology of Organizations,* offer us a sort of typology of motive patterns which cause people to act or behave.[8] These motive patterns are called legal compliance, instrumental satisfaction, self-expression, and internalization.

Legal compliance is based on authority and is reinforced by the threat of penalties. This motive pattern gets results; however, they are usually of a minimally acceptable standard and very little organizational loyalty is ever developed. If people must perform or be fired, it is unlikely that their performance will ever go beyond that which is required or that they will stay long if they get a better offer.

Instrumental satisfaction is based upon rewards and works best when the rewards are immediate, constant, and adequate. Instrumental satisfactions do increase productivity but they do not stimulate innovative behavior. Further, they stimulate intra-group competition, which can hurt the group's ability to work together. Piecework wages are an example of instrumental satisfaction. One thing which is very clear is that very little organizational loyalty is developed: cut off the rewards and see how long anyone produces.

Self-expression is a motive which will only work with certain individuals. This motive provides a constant challenge to the individual through certain types of jobs which increase in complexity, variety, and responsibility. High productivity and strong organizational loyalty are characteristic of the self-expression motive; however, it is limited only to certain jobs and to certain personalities within the organization.

Internalization is probably without question the most effective motivational pattern. It is, however, the most difficult to institute within subordinates. Internalization means the kind of motivation mentioned earlier in the Kelman studies, or more recently in the description of the small, participatively managed industrial firm. It means that managers have managed, motivated, and persuaded their way to a situation where the goals of the subordinates and the organizational goals are one and the same. If managers are able to achieve high internalization, they can expect low absence and turnover, high productivity at low cost, and extremely innovative and loyal employees. Does this sound like utopia? It may be, but something akin to it is possible through proper management and patience.

What seems to be happening when subordinates internalize is a sort of transformation from externally based conformity to an "inner conformity." According to Hovland, Janis, and Kelley, "the individual finds satisfaction in adopting the advocated view even in the absence of the advocate."[9]

It becomes clear that if we are to manage persuasively and motivate effectively we must develop a plan, a set of communication strategies, if you will. In order to accomplish this, we need to examine the available research that could be useful to managers as they set out to motivate their subordinates by managing their individual attitudes.

While it is necessary to develop a persuasive managerial strategy, we must be careful not to formalize our strategies as we attempt to manage attitudes. Ernest Bormann points this out clearly when he states that:

> Formulas are sufficiently attractive that some of us will come to rely upon them excessively. This is the *formula fallacy,* i.e., assuming that formulas alone will do the job of persuasion. They are useful as supplementary and incidental devices. The major problems of persuasion are better solved by application of principles derived from individual psychology, social interaction, and the process of communication.[10]

Managers, in other words, should have a general, planned framework within which they will operate; however, they should never fall into the inflexible trap of seeing that plan as a magic formula or panacea. Bormann suggests a simple framework of basic tasks which must be accomplished if anyone is going to be persuaded. These steps or stages in the process of persuasion are to:

1. Gain and *maintain* attention.
2. Arouse selected desired motives, habits, interests, etc.
3. Connect desires to persuasive purpose.
4. Produce a specific response.[11]

The management of individual attitudes requires that managers begin with a set of attitudes or system of beliefs which they consider ideal for the accomplishment of organizational goals. Of course, smart management allows room for individual flexibility but there still should be a general set of beliefs or attitudes within which an effective, functioning subordinate should behave. This part of attitude management, then, would be motivational, persuasive attempts to either change undesirable attitudes that do not fit the system or the reinforcement of desirable attitudes. Again, we should reiterate that an effective manager will not force every subordinate to fit a mold as if they were wearing a uniform and standing at reveille. On the other hand, a manager must have a set of organizational attitude goals toward which the subordinates must be motivated.

Perhaps the best way to approach the persuasion research that will serve as the basis for our motivational strategies is to divide the topic into smaller research variables. The most common division of available attitude research variables follows the Berlo pattern of source, message, channel, and receiver. Let us now examine the research which we will use to formulate our motivational strategies.

Source credibility

The main source variable which has been widely researched is *source credibility*. Source credibility is actually the credibility which is accorded the source by his receivers. Credibility is really more of a judgment on the part of a receiver or group of receivers than it is a property of the source. Like beauty and truth, credibility is in the eye of the beholder. We have already alluded to the need for managerial credibility before subordinates will be willing to become followers. Interpersonal trust is also closely related to source credibility. We cannot discuss source credibility for long without asking ourselves what personal factors go to make up this concept we call source credibility.

We have seen that source credibility is an attribute accorded, or not accorded, a source by a receiver or receivers. Actually the credibility of a source, according to a particular set of receivers, would properly be expressed in degrees of credibility along a continuum. But what is credibility? It is obviously a derivative of the word "credit." Some synonyms or partial definitions for credibility might be *prestige, attractiveness, sincerity, likeability,* or *general competence*. One term that is actually Aristotelian in origin is *ethos*. According to Aristotle, ethos was the character of a speaker. There is really little difference, for our purposes, between Aristotle's ethos and source credibility, except that the concept of credibility has been expanded considerably over the concept of ethos. Also, source credibility has been researched and applied in a much broader sense than just the public-speaking rubric related to ethos.

In the past few years, quantitative researchers have tested hundreds of subjects and factor analyzed the results to determine the dimensions that add up to source credibility. In early source credibility research, Hovland, Janis, and Kelley speculatively identified "trustworthiness," "expertness," and "intention" as the key dimensions involved.[12] Further computerized research by Lemert uncovered three credibility dimensions. They were "safety" (comparable to trustworthiness), "qualification" (comparable to expertness), and a third dimension, "dynamism."[13] Dynamism in this case includes such things as participation and activity. James McCroskey also ran similar factor analyses and found two credibility dimensions, "character" and "authoritativeness."[14] These different sets of factor analyzed credibility dimensions roughly correspond to each other as shown in Figure 7.1.

Source credibility is thought by many to be similar to a bank account. This strange analogy is a surprisingly helpful explanation of the gain and loss in credibility experienced by individuals from time to time. The banking notion states that a person can behave in certain positive ways and add to, or make deposits, in the credibility bank. Then, just like a checking account, he can draw upon these credits when he needs them, in persuasive situations for instance. Just as in the case of a checking account it is possible to be overdrawn, out of credibility, in your account. Individuals can no more draw upon their credibility without ever replacing it than they can draw money out of the bank indefinitely.

The most common example of the banking concept is the Kennedy-Johnson administration. John F. Kennedy was young, personable, and popular. He spent almost his entire three years in office putting credits in the bank and some critics felt that he did little else. Lyndon Johnson, on the other hand, was a highly credible, consummate politician who possessed great power in the corridors of decision making. When Kennedy was suddenly taken from the scene, the presidency was thrust upon Johnson. President Johnson began pushing such legislation as Medicare, Medicaid, and the civil rights legislation on behalf of the administration. Just as he had suddenly become president, he also found

Researchers	Dimensions			
Hovland, Janis and Kelley	Trustworthiness	Expertness	Intention	
Berlo and Lemett	Safety	Qualification		Dynamism
McCroskey	Character	Authoritativeness		

Figure 7-1 Comparison of source credibility dimensions.

himself suddenly bankrupt in the credibility bank. He had overspent without adequate deposits in return and the public added a new term to their vocabulary. Lyndon B. Johnson had a "credibility gap" and wisely chose not to run for office again.

No matter how we view source credibility, it is clear that the manager with the highest credibility among his subordinates is the one who will be likely to persuade and motivate best. The degree of credibility possessed by a manager source, as viewed by his subordinate receivers, will affect attitudes, behaviors, beliefs, and interpersonal trust. The amount of credibility accorded a manager will also determine how eager subordinates will be to identify with the manager as a role model.

Source credibility, then, is a person's projected image. It is "what you are" or, better still, "what you are perceived to be." In view of this side of credibility, it seems that credibility is like your face—it is whatever it is and you are stuck with it. Such is not necessarily the case, however.

Perhaps the safest and best way to enhance the credibility of a source is to enhance it before a communication transaction takes place. In other words, if a credible image precedes someone into a communication situation, they are way ahead in the motivational game before they start. For instance, evidence of management competency or product knowledge would pave the way for a manager with subordinates as being a credible source.

During the actual communication transaction credibility can be enhanced in much the same way as it can before the fact. The key in enhancing source credibility is first to understand what dimensions of credibility are highly valued by the subordinates. Then determine approximately what degree of credibility is already perceived by the subordinates. From that point, it should be relatively simple to move in on the problem areas and improve total perceived credibility.

Obviously, credibility itself can be a very persuasive tool. Arthur Cohen in *Attitude Change and Social Issues* points out that:

> How the listener perceives the communicator can affect attitude change in numerous ways: the vividness of his personality, his status, the expertise attributed to him, the stake he has in the issue—all of these may make a difference. Many attitudes can underlie the effects: affection and admiration for the communicator, fear and awe of him, trust and confidence in his sincerity, fairness, and credibility.[15]

Apparently, then, there is a high strategic benefit for managers who are concerned about their perceived credibility as a source. One consideration which can definitely raise or lower a manager's credibility is the kind of messages that managers send.

Message and channel variables

Even with a pretransactional credibility that is extremely high, a great deal of time and care must be taken to insure that the message and channel selection communicates the desired meaning and also that it does as little harm as possible to existing source credibility. Perhaps the message may enhance the existing credibility but at least some care should be taken to guarantee that the message should be carefully planned, even if we do often think of it as a simple matter. Killian supports this notion when he says:

> The key to obtaining a satisfactory response to a communication is the care with which it is planned and implemented. The fact that communication can take dozens of forms and still be as simple as a man-to-man conversation misleads many into thinking it is so easy and obvious that it does not require the most meticulous caution, forethought, selectivity, and follow-through.[16]

So it seems that the old song lyric, "It ain't what you say, it's the way how you say it," rings true. The proper balance of verbal and nonverbal cues which complement each other, the most effective choice of word symbols, and a meaningfully receiver-oriented arrangement of these symbols becomes most important.

When David Berlo, in his SMCR communication concept, talks about the message he feels that it is made up of *code, content,* and *treatment.*[17] The code is a group of symbols capable of being structured with meaning for someone. Symbols would normally be such elements as words, syntax, and nonverbal cues. Content is material chosen by the source to express the desired communication goals, such as assertions, inferences, and judgments. Treatment of a message is the decision made by a source concerning the selection and arrangement of code and content.

Meaning. In constructing a message, the source manager must be concerned about meaning because communication itself is the conveyance of meaning. Effective communication which will motivate subordinates must be receiver-oriented and take into account the meaning the receiver probably attaches to a given set of symbols. Berlo points out some helpful facts about meanings:

1. Meanings are in people. They are the internal responses that people make to stimuli, and the internal stimulations that these responses elicit.
2. Meanings result from (a) factors in the individual, as related to (b) factors in the physical world around him.
3. People can have similar meanings only to the extent that they have had similar experiences, or can anticipate similar experiences.

4. Meanings are never fixed. As experience changes, meanings change.
5. No two people can ever have *exactly* the same meaning for anything. Many times two people do not have even similar meanings.
6. People will always respond to a stimulus in light of their own experiences.
7. To give people a meaning, or to change their meanings for a stimulus, you must pair the stimulus with other stimuli for which they already have meanings.
8. In learning meanings, people operate on the principles of (a) least effort, (b) noninterference, and (c) discriminative capacity.[18]

Nonverbal Message Channels. We referred to nonverbal channels in Chapter 2. Because of the special relationship of the nonverbal message channels to the total message, we will give it special attention. There are a number of types of nonverbal language which are cited by Barker and Kibler in their book, *Speech Communication Behavior*. They point out that nonverbal language includes "sign language, action language, object language, space, and time."[19]

Sign language includes such familiar symbols as the thumb of a hitchhiker or the peace symbol which became popular as an antiwar gesture on campuses in the sixties and has since come to symbolize a greeting or parting gesture. Interestingly, that V-shaped peace symbol had another period of popularity during the forties when it symbolized victory in Europe.

Action language refers to body movements such as a manner of walking, facial expressions, and posture. Object language is any material item which conveys a meaning, such as an expensive car, clothes, jewelry, and fashion.

Spatial language refers to social distance such as that between two people when they communicate. Most people have a "sacred" spatial area around them which they do not want violated. Approximately an arms length is a comfortable communication distance for most of us. Time language usually translates as a matter of punctuality. Keeping appointments and being punctual, or the lack of it, usually communicates a great deal in a formal organization. One additional type of nonverbal language is simply silence. Anyone who has ever expected a phone call or a letter and not received it knows what kinds of meanings can be attached to that silence.

These categories of nonverbal language should be useful when developing message strategies. When the accurate transfer of meaning is so vital, we obviously must be careful to have our verbal and nonverbal cues complement one another. If the verbal and nonverbal language is haphazard and even appears to be in conflict at times, we have added to the confusion in meanings and not helped the effectiveness of communication at all.

Logical Versus Emotional Appeals. Whether we are making use of verbal or nonverbal message cues or the usual combination of the two channels, we must also be concerned about message *appeals*. What kind of appeals are apt to be most persuasive? Will people be motivated more by logical, intellectual appeals or by emotional, psychological appeals? First, there is probably a bit of both emotion and logic in any message appeal. Furthermore, like source credibility, whether a message has an emotional or logical appeal tends to depend upon the eye of the beholder. For instance, where there is a difference of opinion, I am likely to see myself as a logical person and you as overly emotional; you will see the situation as being completely reversed.

By the same token, then, if most of us were asked whether we were more persuaded by emotional or logical appeals, the answer would be quick and sure: "Oh, logical appeals, by all means," we would say. In research studies, people have given that exact response but the same subjects could not recognize any real difference between emotional and logical appeals. Therefore, there is little real basis for any claims concerning the relative effectiveness of emotional or logical appeals.

Professional persuaders such as advertising people do, however, place a heavy emphasis on psychological appeals. They have also come to the conclusion that well-organized messages *do not* seem to be any more persuasive than disorganized messages and that good evidence *is* more persuasive in the long run. Taking our cue from the professionals, then, we would want to structure our persuasive message for psychological impact, with good evidence, and with little concern for the orderliness of appeals.

Anxiety-Arousing Message Cues. Another well-researched topic dealing with message construction is the use of anxiety, or fear-arousing, cues. Such an appeal is usually based upon negative reinforcement. For instance, a fear appeal would be pointing out the bad consequences of not complying with a persuasive message. Recent examples in advertising of fear appeals are toothpaste brand versus tooth decay commercials and the cancer societies' antismoking commercials. A mild appeal is one that points out the danger and allows the receivers to supply their own consequences. A strong fear appeal is when the danger is spelled out and a strong, vivid, and explicit set of consequences are provided for the receiver.

Research by Janis and Feshback[20] has told us that it is possible for an anxiety-arousing appeal to be too strong. Apparently when the appeal is directed at the receivers themselves, they will not pay attention to the message when it is too strong for them to handle. The lack of effectiveness of the "quit smoking" messages seems to bear this out. So the milder, more subtle fear appeal is apt to be more effective. An exception to this may be when the message is directed at a "valued other" such as a loved one. In this instance a stronger appeal seems effective, according to research conducted by Powell.[21]

This information regarding anxiety-arousing appeals is especially important to the manager who must, or feels that he must, manage by threats. We spoke earlier in the chapter of motivation by the method of legal compliance. This motivational method is a specific persuasive instance concerning anxiety-arousing appeals.

Resistance to Counterpersuasion. If we are to persuade effectively as managers we must be concerned with messages that will resist future counterpersuasion and therefore have some lasting effect. This is true mainly because managers cannot directly supervise every subordinate all of the time. Since managers cannot be everywhere at once, they must create messages that persuade and motivate with the sort of internalized private commitment effect Kelman wrote about as his goal. The problem, then, is to construct persuasive messages which will last over time and continue to motivate subordinates when the manager is not always present to oversee the lasting effects.

William J. McGuire provides the results of some interesting research in the creation of persuasive messages which will resist counterpersuasive attempts.[22] One approach to inducing resistance which McGuire points out to us is the *behavioral commitment* approach. When the people behaviorally commit themselves to the desired attitude, they find it difficult to switch behaviors later. This is especially effective when the commitment is made by a public announcement of belief and still more effective when the subject actively participates in belief-oriented behaviors. We should, therefore, gear our persuasive message to induce a commitment from our subordinates.

Another resistance-inducing technique presented by McGuire is *anchoring*. Recall that earlier in this chapter we discussed Rokeach's notion of a series of beliefs integrated into one interrelated system of beliefs in which alteration of one belief may very well affect other beliefs in that system or the entire system. Anchoring, then, is a method of inducing resistance to persuasion by anchoring, or linking, the desired new beliefs into the existing system. Anchoring beliefs makes it more difficult to change the new attitude or belief later because it has been linked to other beliefs and would require changes in these other beliefs as well.

Still another approach by McGuire to solidify new attitudes and beliefs, making them resistant to future counterpersuasion, is the *inoculation* approach. Inoculation in this case means a persuasive adaptation of the familiar biological inoculation method of immunization. Biologically, when we inoculate we give the recipient a small dose of the disease they are being inoculated against and their body builds up antibodies to fight off future exposures to the actual disease. Inoculation theory in inducing resistance to persuasion works the same way. The message recipients are given a small dose of opposing arguments to which they might be exposed in the future. The recipients are then either allowed to think up their own defenses against that future counterpersuasion or are more overtly provided with defensive arguments to use when needed.

It is apparent that there are a great many message considerations which are necessary and important to a persuasive manager. The most effective message components and the selection of a channel or combination of channels appropriate to those message components are vital to success or failure in communicative management.

Receiver variables

Naturally subordinates with no prior attitudes on an issue will be easier to persuade and motivate. On the other hand, an adult who is subordinate in an organizational structure is pretty likely to have a position or existing attitude toward any organizational issue. Again, we find ourselves as managers in the position of perhaps having to persuade subordinates toward a totally new set of attitudes, but more likely we are apt to be in the position of having to change existing attitudes and behavior patterns.

The major concern in the motivation of subordinates, or any receiver for that matter, is their persuasibility; that is, how easy or difficult will it be to persuade and influence these individuals. But what receiver personality variables are related to persuasibility? Research has already established relationships between persuasibility and intelligence, sex, authoritarianism, self-esteem, aggressiveness, the need for social approval, cognitive needs, and dogmatism.

Dogmatism. The relationship between persuasibility and dogmatism is of particular interest to organizational managers. According to Milton Rokeach,[23] the term *high dogmatic* is used synonymously with *closed mindedness* and, conversely, *low dogmatic* is synonymous with *open mindedness*. Managers are obviously going to have a great deal more difficulty persuading their subordinates if the subordinates can be characterized as highly dogmatic individuals with minds that are closed to change or new ideas.

One definition of a prejudice is that it is a belief that cannot be changed even in the face of new irrefutable evidence. Predudice of this kind is a stubborn, dogmatic attitude which any manager will find frustrating and disruptive. One key research finding concerning dogmatism should be of special interest here. The research tells us that the dogmatic subordinates will be persuasible on peripheral issues but will be highly resistant to persuasion dealing with issues in which they have ego-involvement. These findings are important to managers because, when they suspect ego-involvement concerning a certain issue on the part of a dogmatic subordinate, they should realize that they are up against a difficult, if not impossible, persuasion task.

Intelligence. As indicated earlier, intelligence of a subordinate receiver clearly has several effects upon the persuasibility of that subordinate. What sort of effects is not so clear. For instance, on one hand, the greater the intelligence of receivers, the better they are able to comprehend a message. On the other hand, the greater the receivers' intelligence, the greater will be their critical ability; a potential source of resistance to persuasive attempts.

Sex. A far more undeniable correlation between a receiver personality variable and persuasibility exists in the sex variable. Females, on the average, seem to be more persuasible than males in such research as that reported by Janis and Field.[24]

Self-Persuasion. Persuasion is really the "selling" of ideas, issues, and practices, so we are all salesmen at one time or another. This point of view concerning persuasion is brought up because the changes in selling techniques in recent years may give us some strategic persuasion clues. At one time, a salesman was called a "drummer" and lived up to the foot-in-the-door, heavy-handed, and hot breath image. Such an image was clear in the character of Harold Hill and his colleagues in the musical "Music Man." This persuasive technique has always been known as the hard sell. Although businesses such as some home improvements, vacuum cleaners, and encyclopedias may still follow the hard sell method, most sales techniques have changed. The change has been to a much softer and more professional style.

Persuasion researchers have a general label for the soft sell approach of modern professional salesmen. The label is self-persuasion, which is generally felt to be a more effective form of persuasion and apt to have a greater lasting effect. In self-persuasion, the receiver is not directly and coercively persuaded. The receivers are, instead, made aware of existing needs or problems, given the necessary information, and then allowed to persuade themselves. Such a technique has similar qualities to participative decision-making techniques and many of the same predictable results. Many modern researchers believe that there is no such thing as persuasion in the hard-sell sense of the word, but rather that people ultimately must persuade themselves in order to be really influenced. If it is even remotely possible, the smart manager will devise persuasive strategies which will facilitate the efforts of individuals to persuade themselves.

Balance Theories. One of the principal ways in which individuals persuade themselves is in the process of attempting to maintain *cognitive consistency*. The theoretical base which is used to explain this sort of self-persuasion is normally known as either *balance theory* or *consistency theory*. Such a conceptual framework operates from several basic assumptions. They are:

1. Our beliefs and behaviors must be perceived as being consistent to others and to us.
2. Inconsistency is a noxious, painful, or hurtful state and must be resolved or reduced.
3. Man is a rational being.

These assumptions imply that our beliefs and behaviors must be not only internally consistent over time, but that there should be consistency between individuals' stated beliefs and their perceived behaviors. The notion that inconsistencies must be resolved or reduced can be extended fairly easily to mean that failure to do so could result in a serious mental disturbance. So we can count on our subordinates to persuade themselves in an effort to reduce inconsistency once it is pointed out to them.

In Chapter 4 we already mentioned another form of cognitive consistency of special interest here known as *cognitive dissonance.* Recall that we pointed out that dissonance theory is a product of the research of Leon Festinger and speaks to the self-persuasive drive for consistency after a decision has been made. In other words, once individuals arrive at a decision such as making a choice they will, according to the Festinger research, enter into self-persuasion in order to confirm their choice. Specifically, Festinger predicts the following self-persuasion process:

1. In a choice situation there is some good and some bad in each choice. After the choice is made, individuals will seek evidence to reinforce their decision.
2. There will, therefore, be an increase in attraction toward the chosen and a decrease in attraction toward the not chosen.
3. The pressure to reduce dissonance resulting from the choice will vary directly with the extent of the dissonance.[25]

What is actually occurring here is that the individual is using selectivity as described in Chapter 2. The individual is selecting "in" reinforcing evidence and selecting "out" discomforting evidence in order to be able to self-persuade. The dissonance-reducing process is exactly what is happening during the innovation-decision process confirmation step described in Chapter 6.

When someone is buying a car and must decide between the Ford, the Chevrolet, and the Plymouth, they are likely candidates for this sort of self-persuasion. According to dissonance theory, once they have chosen the Chevrolet, they will begin to reinforce their decision by selecting all of the persuasive evidence they can find in favor of the Chevrolet and avoiding all of the positive evidence they can concerning the Ford and Plymouth. The smart salesman facilitates the customer's self-persuasion attempt in every way possible through the sales follow-up call.

We have already pointed out that the persuasive manager is certainly a salesman in every sense of the word. Managers must, therefore, be aware of the importance of follow-up persuasion with their subordinates. Having influenced subordinates in a desired direction is not always enough. Some serious thought must also be given to exposing subordinates to follow-up information which will aid them in their dissonance-reducing self-persuasion process.

SUMMARY

In Chapter 7 we have examined the manager as a strategy-oriented persuader and motivator of subordinates. It is apparent that persuasion is very pervasive, in some way and to some degree a part of all communication. We have settled on "a conscious attempt by one individual to change the behavior of another individual or group of individuals' through the transmission of some message" as our definition of an overt persuasion attempt.

An attitude is a predisposition to behave in a certain manner which individuals bring to a communication situation. Attitudes or beliefs are really blueprints for behavior and tend to cluster within each individual in the form of a belief system. The belief system, while it is an integrated whole, is made up of many separate beliefs. Some of these beliefs are very central to the system and relatively unchangeable, while other beliefs are more peripheral and not so closely tied to the system.

It is the business of any effective manager to create and maintain a social work climate of high subordinate morale and interpersonal trust. Strategies such as participative management and a Theory Y management style are helpful. We must manage for the kind of reaction we desire. Interpersonal reflex is apt to cause subordinates' behavior to mirror the style by which they are managed. We have a choice of motivational bases ranging from legal compliance, through instrumental satisfaction and self-expression, to internalization. In short, we must identify subordinate attitudes and needs and manage individual and organizational attitudes with these in mind.

Our approach has been one of looking at source, message, channel, and receiver variables. We first looked at the source and found that the important factor here governing the effectiveness of the persuasive communication is the credibility of the source. In other words, our concern is with the image of the source or how he is perceived by his receivers. The manager source can store up credits in a credibility bank much like a checking account and then draw upon these credits in times of unusual stress.

The channels available are either verbal or nonverbal. In order for a message to have meaning for the receiver subordinates, it must be created with the receivers in mind. Words and things do not *mean,* people do, so we can say that meanings are in people. We have some research at our disposal to help us develop strategies concerning whether to use threats or anxiety-arousing cues. We also have some evidence on the relative merits of emotional versus logical appeals. There is always a concern over whether or not our persuasive message, once it has been accepted, has any staying power against counterpersuasion. We have examined a number of channel and message selection techniques that will build defenses against counterpersuasion into the original message.

Our concerns with the receiver have centered around his persuasibility and the various personality variables that affect that persuasibility. We have examined the relationship between highly dogmatic subordinates and the predictability of their behaviors. Every persuader manager is really a salesperson and would do well to follow the modern soft-selling technique of providing the subordinates with the information, atmosphere, and whatever else is needed to help them persuade themselves. Self-persuasion techniques such as the use of consistency theory and cognitive dissonance are right at the heart of the sort of modern persuasion and motivation which the modern communication strategist manager should be using.

To develop a motivational strategy, then, a manager must take several important steps. They are to:

1. Determine the purposes and goals of each communication attempt.
2. Be familiar with the attitudes and belief systems of the subordinates as well as the organizational setting.
3. Establish subordinate needs and communicate with these needs always in mind.
4. Create a communication plan based upon the above factors as carefully as any other organizational plan is created.
5. Base the plan upon available persuasion research in order to eliminate as much trial and error as possible.
6. Follow up by checking the effectiveness of communication results through feedback channels.

NOTES

1. Willard V. Merrihue, *Managing by Communication,* New York, McGraw-Hill, 1960, p. 36.
2. David K. Berlo, *The Process of Communication,* New York, Holt, Rinehart and Winston, 1960, p. 9.
3. Howard H. Martin and Kenneth E. Anderson, *Speech Communication Analysis and Readings,* Boston, Allyn & Bacon, 1968, p. 126.
4. Erwin P. Bettinghaus, *Persuasive Communication,* New York, Holt, Rinehart and Winston, 1960, p. 13.
5. Milton Rokeach, *The Open and Closed Mind,* New York, Basic Books, 1960, pp. 39–40.
6. Timothy Leary, *Interpersonal Diagnosis of Personality,* New York, Ronald Press, 1957, p. 91.
7. From a poem, "Pershing At the Front" by Arthur Guiterman.
8. Daniel Katz and Robert L. Kahn, *The Social Psychology of Organizations,* New York, Wiley, 1966, p. 389.
9. Carl I. Hovland, Irving L. Janis and Harold H. Kelley, *Communication and Persuasion: Psychological Studies of Opinion Change,* New Haven, Yale University Press, 1953, p. 282.
10. Ernest G. Bormann, *Discussion and Group Methods: Theory and Practice,* New York, Harper & Row, 1969, p. 241.
11. Ibid., p. 225.
12. Hovland et al., op. cit., pp. 19–55.

13. James B. Lemert, "Dimensions of Source Credibility," paper presented to the Association for Education in Journalism, August 26, 1963.
14. James C. McCroskey, "Scales for the Measurement of Ethos," *Speech Monographs, 30* (1966), 65–72.
15. Arthur R. Cohen, *Attitude Change and Social Influence,* New York, Basic Books, 1964, p. 23.
16. Ray A. Killian, *Managing By Design . . . for Executive Effectiveness,* American Management Association, 1968, p. 257.
17. Berlo, op. cit., p. 54.
18. Ibid., p. 184.
19. Larry L. Barker and Robert J. Kibler, *Speech Communication Behavior: Perspectives and Principles,* Englewood Cliffs, N.J., Prentice-Hall, 1971, p. 21.
20. Irving L. Janis and Seymour Feshback, "Effects of Fear-Arousing Communications," *Journal of Abnormal and Social Psychology, 48,* no. 1 (1953) 78–92.
21. F. A. Powell, "The Effects of Anxiety-Arousing Messages When Related to Personal, Familial, and Impersonal Referents," *Speech Monographs, 32* (1965), 102–106.
22. William J. McGuire, "Inducing Resistance to Persuasion: Some Contemporary Approaches," *Advances in Experimental Social Psychology, 1* (1964), 191–229.
23. Rokeach, op. cit.
24. Irving L. Janis and P. B. Field, "Sex Differences and Personality Factors Related to Persuasibility," in I. L. Janis and C. I. Hovland (eds.), *Personality and Persuasibility,* New Haven, Yale University Press, 1959, pp. 55–68.
25. Leon Festinger, *A Theory of Cognitive Dissonance,* New York, Harper & Row, 1957.

8 the small-group leader

> Every human organization—business, educational, service, and political—includes numerous task-oriented groups to carry out the various functions of that organization and other task-oriented groups to coordinate the efforts of all other groups. Perhaps the most interesting of these organizational subgroups are the management groups—those groups charged with the task of organizing the various organizational groups and subgroups into a unitary efficiently functioning organization. B. Aubrey Fisher

OBJECTIVES for Chapter 8

After reading the chapter you should be able to:

1. Define a "group" and discuss the ways it may come into existence.
2. Show the relationship between group functions and systems functions.
3. Describe the characteristics of an effectively functioning group.
4. Discuss the following as they relate to a small work-oriented group in an organization:
    a. Norms
    b. Roles
    c. Power
5. Describe the three ways in which group leadership may be achieved.
6. Compare and contrast the *great person theory* with the *trait approach*.
7. Discuss the positive and negative ways in which a leader may influence his subordinates.

8. Compare and contrast:
    a. Lippitt and White's three leadership styles
    b. Authoritative vs. participative leadership
9. Describe the effects of leadership upon:
    a. group cohesiveness
    b. group productivity
    c. job satisfaction

As pointed out in the opening quote, the formation of small groups within organizations seems as inevitable as communication, change and the other organizational inevitabilities already discussed. Most complex organizations are too large to be efficient without being subdivided into smaller, more workable size groups of some kind. Of course, the most common divisions are such things as sales territories or departments. Since most territories and departments have a manager, we can justifiably look toward small-group research for some of our management strategies. In an article in 1969, *Business Week* pointed out that:

> the manager is going to become a mobilizer of competencies in the emerging knowledge-based industries. The basic job will be to create conditions in which good things are most likely to happen.[1]

They further point out that managers are normally poorly equipped to manage in such small-group, team environments. The prediction is that learning to do this will be a major challenge in the next few years for existing managers and businesses.

SMALL GROUPS AND THE ORGANIZATION

We have seen in earlier chapters, particularly Chapter 7, that management is often the business of influencing individuals strategically. There are, therefore, factors relating to the total organization and, at the same time, other factors relating to the individuals within that organization to be considered simultaneously by a manager.

It has long been a management technique to deal with members of an organization on an individual basis. This has proven to be good for organizational morale and, after all, each individual does have a set of characteristics which make them unique. This individualistic approach to management is still a valid method at times if it is not used exclusively as a panacea and to the exclusion of group considerations. Let us examine this exclusively individualistic approach in greater detail for a moment. As generally pointed out by Katz and Kahn[2] and Borman et al.,[3] the essential weakness of this individualistic approach is the psychological fallacy of concentrating upon individuals without regard to the role relationships that constitute the social system of which these individuals are a part. The individualistic approach is really an oversimplification which neglects the interrelationships of people in an organizational structure and fails to point to the aspects of individual behavior which need to be changed. In recent years there has been a significant change in the methods of managing the modern organization. Now modern managers must think of themselves as working with a team, managing a work group. Borman, et al., point out that, "If a manager fails to supervise his unit as a group, he will not keep informal groups from developing, but he does run the risk of losing control of the groups that do form."[4] Finally in the 1950s, those making a study of organizational management began fully to understand the importance of the group and its relationship to communication and leadership in the modern organization. In 1953 Rensis Likert wrote from the Institute for Social Research at the University of Michigan that extensive studies indicated that supervisor ability to manage subordinates as a group was an important factor in the achievement of managerial success.[5] Clearly, while the individual must remain an important consideration in any organization, such a consideration is worth little unless the individual is also considered as a part of his own milieu, a small group or work team.

The group has a definite effect upon the behavior of individuals in that it sets work norms and behavioral standards. Therefore, such factors as work motivation are apt to be considerably different in groups than they are for the same individual when he is operating alone. That group effect upon work motivation could, of course, be either positive or negative. A basically lazy person will not get away with such behavior when a group forces his conformity to their work norms and insists that he pull his share of the load. On the other hand, the group will sometimes come down hard on an overzealous worker when they have considerably slower work standards. Groups, especially union groups, call such a nonconformist a "scab" and it does not take long for most workers to do whatever they must do to avoid such a label. Whether the effect is positive or negative, it is apparent that the management and evaluation of workers is impossible without considering them as individuals who belong to a group or groups.

A question that often confronts managers is whether to make decisions, set policies, and accomplish productive results through group participation or individual effort. It is believed by some critics that the group method is slow and inefficient. Normally, to be sure, it would seem that a group accomplishes its work slower than does a single individual. On the other hand, a group can be more creative than any individual. The secret is for a manager to influence all group members to work as efficiently as they would individually.

Let us say hypothetically that we have a five-member work group each of whom can produce 20 units of work. Operating at full capacity, the total units of work should be at least 100. The capacity of the group may be even greater than the sum of its parts because of interaction and the exchange of information. If, however, each individual eases off and depends on the other persons because they are no longer personally "on the spot," we have lost our advantage. Let us imagine that when the group members relax in this manner, one person may produce 12 units of work, another 5 units, another 3, and the other two group members contribute nothing. Then we have a total of 20 units of work, have lost our advantage, and really may as well obtain the 20 units of work from one individual and save the time that group action takes. The advantages of group action over an individual effort will be explored throughout the remainder of Chapter 8.

There is considerable research which tells us that groups are capable of inordinate achievement. The old joke about a giraffe or camel being an ordinary animal built by a committee is highly unfair to the group method. While there may be some truth to the joke, the abortive results referred to are functions of the abilities and efforts of a particular group of people and not the group method itself.

Collins and Guetzkow have pointed out that, given instructions and a proper situation, group members often are able to accomplish greater task achievements collectively than any individual members are capable of on their own.[6]

As we mentioned in Chapter 1, Jay Hall tells of similar results from research he has conducted.[7] In his experiments, Hall compared people who were trained to those who were untrained in group methods. Using upper-management people as subjects, the experimenters administered the Lost On The Moon exercise. This exercise calls for people who are presumably lost on the moon to make priority decisions concerning a rank order list from the most important to the least important items on a 15-item list, which they would take with them to a rendezvous with the mother ship. After each person ranked the items on his own list, the subjects were randomly placed into four- to six-person discussion groups and asked to arrive at a group concensus on a single ranked list. The two sets of results were then compared with a master list which is correct according to NASA.

The scores for 75 percent of the trained groups were better than the best individual score in the group. Even 25 percent of the untrained groups achieved more collective success than their top individual. Hall and his associates reached two major conclusions from this research, which were as follows:

1. Groups function as their members make them function.
2. Conflict, effectively managed, is a necessary precondition for creativity.[8]

So we see evidence indicating that the use of group activities in an organization has advantages if it is handled properly. Further, it is clear that if the group method fails, it is usually the fault of the individuals involved and not the method. Hall concludes his analysis by reiterating:

> There is nothing in the group process that makes committees, boards and panels inherently inept.
>
> Ludicrous, ineffective solutions to problems are the product of groups that are pessimistic about their own potential, and have imperfect ways of dealing with conflict.
>
> The horse that is put together by a committee that understands group dynamics won't turn out to be a camel; it may be a thoroughbred filly fit for the Triple Crown.[9]

We as managers must be most concerned that the group method is not simply a scapegoat for avoiding managerial responsibilities. At times managers will throw a decision that should be theirs to a committee in the hope that the responsibility and/or any blame incurred would also belong to the committee. Such actions not only cause slowdowns and inefficient operations, but they also give the group method a bad name. There is no way that the group method can be effective when it is used as a scapegoat.

GROUP DYNAMICS

What is a group? How does it differ from just any collection of people? How is a task group constituted? Where do groups originate? All of these questions and many more can be answered by exploring group dynamics and the psychological implications of constituting a group.

No matter what sort of group we are dealing with, it had a beginning of some kind and may, or may not, have an end. When a group is formed there is usually a set of causal conditions which means that groups spring up because of circumstantial needs. We could set out roughly three basic reasons for groups to come into existence. They are formed, according to Cartwright and Zander, either *deliberately, spontaneously,* or by *external designation.*[10]

Deliberately formed groups are designed by an organization to serve specific functions. Examples of deliberate groups are work groups, problem-solving groups, and social action groups such as the Chamber of Commerce or citizens' committees. These groups are usually highly formalized and structured by the very nature of their tasks.

A spontaneously formed group, while performing just as important an organizational function, is apt to be far more informal than the deliberately formed groups. These spontaneous groups are collections of people with common interests or goals who become acquainted and are attracted to each other on a fairly permanent basis because of particular social-psychological needs. These needs are fulfilled either by group membership or by a certain member or both. Such groups are often formed by mutual consent of the participants through repeated social contact. They are also often formed through an extension of an existing physical closeness to each other. For instance, close-knit groups are often formed in the military service among people who are all in the same disagreeable situation together. Later, under other conditions, they may have no desire to see each other again. More will be said in a moment concerning the fulfillment of needs by a group.

Groups originating through external designation are collections of individuals who find themselves categorized into a group by the generalizations of some outside force. This category would include ethnic and religious groups, women, linguistic groups, artists, the poor, and college students. There are obviously as many ways to segregate and designate people into generalized groups as there are people engaging in the acts of categorization and designation. Perhaps the most interesting point here is the reaction of the person being categorized. Although a few resist being grouped by outsiders because of certain of their behaviors or characteristics, most people being categorized seem to come closer together and transform the outsider's loose generalization into a raison d'être and a sort of group symbol. For example, over the years many persons generalized black people as being different from others but very similar to each other, even to the point of looking alike. Finally, in the 1950s, black persons began to think, "Perhaps we are alike in many ways," then, "I am black," then, "Black is beautiful," then, "Black power." Looking back from this point of strong group identity we must remember that its strength has been reinforced, if not initiated, by outside categorization.

Clearly, we will be more concerned here with groups formed deliberately and spontaneously because they are more prevalent in the organizational setting. But first, what are some of the dynamic considerations involved in the makeup of a small group?

The size of an effective group is often a major concern. Effective group size will vary from situation to situation and group to group, but there are factors that surely designate any number of people as a group. One of these factors is that there must be interaction between group members for any real group activity to take place. Another group-determining factor is whether or not the people in it are aware of each other. Finally, a group does not really exist unless the individuals see themselves as a group.

We can see, then, that group size is not important as long as the size does not prohibit interaction, an interpersonal awareness, and a perceived group unity or "we" feeling. According to Edgar Schein:

> Mere aggregates of people do not fit this definition because they do not interact and do not perceive themselves to be a group even if they are aware of each other as, for instance, a crowd on a street corner watching some event. A total department, a union, or a whole organization would not be a group in spite of thinking of themselves as "we," because they generally do not all interact and are not all aware of each other. Work teams, committees, subparts of departments, cliques, and various other informal associations among organizational members would fit this definition of a group.[11]

Whether the group is a formal organizational work team or a more informal social group cropping up within the formal structure, people become group members and stay in the group because of their personal needs. The small group can often fulfill these personal needs and therefore performs an important psychological function for the individual. Schein points out that groups can provide:

1. Fulfillment for *affiliation needs*.
2. Development of an *identity* and the *self-esteem*.
3. *Establishment and testing of reality*.
4. Increased *security* and *personal power*.
5. *Accomplishment of work* that needs to be done.[12]

It seems clear that in a large, complex organization individuals will occasionally feel frustrated and somewhat lost in the crowd. To the extent that this is true, there is apt to be a constant need for affiliation with smaller groups through which need fulfillment can be attained. The personal needs brought on by large organizations also seem to be of the type outlined by Schein.

George C. Homans, in his book *The Human Group,* explains a conceptual framework for group development known as *social exchange theory.*[13] Exchange theory involves social behavior and is an exchange of goods, either material or nonmaterial goods, such as the symbols of things like approval and prestige. According to the exchange theorists, those who *give* a great deal, may *take* a great deal and so those who take a great deal are under great pressure to give. This give and take is often referred to as a cost and reward system. In any cost-reward structure such as a business, no one will do business with it for long if they continually lose, hence the pressure to give as well as take.

In the cost and reward system we find a sort of mental, psychological accounting going on and most people know whether they are ahead, even, or behind in an interpersonal relationship. Within this cost-reward paradigm may be a variation on the theme we will call simply an exchange of rewards. Although these exchanges must be a two-way street, they need not consist of like rewards. For instance, "friendship" might be returned for "help" in a time of need, or vice versa. The politician rewards, or pays off, his followers with political favors and they reward him in return in the coin of accepted leadership.

No matter how we look at the cost-reward paradigm, we find that it is a good explanation for the people who become group members to fulfill a need or needs. The cost to them, socially at least, is whatever individuality they give up to become a part of the group. The reward lies in the group's ability to fulfill their needs. Social exchange theory, then, is one very valid explanation for the formation and structure of groups.

We can also analyze the formation, development and functioning of small groups within an organization from the standpoint of systems theory. Recall that in Chapter 1 we spoke of a system as a functioning process including inputs, throughputs, and outputs. Relating the facets of a functioning small group as pointed out by Joseph McGrath in his book, *Social Psychology,*[14] to these systems concepts we find the following:

Group Functions	*Systems Functions*
1. Group composition	Inputs
2. Group structure	
3. Task and environment	Throughputs
4. Group process	
5. Group development	
6. Task performance	Outputs
7. Effects upon members	

When we speak of *group composition,* we mean the individuals who come together to form the group and the things each one brings to the group. We refer here to such things as attitudes, unique abilities, expertise, knowledge, work initiative, and so forth. From an input point of view, these are natural resources the group has available.

Group structure refers to the division of labor, degree of formality, and so on. *Task* means the specific objective of the group and *environment* includes situational working conditions such as seating arrangements, light, and heat. *Group process* is the actual interaction and discussion which takes place when the group meets. These are through-put factors in a small organizational group just as surely as they would be in a manufacturing system.

Group development refers to the group growth which takes place in the group as it meets. *Task performance* is evaluative in that it speaks to the quality, quantity, and speed of accomplishment of whatever group product is involved. The *effects on members* refer more to individual growth and personal changes that occur in the individual group members. Again, group development, task performance, and the effect on group members are group outputs just as surely as a car rolling off an assembly line would be.

Another vital factor in considering the dynamics of small groups within the organization is a closer look at the formality and informality of these groups. Often the informal and/or spontaneous group is referred to as a *clique group.* If cliques form to fulfill socialization needs, it is probably neither harmful nor unusual. If, on the other hand, cliques form as substitutes for the structured, formal work groups within the organization, then we may have a problem. The springing up of such a group may serve as an indicator that the formally structured work groups are not functioning properly.

The work group, if it is functioning properly, will probably follow some sort of pattern. The pattern need not always necessarily follow a single format, but it is important for a manager to communicate some sort of mode of operation by which the group members may set their task course and evaluate their progress. A suggested pattern for group work might look like the following:

A. Deciding which decision to tackle first.
B. Defining the exact nature of the problem.
C. Collecting information pertinent to the problem.
D. Ascertaining the minimum objectives any decision will have to achieve.
E. Deciding what is possible and what is impossible.

F. Thinking up many alternatives.
G. Checking the alternatives to see which ones achieve the minimum objectives.
H. Picking the best of whatever alternatives survive Step G.
I. Putting the decision into action.

We have seen that small-group communication causes some loss of individuality, sometimes results in a power struggle, and takes a great deal of time. In spite of these facts, we conversely find that there are counter reasons which serve as advantages for using the group method. Wayne Thompson cites three such advantages or benefits derived from small-group communication when he points out that:

1. Small group communication is conducive to bringing about attitude change in group members.
2. Small group communication can result in improved thinking and decision making.
3. Small group communication usually results in a decision that is superior to that of an individual working alone.[15]

We should add to this list an advantageous factor such as the impetus given to implementation of decisions when those decisions are made participatively. Adding up the advantages and comparing them to the disadvantages, we find the group communication in an organization is not only inevitable socially but is often the most effective way to accomplish necessary work.

According to Douglas McGregor, in his book *The Human Side of Enterprise,* there are some characteristics which exemplify an effectively functioning group in an organization. They are:

1. The atmosphere tends to be informal, comfortable, relaxed.
2. There is a lot of discussion in which virtually everyone participates, but it remains pertinent to the task of the group.
3. The task or objective of the group is well understood and accepted by the members. There will have been free discussion of the objectives at some point until it was formulated in such a way that the members of the group could commit themselves to it.
4. The members listen to each other! Every idea is given a hearing. People do not appear to be afraid of being foolish by putting forth a creative thought even if it seems fairly extreme.
5. There is disagreement. Disagreements are not suppressed or overriden by premature group action. The reasons are carefully examined, and the group seeks to resolve them rather than to dominate the dissenter.
6. Most decisions are reached by a kind of consensus in which it is clear that everyone is in general agreement and willing to go

along. Formal voting is at a minimum; the group does not accept a simple majority as a proper basis for action.
7. Criticism is frequent, frank, and relatively comfortable. There is little evidence of personal attack, either openly or in a hidden fashion.
8. People are free in expressing their feelings as well as their ideas both on the problem and on the group's operation.
9. When action is taken, clear assignments are made and accepted.
10. The chairman of the group does not dominate it, nor on the contrary does the group defer unduly to him. In fact, the leadership shifts from time to time depending upon the circumstances. There is little evidence of a struggle for power as the group operates. The issue is not who controls but how to get the job done.
11. The group is self-conscious of its own operation.[16]

Most of these functions are actually in the domain of the managers as they fulfill the role of task group leader. In the following sections we will take a closer look at the roles and functions of the manager as a group leader.

NORMS, POWER, AND ROLES

The behavior of individuals in organizational work groups is governed to a great extent by group norms, role designations, and the quest for, and maintenance of, power.

Norms

We have seen in Chapter 4 that a *norm* is a sort of social rule which governs the behavior of the members of a social system. It is an expectation shared by the members of a social system for "right action." The members of an organization are expected to behave in ways that are set down explicitly or implicitly by the organization. In many formal organizations a person is expected to follow certain norms, such as mode of dress, what organizations to belong to, and even where to eat and socialize. So there are organizational norms, which people who expect to get along and progress in an organization must follow.

Remember, we have already established that an organization has many small groups, both social and work groups, within it. These small groups also generate their own set of norms in addition to the norms of the larger social system concerning what is right or proper behavior. Such norms can even be extended to include the amount and type of work to be performed. Earlier we pointed out what can happen when people do not adhere to work quality and quantity expectations.

In Chapter 4 we also pointed out that when we speak of norms, we must also speak of *conformity* to these norms. A norm itself is meaningless unless there is some kind of pressure to conform to that norm. Kurt Lewin's Field Theory[17] is a widely accepted explanation of the concept of pressure to conform to group norms. According to the field theory notion, the members of a group tend to cluster around a norm in much the same manner as iron filings will cluster around a magnet in physical science field theory. If there is a deviant member who cannot or will not conform and join the cluster around the norm, there is a group pressure on that member to conform. The deviant member may move toward conformity with the norm insofar as possible, but morals, beliefs, other norms and so on may prevent that deviant member from conforming—at which point the group either accepts the deviant member's position or reverses the pressure to conform and expells the member from the group.

For example, a young man recently took a job as a tool designer in a job shop. While working on a drawing one day, the young man was being badgered by an engineer from the client company. In trying to explain how he wanted the drawing done, the engineer became increasingly hostile until he began to call the young man names. When he finally came to a name which was particularly disagreeable, the young man called the engineer a name sending the enraged engineer straight into the job shop supervisor's office. The young man was called into the the office and told that, since the engineer's firm was paying the bill, he must apologize to the engineer. He refused and was told, "Well you must apologize because that is the way we do things here" (pressure to conform to an organizational norm). The young man said, "I will not apologize so then perhaps I shouldn't be working here" (he was unable to go that far in conforming.) At this point the young man was fired (the organization expelled him as the sort of nonconformist with whom they could not live).

Norms serve a very positive organizational function. That function is a regulatory one which sets behavioral standards. These behavioral standards tell organization members what is expected of them and, at the same time, the standards tell them what they may expect behaviorally from others in the organization. In short, organizational and small-task-group norms can enhance our ability to predict behavior, thereby limiting troublesome uncertainty.

While pressure toward normative conformity is a fact of group life, it can be carried too far. Psychologist Irving Janis points out that an organization which overemphasizes consensus and conformity is a prime candidate for what he calls *groupthink*. Janis says that groupthink is "the desperate drive for consensus at any cost that suppresses dissent among the mighty in the corridors of power."[18] In other words, when we all think alike it is quite possible that none of us think very much. Overconformity and the drive for consensus can cause group members to suppress the sort of important, constructive disagreement which fosters creativity and the critical analysis so important to sound decision making.

Power

Recall from our brief discussion in Chapter 1 that *power* is the driving force behind influence and influence is the ability to induce another individual or group of individuals to behave in a desired fashion. Whether behavior is based upon out-and-out coercion or more subtle types of persuasion, the inducement must gain its impetus from some kind of power. Methods of influence and motivation discussed in Chapter 7, such as fear appeals, are definitely typical sources of power.

In a small group, the group usually has power over the individuals. If the individuals highly value membership in the group, they will be much more apt to subject themselves to the behavioral norms the group sets down for its members. The norms dictating the desired behaviors are the influences and the individuals' need to belong to the group provides the power. On the other hand, occasionally, individuals will have the personal power to influence the group. For instance, if individuals have some particularly needed expertise or if they are prestigious enough people to be sought after, as a famous person is, they could very well influence the rest of the group.

Power of the foregoing variety is certainly ever present in today's organization. An organization is also apt to find power manifesting itself through groups attempting to influence other groups. Management has power over labor and the labor union has power over the organization. Subgroups within an organization will have power over one another at various times. The result of such a power match between groups is inevitably what we usually call a power struggle.

The college students who endure considerable harassment during a fraternity or sorority initiation do so because membership holds a power of attraction over them. Power is every bit as evident when an individual puts up with an ogre of a boss and/or works long, tedious hours because the salary is good or a sought-after promotion seems possible.

Although power is not always manifested verbally and does not always contain a threat of force, it is often an application of some sort of force. As Carzo and Yanouzas point out:

> Power may be described as a latent force. Power is not applied. It becomes manifest through force which is applied. Force is visible and apparent. When an executive applies sanctions to a subordinate, he is using force and showing his power. The application of sanctions also identifies him as a power holder and gives evidence of his willingness to use force.[19]

Perhaps we can sum up some concepts related to power in a small group by listing several power-related propositions presented by Collins and Guetzkow as attempts at some conclusions based upon prior research:

1. Direct control of task-environmental rewards is a source of power.
2. Control of the rewards associated with "friendly interaction" is a source of power.
3. The greater the personal attraction of other group members to a single individual, the greater the power of that individual.
4. The greater the interpersonal attraction among the members of a group, the greater the power of the "group" over the group members.
5. Control of punishment will be a source of power (a) when the conditions of punishment are clearly specified and (b) when compliance can be observed.
6. Punishment-based power (a) will not lead to interpersonal liking and (b) will inhibit the exercise of power based on interpersonal attraction.[20]

Roles

Every position in an organization has a set of duties or tasks which must be carried out by the person assigned to that position. We call this a *role*. Actually, this is the person's formal or technical role. It is entirely possible that the person may at one time or another play many social roles in addition to the formally prescribed role. The role which is a part of an organizational position is usually fixed regardless of who is filling that position. It is, of course, true that the role may be altered slightly to fit the personality of a particular individual; however, in the main, the role will probably remain fairly stable.

Just as we sometimes have conflicts between the norms of groups to which we belong, so do we sometimes find ourselves in a role conflict. Such a conflict usually involves a set of norms that go with a role. For instance, during the late 1960s and early 1970s there were a great many college students who were in the National Guard. The incidence of wig purchasing was high because the hair norm in college was about shoulder length and in the National Guard it was considerably shorter. Even more of a role conflict must have gone on in the minds of these full-time students, part-time soldiers during the period of campus unrest over the unpopular war in Vietnam. The norms governing their student role certainly dictated an attitude set of one kind. The norms and role accompanying their tasks as soldiers called to riot duty would be almost the complete antithesis of their student role, thus causing a serious role conflict.

Each role carries with it a certain amount of *status*. The status will usually vary directly with the hierarchical importance of position. Status, then, refers to a sort of organizational prestige ranking. *Esteem* is also a factor related to various roles but, unlike status, it is not awarded with a position or role. Esteem must be earned by properly carrying out the role prescribed by the position.

Leaders of work groups may find themselves engaged in duties which can cause some role conflict or at least some role confusion. Leadership research over the years, especially that conducted by Robert Bales,[21] points to the necessity of more than one kind of leadership role function to be carried out in a task group. First, there is obviously a need for goal-oriented, task leadership. There is also usually a need for a socioemotional type of leadership which carries on a sort of group maintenance function.

Two facts come through quite clearly from all this research. One fact is that it is often impossible for a group to continue to function concerning task accomplishment until they straighten out socioemotional difficulties that may have arisen. Further, it is equally clear that the task and socioemotional leadership roles as Bales describes them would be very difficult for one person to carry out simultaneously. A definite role conflict and perceived managerial inconsistency is bound to occur when a tough task-master type leader begins temporarily to set aside tasks and minister to the human need of the group members. The opposite of this situation, that is one where an established socioemotional leader comes down hard on task accomplishment, is apt to appear equally inconsistent.

There are, of course, a variety of leadership roles called for in the management of a work group. Some of these roles described by

Thomas Gordon[22] are: counselor, channel of authority, communication facilitator, group therapist, upward spokesman for fellow manager leaders, and as an information storage and retrieval center.

EFFECTIVE LEADERSHIP

While effective leadership alone will not guarantee an effective group, it is an indicator and predictor of potential effectiveness. In a formal organization there is a particular need for leadership from an organizational health and maintenance point of view alone. Because leadership in an organizational task group is so vital, we should examine how a person rises to a position of leadership.

First, we must note that every effective group has leadership functions that must be performed, such as task orientation, summaries, facilitation, and so forth. These leadership functions can be provided either by a particular designated leader or by anyone in the group who can and will handle the functions. It is not always necessary, then, to have one designated leader in a small group; however, in an organization it is highly likely that leadership will be designated.

There are several ways for a group member to achieve a designated leadership role. One view is that a leader will become a leader either by appointment, selection, or emergence. When a leader is *appointed,* the appointment normally comes from outside the group and does not necessarily include the group members in the decision. A *selected* leader is chosen by election or some type of consensus agreement among the members of the group. In an *emergence* situation, the group is initially leaderless in terms of a designated leader but will have its leadership needs fulfilled by whoever in the group is capable or desirous of fulfilling them at any given time.

Clearly, the method of selection should provide a group with leadership that can function smoothly. An emergent situation allows for different individuals to emerge to commit a leader act of some kind and then fade back into the group. One major advantage is that people can provide leadership whenever group needs seem to call for their particular situational needs. Another advantage is that leadership in an emergent situation is seldom ever forced upon a group. On the other hand, an appointed leader is put in that position as a group outsider of higher authority and might therefore feel compelled to lead whether it is necessary or not. Of course, the leaders of small task-oriented groups within organizations are nearly always appointed. Normally, the hierarchy of an organization will insist upon leaders appointed by them for control purposes.

Perhaps even more basic than *how* a person becomes a leader is the question what kind of person will normally lead. Whether the leader emerges, is appointed, or is elected, it could be through behavioral reasons. In other words, one might be found suitable to lead based upon what one does and/or can do.

Other more predominant theories concerning how a person becomes fit to lead are *the great person theory* and *the trait approach.* The great person theory simply says that leadership qualities are inborn and, therefore, that leaders are born rather than made. On the other hand, the trait approach says that there are certain qualities which lead ultimately to leadership and that, if they can be identified and duplicated, we will have leadership. Whatever the origin of leadership may be, any leader will certainly possess at least some characteristics which are common to most leaders. R. M. Stodgill points to the following characteristics associated with leadership:

1. Capacity (intelligence, alertness, verbal facility, originality, judgment).
2. Achievement (scholarship, knowledge, athletic accomplishments).
3. Responsibility (dependability, initiative, persistence, aggressiveness, self-confidence, desire to excel).
4. Participation (activity, sociability, cooperation, adaptability, humor).
5. Status (socio-economic position, popularity).[23]

H. H. Meyer reports that certain factors seem to affect effective supervision and that others do not seem to matter.[24] The effectiveness of supervision, according to Meyer, is related to such factors as the ability to make social judgments, to problem-solving skills, to work fluency, and to the leader's personal background. However, such things as age, sex, experience, social attitudes, and personality traits do not seem to have much bearing upon the situation.

Leader influence

The goal of any leader, particularly one in a formal organization, is to influence behavior within their group; to motivate the members of that group as discussed in Chapter 7. Of course, leaders in organizations have the formal authority that goes with their assigned position at their disposal. *Authority,* as pointed out in Chapter 1, refers to rights, privileges, domains, and responsibilities delegated to an individual along with a formal position. Power would then derive from the proper use of this authority. The real problem facing most managers or supervisors is the constant search for new and better strategies to extend the scope of their sources of influence over subordinates. No matter how broad the formal authority may be, it is still often too narrow to accomplish some tasks. Perhaps the extension of formal authority becomes one of the true tests of leadership abilities.

One way of extending authority is by authoritatively designating subordinate roles; however, that requires very little imagination. Such a technique is really only the legal compliance work motive discussed earlier. The danger, of course, in such an authority extension strategy, is the possibility of an all-out subordinate rebellion. Most subordinates can live with managers who are sometimes unpleasant as long as they always are within the confines of the formal authority issued to them. There seems to be a reluctance to cross swords with the formal authority stemming from organizational policy. On the other hand, subordinates whose main work motive is legal compliance will be quick to sense the absence of the legality factor when managers extend their authority beyond the limits of formal authority to self-designated informal limits.

A far more challenging use of leadership would be to assist subordinates in extending their capacities. Managers, because of their leadership position, have many advantages. For instance, we pointed out in Chapter 3 that the leaders of groups are naturally a focal point for information and are, therefore, more apt to have information directed at them than anyone else in the group. Leaders also can expedite needed supplies, they can defend their group in a conflict with other groups, and, because of their unique position as leader, they can provide personal favors for subordinates. These are only a few of the advantages that managers have at their disposal to create unique manager-subordinate relationships based upon a sort of obligatory loyalty. From a cost-reward point of view, we find a manager leader who does favors for subordinates which, in the long run, facilitate task accomplishment. In return, we find subordinates repaying the manager for the favors in the coin of accepted leadership and increased loyalty. Such a strategy appears to be double edged with accompanying doubly positive outcomes.

Research by John French and Richard Snyder bears out the prediction of such positive results.[25] They found that managers who commanded loyalty from a group of subordinates, that is managers who were respected, liked, and accepted, seemed to have more control over the subordinates than other managers did. This is true, at least in part, because in these cases there was greater subordinate confidence in the manager's authority to give orders. The ultimate criteria for effective exercise of authority by a leader must, of course, be the level of subordinate performance. In that regard, the French and Synder research seems to imply that managers who command subordinate loyalty will be leading more highly productive groups than managers without subordinate loyalty.

The interface of attitudes, beliefs, and general points of view between the manager and the subordinate are of prime importance when deciding what kind of management will work best. Robert Tannenbaum and Warren H. Schmidt point to four key questions related to subordinate-focused selection of the proper management style. These questions are:

Q-1. *Can a boss ever relinquish responsibility by delegating it to someone else?*
  A. Not really, since the organization will ultimately hold the boss responsible. Because of this, delegation to subordinates carries with it a risk which must be recognized. Anyone can delegate duties to another but delegating the accompanying right to be wrong occasionally is not so easy.

Q-2. *Should the manager participate with his subordinates once he has delegated responsibility to them?*
  A. Managers must decide before delegating what their postdelegation role should be. If it seems appropriate to participate, then managers should make it clear that they see themselves as just another group member and not an authority figure.

Q-3. *How important is it for the group to recognize what leadership behavior the boss is using?*
  A. It is very important for managers to make it crystal clear just how they plan to use authority. They need to make it clear which decisions they will make and which ones the subordinates will be making. Managers should definitely avoid making the decisions in advance and then pretending to solicit subordinate participation.

Q-4. *Can you tell how "democratic" a manager is by the number of decisions his subordinates make?*
  A. The number of decisions alone is not necessarily significant. It is the magnitude of the decisions delegated to subordinates in a far more revealing measure. For instance, one major decision made by subordinates may be more of an indicator of a democratic style of management than a dozen little insignificant decisions.[26]

Deciding how to lead is never definite. It will vary from subordinate to subordinate and situation to situation and so it is most important that the leadership style be flexible. In the short run, a manager must do whatever is necessary to accomplish immediate goals and meet immediate needs. In the long run, most managers can take the time to develop strategies and shift their attention to assignments with less immediate pressure attached to them. According to Tannenbaum and Schmidt, the following are examples of such assignments:

1. To raise the level of employee motivation.
2. To increase the readiness of subordinates to accept change.
3. To improve the quality of all managerial decisions.
4. To develop teamwork and morale.
5. To further the individual development of employees.[27]

Leadership patterns and styles

The choice of a proper leadership style at the proper time is vital. The proper style is that which fits the personalities of the manager and the subordinates and whatever style fits the situation. However, no matter how participative the management's leadership style may be, the final decision still may rest with *the person* in charge. Not long ago a magazine carried a cartoon which depicted King Arthur in his crown and tall, kingly chair sitting at a round table with his knights. The king says, "While the round table is a symbol of our equality, my gold crown and fancy chair signify that I am perhaps just a smack *more* equal." The cartoon and its caption describe manager-subordinate "equality" the way it often must be no matter what the ideal might be. In other words, no matter how equal the managerial style might be, it is still necessary for someone to be in charge.

In addition to the difficulty of achieving any real equality between organization levels, it is also difficult to manage people equally or with identical leadership styles. Oddly enough, many successful managers tell us that the most unequal thing a manager can do is to treat all people equally. Different people require different management strategies or, as the transactional psychologists put it, we must use "different strokes for different folks."

On the other hand, most subordinates tell us that their biggest single problem with their managers is inconsistent management behavior. One particular fellow tells of the frustration brought about by a manager who "talks out of both sides of his mouth" from one moment to the next. For example, a report is due to a superior and it is classified as being important enough for the subordinate to wait around and make sure the superior gets the report, reads it, and OK's it. The superior becomes annoyed, informing the subordinate that he is too busy, that he will tell him when he has the time, and to stop "bugging" him about the report. Following this cue, the next time such a report is due the subordinate just holds the report and waits patiently. The superior then gets even more angry and says to the subordinate, "You should have bugged me on this. It's your job to bug me." Not only is the foregoing story true, but it is a highly frustrating spot for the subordinate to be in.

There seems to be a paradox here. On one hand, we say that all people must be managed and led differently. On the other hand, we point to the frustration arising from inconsistent leadership. What we are seeing is really not a paradox, but rather the nucleus of a general strategy for leading a task-oriented group of individuals. Both notions are true and valid. All people must be managed differently because of their own highly individualized motivations and personality. However, single individuals must be managed very consistently and with a great deal of predictability or they will quickly become frustrated and confused through uncertainty. So the strategy is to manage different individuals differently and always treat an individual case in a clear, consistent, and predictable manner.

Peculiarly, many managers try to lead their work group with a strategy which is the exact reverse of this suggested strategy. In an effort toward equal treatment of all individuals, these managers will treat each subordinate the same in a single situation but they will vary their treatment of similar situations from one time to the next. Although this reversal is quite common, it is not the way most subordinates want to be led. The importance of gaining maximum output by leading and managing subordinates the way *they* want to be led and managed should be reinforced again here.

Now let us turn our attention to some actual leadership styles that are available to managers and to what research tells us about the relative merits of those styles. Among the earliest, and still landmark, studies concerning group leadership styles were the White and Lippitt studies.[28] In these studies they experimentally compared the effectiveness of various leadership styles. Basically, the comparison was between the *authoritarian, democratic,* and *laissez-faire* styles. The *authoritarian* style was characterized by the leader determining all group policy, techniques, and steps as well as dictating the tasks. Authoritarian leaders were very personal in their praise and criticism of the subordinates. The *democratic* leaders opened up all policies, decisions, techniques, and steps to the group and all subordinates chose their own tasks. They were objective in their praise and criticism. The *laissez-faire* style leaders did not participate, let the group have complete freedom, and made no attempt to praise or criticize.

Many of the results connected with these studies have implications for managerial styles in small work groups. For instance, the laissez-faire style was characterized by play and produced a poorer quality of work as well as less work than did democratic leadership. Experimental subjects expressed a preference for the democratic over the laissez-faire style of leadership. The democratic style was characterized by the most sharing, friendliness and group-mindedness of the three.

Perhaps most important were the results that emerged from the examination of the authoritarian style. Authoritarian leadership created hostility, aggression, and often discontent which did not always manifest itself immediately. The authoritarian style had a tendency to create a dependency upon the leader, hence thwarting subordinate individuality and creativity. Such an outcome is fairly predictable because the oppressive behavior of an authoritarian, over time, will cause a subordinate either to drop out of the group or stay and endure the authoritarianism by becoming submissive. Submissiveness will usually lead to a loss of identity, creativity, and eventually, self-esteem. These negative results alone are enough to make a smart manager avoid an authoritarian style of leadership, at least for any prolonged period of time.

Authoritarianism versus participation

Earlier we pointed out that one of the long-range goals of most managers was "the individual development of employees." It is also clear now that the authoritarian leadership style is apt to produce just the opposite. The sales manager who philosophically stated that a manager "Could only *expect* what he *inspects*" was admitting that his men would only produce when he was there to see to it that they produced. It is possible that the manager may have also been admitting an authoritarian style of management, since his workers depended so heavily upon him to get them going. The problem here, of course, is that managers with subordinates spread over half a state are always partially absentee managers. They are always away from some of their subordinates and must depend upon them to be self-starters and at times even develop their own subleaders. Of course, participative, group-centered leadership is risky for paranoid managers. There is always some danger of a threat to the managerial rights and prerogatives of insecure managers when they move away from an authoritarian style.

According to Tannenbaum and Schmidt, there are several managerial behaviors along a continuum which depict the varying degrees of participativeness which might occur in small-task-group decision making. These managerial behaviors are that a manager:

Makes the decision and announces it
"Sells" his decision
Presents his ideas and invites questions
Presents a tentative decision subject to change
Presents the problem, gets suggestions, and then makes his decision
Defines the limits and requests the group to make a decision
Permits the group to make decisions within prescribed limits[29]

The foregoing list of management behaviors moves from a highly authoritative style to a highly participative one in which group members are very involved in the decision-making process. Perhaps we should take a closer look at the participative and authoritative approaches mentioned briefly in Chapter 4.

Participation is the engagement of individuals in the group so that they are involved in decisions which affect them as a group member. In a totally participative organization, individuals have both a voice and a vote in the small group in which they function as well as a voice and a vote in the representation of that group in the larger structure. Such participation also guarantees them an opportunity to share through their own involvement the rewards of the group cooperation that constitutes the organization. As Coch and French point out, research shows that industrial workers who were given such opportunities for discussion accepted decisions in work procedures much more readily than did workers in situations where no discussions were allowed.[30] It seems clear that the more participative a system is, the more integrated the communication will be.

The *authoritative approach* to decision making is the opposite of the participative approach, in that the group is not involved in the decision. Decisions are made unilaterally and flow down from the top of the hierarchy in the form of rules and policies. Because reaching a group decision is normally a frustrating and time-consuming process, decision making usually seems faster when achieved by the authoritative approach than by the participative approach. Decisions brought about by the authoritative approach, however, are more likely to be discontinued than those brought about by the participative approach, because of the lack of individual involvement and commitment to the final decision missing in the authoritative approach. According to Cartwright and Zander, "A belief by the membership that they have a reasonable control over group decisions seems to generate an interest on their part in the goals."[31]

In addition, there is evidence that, in practical organizational applications, the group method is really the fastest and most efficient decision-making method in the long run. A group of industrial managers recently pointed out that although the group method may take time, it often takes less time than other forms of decision making. The consideration here, according to these managers, is that a number of individuals affected by a decision will have to be informed of a unilateral decision and perhaps even persuaded. This process of informing and persuading is often more drawn out than simply taking the time initially to involve all affected persons in the decision-making process itself.

In an organization where the pattern and expectation has always been for decisions to be reached participatively, a situation occurred recently where they were reached unilaterally. The results were almost violent. When the expectation is participative decision making and a decision is made unilaterally, member satisfaction is apt to be low. In this particular instance the manager either made a decision, or appeared to have made a decision, on an issue. The group members were not even aware that a decision had to be made. To further compound the problem, the group members were eventually called together to discuss the issue in a way which was perceived as being a request for a "rubber stamp" on an already completed decision. There was a great deal of tension for a while in the organization until the opportunity arose to straighten out the problem.

Despite the knowledge that the participative method is highly effective, and the reinforcement of excellently devised training programs, managers will still often reach a decision unilaterally and then attempt to persuade the subordinates to adopt their solution. When the manager has a preferred solution, he naturally experiences difficulty in not pushing his own bias. Other barriers to participative leadership are that leaders sometimes have a tendency to:

1. have feelings of personal inadequacies. To these leaders, the allowance of participation might be perceived as a sign of weakness.
2. fear evaluation and rejection if the subordinate is made to feel free to speak up.
3. rely far too heavily on the authority that goes with the position or perhaps whatever extra authority he can gather.
4. engage in an ego trip which manifests itself as an "I am the boss and make no mistake about that" syndrome.

Conversely, there are many advantages stemming from participative leadership and management. Some of these are as follows:

1. There will be less subordinate negativism concerning decisions.
2. There will be an increased openness to change.
3. There will be a stronger tendency to implement the decisions.
4. There will be less labor grievances.
5. There will be a higher quantity and quality of output.

THE EFFECTS OF LEADERSHIP

Sound leadership in a small group can enhance other important related organizational factors. For example, there are strong ties between effective leadership and such factors as group cohesiveness, productivity, and job satisfaction.

Leadership and cohesiveness

What do we mean when we say a group is cohesive? The cohesiveness of a group refers to the group's unity, loyalty, "we" feeling, or solidarity. In a nonorganizational setting cohesiveness includes whatever factors draw and hold a group of individuals together. Obviously the members of an organizational work team are often constituted as a group through no choosing of their own. Collins and Guetzkow point out that, "Under conditions of common fate, the individuals will develop interpersonal attraction."[32] Although the development of such an interpersonal attraction and the eventual cohesiveness which develops from that attraction are possible, someone like the leader must usually make cohesiveness happen and control it. In such a group, then, the manager leader should create a work climate which will nurture the cohesiveness of the group.

One way for a leader to develop group cohesiveness is to keep the communication channels open, especially for feedback and interaction between group members. Some other methods of creating cohesiveness are described by Borman et al., when they present eight steps to greater cohesiveness in a work group. These are as follows:

1. Give your group an identity
2. Build a group tradition
3. Stress teamwork
4. Recognize good work
5. Set clear, attainable group goals

6. Give group rewards
7. Keep psychologically close to the group members
8. Treat group members like people.[33]

It is important for leaders to do whatever they can to create cohesiveness in their work group for a variety of reasons. For instance, members of highly cohesive groups have far less anxiety, they are less nervous, and feel less pressure than members of less cohesive groups. Also, a highly cohesive group will normally have a much steadier rate of output because it will have a more effective work standard with all members doing their part. Normally, in a highly cohesive work group, if someone is ill or has a work impairment of some kind, the other members are more apt to take up the slack and help out by producing more. Of course, it goes almost without saying that small, highly cohesive work groups in a large organization will have strong team feelings, which for the most part is a desirable behavior.

There is one danger in the indiscriminate development of a highly cohesive team feeling. If carried to extremes and handled improperly, such small-team-building can backfire and cause divisive influences within the larger organization. In other words, if the "we feeling" becomes a highly competitive sort of "we," it is an open invitation to the development of an antithetical "they." In this case the they would unfortunately include all other small work teams in the organization as well as the organization itself. It would be wise at this point to recall the discussion of the suprasystem, system, and subsystem in Chapter 1. Recall, if you will, that we pointed out that the members of any subsystem (small work group in this case) were at the same time members of a larger system and even a suprasystem. To use the same example as we used in Chapter 1, a member of an axle assembly team (subsystem) at Pontiac Motor Division is also a member of Pontiac Motor Division (system) and General Motors Corporation (suprasystem). Therefore, any leadership strategies which go so far as to develop a small-group team that is cohesively working for themselves and against the larger organization is, in the long run, counterproductive.

Leadership and productivity

Group productivity can best be measured by examining the degree to which a group is able to approach or accomplish the optimal performance level of a task. Of course, the optimal level of performance may be preset, varies from task to task, and should vary from subordinate to subordinate.

Many researchers and authors feel that the cohesiveness of a group is central to the predictable level of productivity. Most research points to the fact that people working in a group must work together and get along fairly well or they may never become a productive group. For instance, the *dissipation of power* notion tells us that we only have so much individual and collective power. If we are an incompatible group and lack cohesiveness, we are apt to waste all of our power and energy on each other, leaving little or no power and energy to expend on the task.

Obviosuly leadership is closely tied to productivity. If we again look back to Chapter 1 and our discussion of Theories X and Y as well as our discussion in this chapter of the leadership style research, we can find some information pertinent to the relationship between leadership and productivity. We have seen in a number of different ways that a Theory Y style manager would be apt to adopt a democratic leadership style and a participative type of decision making. He would do whatever he felt necessary to create a work climate in which people could produce. Research and practical application does tell us that, in the short run, the authoritarian style of group leadership appears to be highly productive. However, in the long run, with the continued use of an authoritarian leadership style, a continuing, ongoing group will suffer such debilitating effects as low morale, loss of individual creativity, and a very tense social climate, completely lacking in cohesiveness. In short, the selection and application of the proper leadership style has a great deal to do with productivity.

Leadership and job satisfaction

The quantity and quality of work produced by an organizational work group depends to a great extent on the degree of subordinate satisfaction with the group and the job. We have already seen that the manager leader can have an effect on group cohesiveness and productivity. A leader can certainly have just as great an effect on member satisfaction, whether that effect be direct or indirect. Collins and Guetzkow point out the direct and indirect effects that leadership has on member satisfaction.[34] Some of them are as follows:

1. Success on the group task will produce satisfaction.
2. Success in solving problems of interpersonal relations will produce satisfaction.

3. Congruence of member motivation and a lack of self-oriented needs will produce satisfaction.
4. Agreement on leadership will produce satisfaction.
5. Interaction with persons we like and persons who like us will produce satisfaction.
6. A position of high power will produce satisfaction.

The leader manager is responsible for creating all work environments and standards that will produce satisfied workers. An example of the effect that task success can have upon satisfaction is a winning athletic team. During the early 1950s there was a large midwestern university with a football team sporting a 28-game winning streak and ranking number one in the nation. The coach was a tough taskmaster who was not necessarily loved by all his players. He was, however, highly respected. According to the players, the coach was most respected for his ability to pull all of their individual hard work together and make a winning combination out of them on Saturday—nothing more nor less than member satisfaction due to group success.

Managing and leading people according to the style by which they want to be led should produce high member satisfaction. The productive outcomes of high member satisfaction are really the difference between a group that will stay an extra five minutes or work on Saturday and a group that does just what it has to and no more.

It should be obvious by now that leadership strategies and such factors as cohesiveness, productivity, and job satisfaction are all inextricably interdependent.

SUMMARY

We have seen that an understanding of the place of the small work group in a large organization is important to the development of a total managerial communication strategy. It is also important to realize that the norms of an organization will designate appropriate leadership roles and the power that goes with them.

Small groups within large organizations are, other things being equal, easier to manage, more cohesive, and more productive than larger organizational groups. The small group within an organization can fulfill the production needs of the organization as well as the social-psychological needs of the group members.

Of the leadership styles or patterns available and examined in this chapter, it should be clear that the style most often effective is one that is democratic and participative in nature. A leader who manages and motivates his subordinate work group on their terms, but still with solid control, is apt to be the most influential force in that work group.

The effects of sound leadership on the organizational task group are far-reaching indeed. There is no more highly researched group variable than leadership, which is another indication of the pervasiveness and importance of this factor. Leadership in a small group has a strong effect upon such variables as group cohesiveness, group productivity and group member satisfaction. These variables in turn have an effect on nearly everything the group is and does.

The manager as the leader of a small work group within a larger organization is operating right at the organizational level where everything is really happening. The functions in which the organization engages really begin and end at this level. It is at this level that inputs are received, workers are brought together to accomplish the throughputs, and the outputs of the organization are produced. The importance of effective leadership and management at this small-group level cannot be overemphasized.

NOTES

1. "The Managers," *Business Week* (December 12, 1969) 146.
2. Daniel Katz and Robert L. Kahn, *The Social Psychology of Organizations,* New York, Wiley, 1966.
3. Ernest G. Bormann, William S. Howell, Ralph G. Nichols, and George L. Shapiro, *Interpersonal Communication in the Modern Organization,* Englewood Cliffs, N.J., Prentice-Hall, 1969.
4. Ibid., p. 52.
5. Rensis Likert, *New Patterns of Management,* New York, McGraw-Hill, 1961.
6. Barry E. Collins and Harold Guetzkow, *A Social Psychology of Group Processes for Decision-Making,* New York, Wiley, 1964, p. 45.
7. Jay Hall, "Decisions, Decisions, Decisions," *Psychology Today* (November, 1971), 86–88.
8. Ibid., 88.
9. Ibid., 88.
10. Dorwin Cartwright and Alvin Zander, *Group Dynamics: Research and Theory,* New York, Harper & Row, 1968, p. 54.
11. Edgar H. Schein, *Organizational Psychology,* Englewood Cliffs, N.J., Prentice-Hall, 1970, p. 81.
12. Ibid., pp. 84–85.
13. George C. Homans, *The Human Group,* New York: Harcourt Brace Jovanovich, 1950.
14. Joseph E. McGrath, *Social Psychology: A Brief Introduction,* New York, Holt, Rinehart and Winston, 1964, pp. 63–71.
15. Wayne N. Thompson, *Quantitative Research in Public Address and Communication,* New York, Random House, 1967, pp. 97–105.
16. D. McGregor, *The Human Side of Enterprise,* New York, McGraw-Hill, 1960.
17. Kurt Lewin, *Field Theory In Social Science,* New York, Harper & Row, 1951.

18. Irving L. Janis, "Groupthink," *Psychology Today, 5,* no. 6, (November, 1971), 43.
19. Rocco Carzo, Jr. and John N. Yanouzas, *Formal Organizations: A Systems Approach,* Homewood, Ill., Irwin, 1967, p. 187.
20. Collins and Guetzkow, op. cit., p. 139.
21. Robert F. Bales, "Task Roles and Social Roles in Problem-Solving Groups," in T. M. Newcomb and E. L. Hartley, *Readings in Social Psychology* (3rd ed.), New York, Holt, Rinehart and Winston, 1958.
22. Thomas Gordon, *Group-Centered Leadership,* Boston, Houghton Mifflin, 1955, p. 318.
23. R. M. Stodgill, "Personal Factors Associated With Leadership: A Survey of the Literature," *Journal of Psychology, 25,* (1948), 35–71.
24. H. H. Meyer, "Factors Related to Success in the Human Relations Aspect of Work Group Leadership," *Psychological Monographs, 63,* no. 3 (1951).
25. John R. P. French, Jr. and Richard Snyder, "Leadership and Interpersonal Power," Darwin Cartwright (ed.), *Studies in Social Power,* Ann Arbor, Institute for Social Research, University of Michigan, 1959, pp. 118–149.
26. Robert Tannenbaum and Warren H. Schmidt, "How To Choose A Leadership Pattern," *Harvard Business Review, 36,* no. 2 (March–April, 1958), pp. 95–101.
27. Ibid., pp. 95–101.
28. Ralph White and Ronald Lippitt, *Autocracy and Democracy,* New York, Harper & Row, 1960, chapters 3 and 5.
29. Tannenbaum and Schmidt, op. cit., pp. 95–101.
30. Lester Coch and John R. P. French, Jr., "Overcoming Resistance to Change," *Human Relations, 1,* no. 4 (1948), 512–532.
31. Cartwright and Zander, op. cit., p. 407.
32. Collins and Guetzkow, op. cit., p. 151.
33. Bormann, et al., op. cit., p. 101.
34. Collins and Guetzkow, op. cit., p. 209.

9 the total organizational communicator

> The world we live in is basically a world of people. Most of our actions toward others and their actions toward us are communicative acts in whole or part, whether or not they reach verbal expression.
>
> Daniel Katz and Robert L. Kahn

OBJECTIVES for Chapter 9

After reading the chapter you should be able to:

1. Discuss the interrelationship between internal and external communication in an organization.

2. Discuss the advantages and disadvantages of the written and oral communication channels.

3. Demonstrate the skills involved in honest, accurate, organizational reporting.

4. Describe the similarities and differences between the various basic types of interviewing.

5. Discuss organizational conferences and describe the specific features of problem solving, information, and change of attitude conferences as well as brainstorming and buzz sessions.

6. Be able to create and deliver a manuscript speech according to the guidelines set down in this chapter.

7. Discuss the relationship between advertising, promotion and public relations in an organization.

Thus far in Part II we have explored strategies for the manager acting as a change agent, an interpersonal motivator, and a small-group leader. Although these are unquestionably key management functions, our discussion of organizational communication in Part I reveals that there must be others. We have pointed out that communication is highly pervasive and the quote at the beginning of this chapter reiterates that "most of our actions toward others and their actions toward us are communicative acts."

In Chapter 2 we discussed internal and external communication. We said that organizational management must realize that communication relating to that organization includes a much broader scope than the formal organizational boundaries and that internal and external communication are inextricably tied together.

In this chapter we will deal with some of the pervasively based settings for communication in an organization in more detail. Although we have already dealt with many functions in the management of internal commuication, we will touch upon it again in this chapter. Additionally, we will take a much closer look at such factors of external communication as advertising, public relations, sales, and recruiting. We will also examine areas that could apply to internal or external communication, such as interviewing, public presentation, and conferences, as well as the oral and written style of message presentation. Although we are touching on these important topics, the treatment is necessarily limited; entire books have been devoted to each of them, and they are not the main focus of this book.

INTERNAL COMMUNICATION AND TOTAL COMMUNICATION

A large portion of Part I of this book dealt with internal communication and its directionality, its formal-informal aspects, and its association with productivity and subordinate morale. A still larger portion of Part II has dealt with various communication strategies that managers might employ to accomplish their internal communication goals. While it is true that these communication problems and their strategic remedies are general and may be applied to any communication situation, the basic focus up until now has been upon internal communication applications.

One area not really covered until now has been the interrelatedness of internal and external communication. First, produced goods which are quantitatively or qualitatively weak due to internal communication breakdowns cannot be effectively marketed in the external marketplace, regardless of how well-planned the external communication may be. All the intricate advertising campaigns and high-powered sales teams in the world cannot make up for an inferior or poorly produced product for very long. Also, the externally communicated public image so jealously guarded by organizational public relations, advertising, and sales promotion people can be destroyed almost overnight by a faction of subordinates who have low morale and a poor relationship internally with the company. Who are you, as an outsider, going to believe when forming your own mental image of an organization? Will you believe the person on television or billboards or in magazines who tells you how great and philanthropic Acme, Inc. is, or will you believe the person next door who works there and says, "they stink," or "no one ever tells me anything," or "my boss is unreasonable" or "the orders from above are so screwed up nobody knows what they are doing." The chances are that you will believe the neighbor, if he has any credibility at all, and that all that money and time spent promoting Acme, Inc. to the external world could be shot down by a few dissident employees with whom no one had taken the time to communicate internally.

From these very real examples we can see that the organizational subordinate is, either positively or negatively, an organizational public relations person in their own right. It further becomes obvious, then, that the subordinate who is communicated with properly and strategically internally is far more apt to present the external, public image the organization wants. The use of many of the internal communication strategies already presented in Part II will have a great effect upon the external communication system of the organization. In fact, it should now be apparent that internal and external communications are really very closely interrelated subsystems in a system of total organizational communication.

EXTERNAL COMMUNICATION

Our discussion of external communication will not be a course in advertising or sales. It will, however, encompass an examination of the external communication factors with which an organization manager must be familiar.

It is a major function of external communication to paint the kind of organizational picture desired by the organization in the minds of the public. External communication obviously includes public relations, sales promotion, advertising, and sales. But it also would include such less obvious functions as customer relations, service, personnel recruiting, company service, and a whole myriad of other communication functions. In short, external communication includes all contacts an organization might have with its outside environment.

As we mentioned at the beginning of this chapter, every person in an organization is really a member of the public relations and customer relations staff. In these highly competitive days, the token public relations person with the carpeted office in the executive suite cannot do the job alone. The subordinates at the lower levels see more of the public on an interpersonal communication basis every day than the "PR people" and their colleagues in the executive suite do in several months. Such a realization has caused modern organizations to strive for better, more accurate internal communication and to do everything within their power to cause each lower-level subordinate to think of themselves as *the* organizational representative. They may be just that, since the public they meet daily may never see any more of the organization than that individual organization member. Consequently, how the public perceives the attitudes of that subordinate, whether positive or negative, is pretty apt to be the way they perceive the total organization.

Managers must instill in their subordinates, therefore, the notion that public relations and customer relations do not stop with a piece of trade advertising or a donation to the United Way. These things, essential as they may be, are only beginnings and perhaps even a little peripheral. The subordinates must understand that real public and customer relations consists of people just like them doing interpersonal things for other people and communicating with these others interpersonally. In the insurance business, for instance, there are far more new policies sold because someone handled a claim personally—fast and fair—than as a result of all the national advertising and public relations campaigns ever devised.

The organizational hierarchy, especially in the industrial setting, now has many other public relations concerns that fall directly in its domain. A public, too long silent, now demands to know what large complex organizations are doing about the newly discovered problems of the 1970s, such as pollution and energy conservation. It is no longer enough to build a good-looking, high-quality automobile. Today's cars must also be economical in their use of gas and oil and must not only be made in pollution-free factories, but themselves not pollute our atmosphere when we drive them down our streets and highways. If the task of bulding low-cost, high-quality products that look good, ride good, do not waste fuel and do not pollute in factories that in turn do not pollute the atmosphere sounds like a huge engineering problem, it is. But this multifaceted dilemma is even more of a dilemma to the organization's external communication subsystem, mainly the public relations people. This dilemma can be solved only in part by the individuals at the lower levels. This is an organizational problem which must be solved by top management and the solution must be communicated to the external public as rapidly as possible. As we said a moment ago, the days of the silent majority are gone, perhaps forever, and an aroused public demands: "Executive, do you have a solution or are you part of the problem?" This aroused public is even in the position, through pickets, boycotts etc., of running a counter campaign which could be very damaging to the public image of organizations.

We can see now that the success of external communication functions such as advertising, sales, and the recruitment of top-notch personnel are heavily dependent upon the organizational image communicated externally. We will discuss these other external communication functions throughout the remainder of the chapter but for the moment let us agree that the public image of the organization, both from the executive level and from the bottom-level subordinate, is the broad base from which all external communications functions must operate.

WRITE IT OR SAY IT?

Whether communication is internal or external, the communicator must decide whether to use a written or oral channel. There are no doubt communication situations that call specifically for either written or oral communication. However, the choice may also involve factors of cost, availability and personal preference.

Generally, we can attribute certain advantages and disadvantages to both types of channels. Written communication, for instance, can be much more carefully planned than oral communication. When a message is written the receiver can reread it and examine it more carefully than he can oral communication, which is sometimes presented only once. As a source prepares a written message he will cross out words and phrases in the rough copy and substitute more accurate or more tactful wording. These crossed out words and phrases are never really communicated and represent the sort of thing which *are* communicated orally and get us into trouble because we cannot cross them out orally. Of course, in the courtroom, the judge will admonish the jury to "disregard the last statement." But we have already seen sufficient evidence in this book alone indicating the futility of such a directive.

On the other hand, oral messages have several advantages over written messages. In oral communication the source and receiver are usually face to face so they have the advantage of nonverbal channels, such as the tone of voice and facial expressions, as aids in interpreting the message. Additionally, the receiver of oral communication can ask questions for clarification thereby giving immediate feedback to the source.

There are, of course, other minor advantages and disadvantages as well as the possibility that in certain situations an advantage may be seen as a disadvantage. For example, in certain socially uncomfortable communication situations, face-to-face oral communication may be less desirable than the built-in ambiguity of the written message. In any case, normally the choice between an oral or a written message and the choice of a particular channel is highly situational.

In a study reported in *Personnel,* Thomas L. Dahle tested the most effective method of transmitting information to employees when the information was of interest to those employees. The comparison was between the following methods:

Oral only
Written only
Combined oral and written
Bulletin board
Grapevine

The results showed that the least effective methods were the grapevine and bulletin board method. More directly the research suggests that:

> On the basis of the foregoing experiments, it appears probable that if management wished to transmit certain types of factual information to its employees, the best results could be obtained if the material was presented orally at the same time that written material on the subject was made available. The combined method was definitely better than relying solely on an oral presentation, a written presentation, or the posting of material on a bulletin board.[1]

It is true, of course, that when other factors are taken into account, other methods may be more effective. For instance, it may not seem feasible cost-wise or time-wise to pull subordinates from productive endeavors in order to provide them with an oral presentation. On the other hand, the least expensive method of presenting material could be the most costly in the long run if misunderstanding and ineffective communication cause wasted time and lost productivity.

REPORTING

Reporting is an area of organizational communication which has become increasingly important as a skill necessary for people wanting to be considered for promotion in today's technologically confounding society. Again, the reporting method may be either oral, written, or a combination of the two. The oral style will be covered more extensively later in this chapter when we discuss public performance. We will, then, concentrate our efforts in this report section upon reports in general and the written style in particular.

The importance of the ability to report organizational facts clearly and concisely cannot be stressed too strongly. Many otherwise highly qualified young executives have reached the point of their final promotion long before they should have because of weak writing skills. Further, if you ask any teacher or college professor what is the one skill that even their best students lack, they would invariably answer, "They can't express themselves clearly in writing." In short, they cannot write. Such a high need and accompanying low skill area definitely calls for added concentration in the training of a manager.

The problem of poor reporting seems really to be twofold. Either people are unable to express themselves well, which leads to inadequate reporting, or they express themselves well enough but see the whole business as a game and therefore are apt to produce reports which are inaccurate.

The lack of ability to report adequately seems to be a standard problem in our basic educational format. Many people, otherwise well educated, have never really learned to communicate effectively in writing. If they have learned to write, it has tended to be the development of a skill in writing English themes and not the simple, direct reporting of vital facts so important to an organization.

The person with some writing skill may still not report accurately and dependably for the same reasons that any form of communication can be distorted. For instance, an organizational report may be defensive and say what the subordinate thinks the superior wants to hear rather than stating the facts. In his book, *Why Am I Afraid to Tell You Who I Am,* John Powell speaks about this kind of defensiveness. He says that I am afraid to tell you who I am because I am afraid you will not like who I am. Instead, I try to be who I think you would like me to be. As Powell puts it, "These patterns eventually become so self-deceptive that we forfeit all sense of identity and integrity. We act 'roles,' wear 'masks,' and play 'games.' "[2] The worst part of all this is that in time it may be difficult for us to distinguish who and what we *really* are from any of the many poses we strike for the myriad of individuals with whom we have daily contact. In short, what is real becomes blurred with the unreal.

Certainly this role-taking sort of defensiveness has an effect upon all of our communication. When we are asked by the supervisor to report on some organizational project, we may have a tendency to think that a straight reporting of the facts is unimpressive and instead report what we think will impress him. College students are no different. When describing a term paper, the instructor says very clearly: this project is for you, it must be something that interests you, and will be of personal value to you. Invariably, at least one student will say to the teacher, "What do you want on this term paper?"

Defensive report writing may even contain purposeful ambiguity based upon an "if you can't convince them, then confuse them" premise. One example is the tongue-in-cheek buzz phrase projector which has made the rounds of nearly every office. The directions for the "projector" read as follows:

> Because we must all, at various times, develop reports for our superiors, the following work-aid has been written after much "after-hours" deliberation and research.
>
> The system is guaranteed to fulfill basic frustrations that may develop while writing reports that are to be on high etymological planes. The procedure is simple; think of any three-digit number, then select the corresponding word from each column. Any combination of words from each column can be dropped into any report with that ring of decisive and knowledgeable authority.

Column I	Column II	Column III
0. integrated	0. management	0. options
1. total	1. organizational	1. flexibility
2. systematized	2. monitored	2. capability
3. parallel	3. reciprocal	3. mobility
4. functional	4. digital	4. programming
5. responsive	5. logistical	5. concept
6. optional	6. transitional	6. time-phase
7. synchronized	7. incremental	7. projection
8. compatible	8. third-generation	8. hardware
9. balanced	9. policy	9. contingency

Examples:
131—total reciprocal flexibility
769—synchronized transitional contigency
970—balanced incremental options
698—optional policy hardware
806—compatible management time-phase

No one will have the remotest idea of what you are talking about, but the important thing is that they are not about to admit it!

While this advice is a clever bit of wit, many people in organizations have been writing reports full of the same kind of phrases for years without the aid of even such a device.

The readability of a report is really only a function of a clear writing style that communicates to the reader. This depends not only on such mechanical things as grammar and the avoidance of long, run-on sentences but also the actual content of the report; if the message is not clear there is no point in writing the report in the first place. As report writers we must stop trying to impress our readers with our immeasurable wit and intellect and try simply to communicate. Students frequently complain that a given textbook is deliberately obscure and highly unreadable. Certainly textbooks, just like organizationl reports, are sometimes deliberately confusing. But the written message in either case must be readable without having to take a course of required reading to understand it. We need to become infinitely more aware of the ingredients of better and more accurate reporting and turn these ingredients into better and more accurate reports. John Fielden of Harvard University suggests an inventory of written reports (see Figure 9.1), which provides some guidelines for better reporting.[3]

Such a large set of guidelines may be a bit awkward but there are clues and reminders that help to point out areas in our writing style that need improvement. If we are honest with ourselves, such an inventory can work wonders in our reporting style through an increased awareness alone.

We can say, then, that since upward communication in an organization is so important, we must do our best to develop and train all our reporting skills, both oral and written. Fancy language and the distortions it brings about must be eliminated. In short, we must adopt the philosophy of television's Jack Webb on the old "Dragnet" television detective show when he used to say, "Just the facts, ma'am. Just the facts."

INTERVIEWING

The interview, because it is such a basic, interpersonal, often one-to-one communication setting, is used constantly throughout an organization. There can be little doubt that the interview is the best pragmatic example of interpersonal communication existing today. On the other

Exhibit II. Written performance inventory

1. Readability

Reader's Level
☐ Too specialized in approach
☐ Assumes too great a knowledge of subject
☐ So underestimates the reader that it belabors the obvious

Sentence Construction
☐ Unnecessarily long in difficult material
☐ Subject-verb-object word order too rarely used
☐ Choppy, overly simple style (in simple material)

Paragraph Construction
☐ Lack of topic sentences
☐ Too many ideas in single paragraph
☐ Too long

Familiarity of Words
☐ Inappropriate jargon
☐ Pretentious language
☐ Unnecessarily abstract

Reader Direction
☐ Lack of "framing" (i.e., failure to tell the reader about purpose and direction of forthcoming discussion)
☐ Inadequate transitions between paragraphs
☐ Absence of subconclusions to summarize reader's progress at end of divisions in the discussion

Focus
☐ Unclear as to subject of communication
☐ Unclear as to purpose of message

2. Correctness

Mechanics
☐ Shaky grammar
☐ Faulty punctuation

Format
☐ Careless appearance of documents
☐ Failure to use accepted company form

Coherence
☐ Sentences seem awkward owing to illogical and ungrammatical yoking of unrelated ideas
☐ Failure to develop a logical progression of ideas through coherent, logically juxtaposed paragraphs

3. Appropriateness

A. Upward Communications

Tact
☐ Failure to recognize differences in position between writer and receiver
☐ Impolitic tone—too brusk, argumentative, or insulting

Supporting Detail
☐ Inadequate support for statements
☐ Too much undigested detail for busy superior

Opinion
☐ Adequate research but too great an intrusion of opinions
☐ Too few facts (and too little research) to entitle drawing of conclusions
☐ Presence of unasked for but clearly implied recommendations

Attitude
☐ Too obvious a desire to please superior
☐ Too defensive in face of authority
☐ Too fearful of superior to be able to do best work

B. Downward Communications

Diplomacy
☐ Overbearing attitude toward subordinates
☐ Insulting and/or personal references
☐ Unmindfulness that messages are representative of management group or even of company

Clarification of Desires
☐ Confused, vague instructions
☐ Superior is not sure of what is wanted
☐ Withholding of information necessary to job at hand

Motivational Aspects
☐ Orders of superior seem arbitrary
☐ Superior's communications are manipulative and seemingly insincere

4. Thought

Preparation
☐ Inadequate thought given to purpose of communication prior to its final completion
☐ Inadequate preparation or use of data known to be available

Competence
☐ Subject beyond intellectual capabilities of writer
☐ Subject beyond experience of writer

Fidelity to Assignment
☐ Failure to stick to job assigned
☐ Too much made of routine assignment
☐ Too little made of assignment

Analysis
☐ Superficial examination of data leading to unconscious overlooking of important pieces of evidence
☐ Failure to draw obvious conclusions from data presented
☐ Presentation of conclusions unjustified by evidence
☐ Failure to qualify tenuous assertions
☐ Failure to identify and justify assumptions used
☐ Bias, conscious or unconscious, which leads to distorted interpretation of data

Persuasiveness
☐ Seems more convincing than facts warrant
☐ Seems less convincing than facts warrant
☐ Too obvious an attempt to sell ideas
☐ Lacks action-orientation and managerial viewpoint
☐ Too blunt an approach where subtlety and finesse called for

Figure 9-1 Written performance inventory.

hand, it is more than just synonymous with communication. Interviewing is a unique communication event and will be treated as such here.

The uses of interviewing are varied in most organizations. Generally speaking, these uses include *personnel interviews* in such situations as hiring and firing, *evaluation interviews,* and *persuasive interviews,* such as in the sale situation. No matter to what use it is put, the interview is a prevalent communication event and basically the components are the same in any situation. James Lahiff makes the following statements in an essay found in *Readings in Interpersonal and Organizational Communication:*

> It is these components, and the influence which they exert in an interview, which make the interview distinctive. The universality of these components renders this consideration of the process equally meaningful to anyone, regardless of occupation, who engages in interviews. These major components are control, objectives, questions, situational instability, crucial junctures, and receiver involvement.[4]

While an interview must be kept flexible, it is always necessary to control the interview and follow some sort of predetermined, goal-oriented plan. The interviewer must decide how much control is needed in each situation. The control should usually take the form of keeping the interview tangent-free and task oriented so that both parties may gain the maximum information in the allotted time.

Control will be enhanced considerably by having a clear set of objectives in the interview and by clearly communicating these objectives to the interviewee. Not only does this behavior cut down on wasted words and time but should help in eliminating "games." The same defensive role-playing and gamesmanship discussed in the previous section on reporting is apt to creep into the interview. Sometimes the interviewer is playing a game or appears to be playing a game because he has not clearly communicated the objectives to the interviewee. No matter what the reason, the interviewee may then begin to play a game of his own and the interview can be reduced to one big game. Such a reduction to mere gamesmanship is not apt to produce satisfactory results for either party.

The outcome of an interview is controlled to a great extent by the kind of questions asked. Interviewing is a business of inquiry, so the most effective initial questions and probing subquestions will probably control the interview and be most apt to determine the degree to which the objectives will be accomplished.

Interviewing typically has some role instability because the interviewees have no role model to follow, no other person or standard to which they can conform. Such instability may even cause the participants to start a game. In other words, when the interviewee cannot be sure what sort of behavior will optimize his position, he will begin to search for a comfortable role which he hopes will be what the interviewer is expecting of him. In the absence of a clear behavioral standard, the interviewee will probably make up his own standard and take a chance. Even though it would seem smarter to be oneself in the absence of any real clue as to what the interviewer's expectation is, the interviewee will still often take that chance.

Given the juxtaposition of a certain set of questions, the interview may reach certain junctures which literally determine whether or not it will continue. For instance, during this author's stay in the U.S. Army, he was interviewed for a possible placement into the Counter Intelligence Corps (a sort of investigative undercover function). During the course of the interview, the questioning led to a purposely created stressful situation. The interviewee reacted badly and "blew his cool" altogether. In retrospect, that was a crucial juncture and although the interviewer was polite enough to ask a few more questions, the interview was really over after the interviewee failed to clear the hurdle that had been deliberately set up at the point of crucial juncture.

There is perhaps nothing more characteristic of an interview than a high degree of receiver involvement. An interview is not a lecture; it is an interactive situation. The word interview does, in itself, indicate an interface of points of view which should indicate an exchange of information. The purpose of an interview, however, is to draw out as much as possible from the interviewee. Therefore, the interview at its communicative best would deeply involve the receiver, or interviewee in this case.

The personnel interview

As stated earlier, the personnel interview includes both the employment (or hiring) interview and the exit interview. The exit interview is usually geared to gain information from those who are leaving the organization voluntarily. The information about the organization gained through interviews with people who are leaving, especially concerning why they are leaving, can be invaluable. Obviously such an interview requires a great deal of sensitivity and trust on the part of both the interviewer and the interviewee. The reward for successful exit interviews is an excellent body of constructive negative feedback to be used in correcting the system. If we can learn why people leave the organization and can correct the problem, then we may be able to cut down our personnel turnover considerably, for example. Some firms reportedly provide their top management with an exit interview results summary list.

One thing which must be reemphasized is the building of a climate based upon interpersonal trust and the use of very skillful interviewing in order to insure success. Remember, the interviewer is asking a person who is perhaps already not happy with the organization and who may want a letter of recommendation from the organization. That person could take an attitude that says, "Why should I help them when I don't even like them or care what happens to them?" Or the departing person might be even more likely to say to himself, "I may need a recommendation from them later so I'd better not tell them how I *really* feel." Further, if the employees are leaving on good terms they may be hesitant to be too frank in order to avoid being offensive in case they ever want to return to the organization. In most cases we find the same type of hesitancy to provide any real negative upward communication from these exiting people as we do from those still with the organization. Therefore, it probably takes the most skillful interviewer an organization has to make the exit interview plan work. It would appear that many firms have a tendency to feel that if a person is leaving they are already a lost cause. Perhaps they even say egotistically, "If they don't like us, they can't be much of a loss." Whatever the reasoning, there may be a strong tendency to forget about those who have fallen by the wayside and concentrate the really heavy artillery and top interviewers on the employment of new people.

The employment interview is, to be sure, an extremely important communication function in an organization. During the sales management career of this author, a great amount of time was spent screening and interviewing prospective employees. It is probably fair to credit a great deal of the following information concerning interviewing techniques to the management training at Allstate Insurance Company.

We learned in Chapter 1 that if a system is to survive the entropic process, it must remain open to its environment and constantly have new inputs. There is no better way to keep up with change in the environment and to keep the organization active and vital than to recruit and hire top new talent with fresh ideas. Many firms spend a great deal of time, money, and effort on their personnel recruitment. They advertise, encourage "bird dogs" to give them leads, and follow up every lead in much the same way as an effective salesman would. Once the fresh, new people are recruited, they must be screened to see whether or not the organization and the individual are suited to one another. For instance, a sales manager once told this author that every organization has a collective personality just as individuals have a personality. If there is a personality clash between the organization and the individual, then that individual should find another organization just as they would seek other friends when they found that their personality clashed with the personality of the old friends. The employment interview, then, is an attempt to avoid a clash before it even begins.

In order to be successful, however, the employment interview not only requires high-quality interviewing generally, but very specific, direct, honest communication. Earlier in this section of Chapter 9 we mentioned that people might be apt to play games in the interviewing situation. The game-playing phenomenon is likely to occur in the employment interview. In such an interview we should find two people communicating in an attempt to find a good personality fit between an individual and an organization. Instead we might find an interviewer trying to get information about the real interviewee through games and trickery, or an interviewee trying to get the position by playing the game of being whatever he thinks the interviewer is looking for, or both playing their respective games at the same time. It is definitely to the advantage of the organization for the interviewer to play it very straight, and level with the interviewee about the good and bad of the organization and the purpose of the interview. On the other hand, there is no long-run advantage to the prospective organization member who lies to himself and to the interviewer about who he really is and how he will fit into the organization. If an interviewer asks the question: "Are you willing to work long, hard hours away from your family?" and an interviewee is not really willing but says, "Oh, yes," and gets the position, neither has really done themself or the organization any favor. Sooner or later the real individual-organizational personality clash will rear its head and there will be personnel turnover. Honesty and the open exchange of personalities, then, is vital in the employment interview.

Once the individual is recruited and the screening procedure is set up, the interviewer steps in. The interviewing procedure should be conducted approximately like this:

1. *Preliminary Preparation.* Study the completed personal history supplied by the applicant. Note any areas on which you wish additional information before actually meeting the applicant. In other words have a plan before going in.
2. *The Interview.* Put the applicant at ease. Tact and consideration of the applicant's feelings are essential. Change your approach and

phrasing as the needs of the interview indicate. Ask additional questions as desired. Record your reactions as the applicant answers your questions, if possible.
3. *The Evaluation.* Immediately after the interview, rate the person. Summarize your impressions and recommendations.
4. *Follow-up.* Your next step is to communicate your decision to the applicant. If they do not measure up, courteously advise them of this. If you decide to proceed further, make specific arrangements for testing. Also, contact management so that their responsibilities in the selection process can be planned and coordinated.

Generally, an interviewer will have an interview form, complete with questions to ask and a plan to follow. This is a very useful tool if it is used properly. Proper use in this case means to be so familiar with the form that it is not necessary constantly to be looking at the next question or writing while the applicant is talking. As much as possible of the written evaluation should be done immediately after the interview. Some organizations provide their interviewers with a form for post-interview evaluation which might look something like the following:

1. Is applicant shopping for just *any* job? YES_____ NO_____
2. Does applicant have a successful work background? YES_____ NO_____
3. Can the applicant handle money well? YES_____ NO_____
4. Is applicant physically fit for the job? YES_____ NO_____
5. Will applicant's family back them up in the job? YES_____ NO_____
6. Is applicant likable? YES_____ NO_____
7. Is applicant a self-starter? YES_____ NO_____
8. Are applicant's goals realistic? YES_____ NO_____
9. Is applicant willing to work to achieve those goals? YES_____ NO_____
10. Does applicant's past indicate stability? YES_____ NO_____
11. Do applicant's family relationships seem favorable? YES_____ NO_____
12. Does applicant have the personality to sell others? YES_____ NO_____
13. Does applicant inspire confidence? YES_____ NO_____
14. Is applicant capable of learning our business? YES_____ NO_____

15. Does applicant's background show growth? YES____ NO____
16. Would you like to work with applicant? YES____ NO____
17. Will applicant be a problem for supervision? YES____ NO____
18. Will applicant background check out favorably? YES____ NO____
19. Subject to tests, background check, and the physical, do you recommend employment? YES____ NO____

The object, of course, is to compare the interviewee with the people in the organization who are already successful in a sort of overlay fashion. If an applicant fits the pattern for success in this particular organization, then they should be pursued further.

The employment interviewer, like any other interviewer, must be a total communicator with the strong receiver orientation discussed in Chapter 2. The interviewer must bear in mind the goals to be accomplished in an interview. We have seen that these goals are to find out as much about the interviewee as possible and at the same time see to it that the interviewee finds out as much about the organization as possible. We might also add the goal of the creation and maintenance of organizational good will. If, for some reason, the interviewee is not acceptable to the organization, perhaps the interviewer will be the only contact with the organization. It obviously requires a high degree of communication skill to reject an applicant and still have that applicant hold a favorable opinion of the interviewer and the organization. It is, however, done everyday by top-notch interviewers.

The evaluation interview

Communication within an organization can be enhanced considerably by the creation of a climate in which all organizational members feel like full participants with a real chance to improve themselves. In many organizations this climate is accomplished through performance evaluations and personal follow-up interviews on a regular basis. Even if it is necessary to be highly critical in the interview, through proper communication the evaluation can be helpful to the employee. If handled positively, the interview can point out areas of strength to be continued and areas of weakness to be improved.

A performance evaluation in this sense means a system of regularly scheduled reviews of each organization member's work and the opportunity to discuss the individual's performance in terms of desired organizational standards. Such a performance evaluation system should include:

1. A review of the individual's performance.
2. An evaluation of the performance using a standard organization form.
3. An interview with the individual to discuss the evaluation.
4. A follow-up when indicated by the recommendations made on the form and brought up in the interview.

A performance evaluation system can provide additional avenues of communication between managers and subordinates. It can also assist in building employee morale. The evaluation system can help with organizational development in several ways because:

1. Specific time is provided for subordinates and their supervisors to discuss the progress of the subordinate.
2. Subordinates are given individual attention which they might not otherwise receive.
3. Subordinates are given a chance to ask questions and express their feelings.
4. A formal opportunity is provided for managers to compliment their subordinates for good performance and to discuss unsatisfactory performances with them. It also provides an opportunity for managers to discuss an improvement plan with subordinates.

With these purposes for the performance evaluation clearly in mind, let us examine a few of the possible uses or byproducts of such evaluations. For instance:

1. Performance evaluations can be of help in discussing and communicating subordinates' promotion potential.
2. The evaluation can serve as an opening for communicating to subordinates whether or not they have earned a merit pay increase.
3. Evaluations and interviews can provide an opportunity for an appraisal of subordinates' training and other needs.
4. Interviews give managers and subordinates a chance to discuss the things subordinates will need to do if they are to achieve their goals.

As indicated earlier, the manager, must first review the performance of the subordinate and then make an evaluation with some kind of standard performance evaluation form. At that point the subordinate is ready to be interviewed. The interview is the most important part of the whole evaluation. Just as in the case of the employment interview, the performance evaluation must be well planned with the evaluation or some other guideline to follow. There are some other preparations which can be made to insure a fully useful interview. First, managers should prepare themselves by briefly reviewing the job, the subordinate, and the reasons for evaluating the performance in the first place. Managers should think of ways to illustrate and personalize the points which they want to make clear to the subordinate. Also, managers should predetermine what it is that they want to accomplish during the interview and include that in their interview plan. Further, managers must allow enough time for the interview so that neither they nor the subordinate feel rushed. The impression of superficiality must be avoided. Finally, managers should select a place for the interview which will provide the proper physical surroundings and afford uninterrupted privacy: no phones, no open doors, and so on.

When a manager sits down with a subordinate for the actual interview, the manager should anticipate some degree of anxiety, tension, and curiosity on the part of that subordinate. A manager should try to put subordinates at ease by talking about some of the things the subordinates have done well first. Then the manager should try to get the subordinates to talk about themselves. This will give the manager a chance to find the right opening for a full discussion of the subordinates' performance and the management evaluation of it. The more positive aspects of the performance evaluation will be better maintained if the interviewer tries to keep the discussion in terms of the subordinates' personal growth and development. Other positive factors to communicate are the value of the subordinates' individual contribution to the organization and their future possibilities, based on past and present performance.

In conducting the interview the interviewer would do well to keep in mind some of the basic reasons for holding the interview such as:

1. Giving subordinates a clear picture of how they are doing in their position and where they stand with the organization.
2. Encouraging subordinates to do a better job.
3. Building a personal relationship between managers and the subordinates.
4. Eliminating or reducing the anxieties of the subordinates.
5. Providing an opportunity for subordinates to discuss any facets of their work that they feel they do not fully understand or in which they feel they need training.

We should call special attention to the first notion above and re-emphasize the importance of clarity and fairness through the use of honest, open communication. If the evaluation and discussion of the evaluation are seen by the subordinate as so much "baloney" or as an exercise in futility, the whole purpose will be destroyed. If one has ever listened to the comments of an individual who feels like that about the evaluation procedures of the organization, one understands what a bad impression can be made in the mind of the subordinate and how worthless the whole evaluation procedure can be.

Aside from answering the questions of interviewees, it is extremely important to let them talk as much as possible. Through clear communication and a mutual exchange of information the manager can be sure that the subordinates end up with:

1. As much knowledge of their strengths and weaknesses as their personality can take.
2. The will to improve upon their past performance no matter what it was.
3. A definite plan of action for both the subordinate and the manager.

The persuasive interview

Everything we have said concerning interviews in general and the personnel and evaluation interviews in particular certainly applies equally to persuasive interviews. There is, of course, an element of persuasiveness to all interviewing but we probably could find no better example of a truly persuasive interview than the sales interview. It is not the purpose of this book or this small section of Chapter 9 to provide any substantial amount of sales training. We will, however, briefly examine the sales interview as an example of the persuasive interview.

The sales interview is a combination of the persuasive techniques described in Chapter 7 and the interviewing principles discussed in this chapter. It is perhaps even more important for the interviewer to control the interview in a sales situation than it is in others. The interviewer must know as much as possible about the interviewee (customer in this case) before coming into the interview. While control is important, it is a peculiar type of control. The control in a persuasive interview is best accomplished by asking questions which will draw the interviewees out and then just listening. If the right questions have been asked, the interviewees will usually tell the interviewer how they want to be persuaded. For instance, if an automobile salesman is interviewing a customer and the customer remarks how much he or she likes the new designs, the customer has made it clear how they want to be sold. The customer will buy for aesthetic reasons and the salesman who sells horsepower or economy will probably fail. Therefore, the control is in listening and reacting to what is heard.

The only other control method is moving the interview along at the rate of speed desired by the interviewer. A sales manager once told this author that whenever a salesman and a client engage in a sales interview there will always be a sale made. Either the salesman will sell the client that the client needs the product or the client will sell the salesman that the product is not needed. It is all a matter of who controls the interview.

The persuasive interview, like all forms of interviewing, plays a major role in the communication system and in the very wellbeing of all organizations. The interview is an excellent source of vital information, both internal and external, to the organization and requires a high level of communication skill.

MANAGING THE CONFERENCE

The conference has become an institution in organizational management. Conferences of one kind or another make up a major portion of the internal communication which goes on in today's modern organizations. These conferences may range in size from a small group of three to ten all the way up to an almost infinite number of people at a large mass meeting.

The manager functioning as an organizer of such a meeting will make arrangements for such details as the meeting place, who will participate and so on, as well as managing the actual conference. Throughout the entire process sensitivity to such subtle but important things as the appropriateness of the time, place, and conference procedures, and the human relations between the participants must be maintained. Many organizations make conference planning and management positions, such as training director, a sort of training or trial position. If young executives handle themselves well under these conditions of stress, they may be more surely eligible for advancement in the organization.

Perhaps the best way to begin an examination of conference management would be to take a quick look at some of the major organizational uses of the conference. Many of the following conference planning ideas were also taken from a conference management training course given by Allstate Insurance Company. In any conference situation, the managers must first ask themselves if a conference really is needed enough to justify the time, expense and trouble it will take to put one together. If the answer is "yes," it must then be determined what the general objectives of this conference or meeting will be. If the objective is to solve a problem then a *problem solving conference* must be planned. If, on the other hand, the object is to disseminate information, then the manager will be planning an *informational conference*. Should the need be a change in the attitude of the conference participants, the plan will call for a *change of attitude conference*. If the aim of the conference is to gain a large quantity of ideas in a short time, then a *brainstorming session* is probably needed—and perhaps a "buzz session" if full discussion participation from a very large group of people is desirable. The foregoing types of conferences or meeting styles, to be discussed now in greater detail, will generally cover most organizational conference communication situations.

Planning steps

After deciding what sort of conference will be planned, depending upon the particular needs at the time, the manager must begin a whole series of considerations. Consideration should begin by setting up criteria for what will be an effective conference when it is evaluated later. These criteria should be based upon the initial needs for a conference and should also serve as guidelines for planning along the way.

The conference manager should then select who the conferees will be. If the group is to be small, such as a normal problem-solving group, the conferees should be chosen for their qualifications for the conference topic; this will include such factors as their training, experience, mature judgment, and creative ability. In any conference, large or small, a major criterion for selecting conferees should be that they have a strong interest in the subject matter.

Next the conference manager must plan a conference strategy for dealing effectively with the participants. The conference topic, the objectives, and the participants should be analyzed simultaneously to determine the best conference strategy. For instance, the manager should try to anticipate some of the problems and formulate plans for handling them. Once the conferees are selected and the basic strategies are set down, the conferees should be notified of the time, place, and purpose of the conference. Notification should be made as explicitly and as far ahead of the conference as possible.

The final preconference step is for the manager to plan an agenda that is flexible and yet will give the conferees a sort of schedule and track on which to run. How much of the plan can be left flexible depends upon the size of the conference. A very small conference can afford a great deal of flexibility, while the larger conferences must be more structured in order to maintain control.

Each conference should include a follow-up and evaluation plan. The conference leader should follow up every conference in some way. Such a follow-up is especially essential for a problem-solving conference. The conference leader is, first of all, responsible for seeing that the conference decisions or results are implemented if called for. However, follow-up of any kind will give the conferees more of a sense of accomplishment.

Postconference evaluation must take place using the predetermined criteria. The evaluation will tell us how clearly we have met our conference objectives and give us invaluable insight into producing better, more effective conferences. For instance, managers must look at themselves as conference leaders in an evaluative way. They might want to ask themselves questions such as:

1. Was a conference the best method for approaching this subject?
2. Was my problem–question real and specific? Was it understood and accepted by the conferees?
3. Was the agenda adequate?
   a. Did the introductory remarks set the right tone for the meeting?
   b. Were the questions well planned, and properly presented? And did they provoke discussion?
      i) Were there any that should have been omitted or rephrased?
      ii) Were there any others that should have been included?
4. Did I deal effectively with the participants?
   a. What was the participants' general attitude toward me?
   b. What was the degree of participation by each conferee?
      i) Amount?
      ii) Quality?
   c. Did I refrain from: offering my personal opinions? lecturing? dominating the conference?
   d. Did I maintain control over the conference at all times?
   e. Did I keep to the time schedule: begin and end on time, and did I allow enough time for each phase of the conference?
5. Did I make any serious mistake in dealing with the participants?
6. What disadvantages did I have to work against?

7. Was there a feeling of accomplishment after the meeting?
8. Have I followed up the conference?
9. Where have I improved my techniques and skills in leading a conference?
10. How can I improve my next conference?

Audio-visual communication

Research indicates that the average person can recall only 10 percent of any oral presentation after three days. But the same person can recall 65 percent of a similar presentation if it is given with the help of visual or audio-visual aids. Audio-visual aids will be needed more in some types of conferences than in others. As a reminder, audio-visual aids which can be used most effectively in a conference are:

Visual Aids	*Audio-Visual and Audio Aids*
Blackboard	Films
Chart easel	Filmstrips
Flannelboard	Records
Handouts	Tape recorders

Filmstrips, films, records, and tape recordings are particularly helpful in an informational conference and, occasionally, in a change of attitude conference. The manager must choose the audio-visual aids needed, if any, very carefully. The manager must make sure that the aid ties in with the particular presentation. The manager also must be sure to see the films, listen to the records, and try out all equipment before using it. While audio-visual aids can be helpful, they can also let one down if they fail and one has no alternative plan. The wise conference leader will always have an alternative to such things as films and so on, so that a broken film or a burned out bulb cannot put the conference out of business. It is also possible to overdo the use of audio-visuals. The only use for such aids is as a supplement to a presentation and the minute the aids become more important, the presentation has been distorted or perhaps ruined.

The problem-solving conference

The problem-solving conference is normally limited to a fairly small group of about three to ten. Research reveals that a group size of five is ideal. There are a variety of objectives other than those basic to solving problems for a problem-solving conference. The leader might use such a conference for coordinating an activity or for reviewing routine operations. The manager leader may also use the problem-solving conference to help in formulating a policy or in making recommendations. In such an application, the conferees would not be expected to make the final decision.

The problem-solving conference requires a special format which would probably look something like the following:

Steps in a Conference	Conference Leaders Are Responsible for
1. Define the problem	Defining and identifying the problem, and for setting the tone for the meeting.
2. Analyze the problem	Guiding the conferees—through questions—toward a thorough analysis of the problem.
3. Solutions are proposed	Making certain that the conferees propose all of the solutions they can think of.
4. Best solution is reached	Helping the conferees to choose one solution. If they have done a good job in leading the conference, the moment of decision will probably be easy and agreeable.
5. Summarize	Summarizing the conference and making certain that all conferees are aware of any assignments they may have as a result of the decision.

The informational conference

The general objective of an informational conference is to inform the participants. The specific objectives are the main points of new information which the manager wants to tell the conferees. These are really educational or training sessions, so the manager should prepare carefully by determining exactly what main ideals the conferees should gain from the conference and exactly how they should be presented. In this type of conference, the use of audio-visual aids can greatly increase effectiveness. The size of the conference can vary greatly.

A suggested format for the informational conference might be similar to the following:

Steps in a Conference	Conference Leaders Are Responsible for
1. Introduction	Presenting the new information. They can spend half the conference time in this beginning phase.
2. Drawing out	Guiding the conferees through questions to analyze the new information. Managers are, more or less, the authority and can accept or reject the conferees responses.
3. Agreement	Guiding the conferees to accept the new information and understand it.
4. Application	Guiding the conferees toward discovering ways in which the new information can be applied and used.
5. Summary	Summarizing the main ideas presented in the introduction and giving credit to conferees for contribution.

The change of attitude conference

The general objective of a change of attitude conference is to get the participants to accept new information, a change in procedure, a new plan, or a change in company policy. This type of conference is normally used only when managers anticipate that they will meet with resistance when presenting new information. The objective is to change the attitudes of the conferees. Such a change objective falls into the highly persuasive category and a great deal of strategic help in achieving it may be found in Chapters 4, 6, and 7 of this book.

As we have seen in Chapters 4 and 6, it is difficult to change the attitudes of individuals by talking *at* them; a demonstration sometimes can get the point across much more clearly. The manager in such a conference might assume almost the same position as a defense attorney trying to sway a jury. The defense attorney begins with the assumption that the jury is pro-prosecution and that their attitude must be changed.

The change of attitude conference is applicable in such organizational settings as an annual sales kick-off meeting, a training session for a new product line, or a change in office procedure. Those conferences are often quite large. A general format which would be useful in such a conference might resemble the following:

Steps in a Conference	*Conference Leaders Are Responsible for*
1. Introduction	Introducing the new plan and logically justifying why this plan was adopted and why others were rejected.
2. Drawing out	Drawing out the participant's opinions carefully by asking questions, or by inviting the conferees to ask questions. The amount of discussion that the leader should allow is determined by the resistance met.
3. Summary	Summarizing the main ideas established in the introduction.

The brainstorming session

The brainstorming session is really more of a method or technique than it is a type of conference. The technique was invented some years ago by Alex T. Osborn,[5] a member of the Batten, Barton, Durstine, and Osborn advertising firm. The brainstorming method encourages creativity by discouraging any on-the-spot disagreement or criticism. The purpose is to get as many ideas as possible out into the open, as rapidly as possible, by the participants around the room encouraging each other. The ideas are weighed and evaluated later, perhaps by another body, but during the session the participants are made to feel that there is no such thing as a "dumb" idea. Once this author created a list of 125 group discussion topics in ten minutes with a class of only 25 students by using the brainstorming technique. To be sure, there were some very strange topics on that list, however, there were also some very useful ones.

The rules for brainstorming are quite simple. They are as follows:

1. Criticism is ruled out.
2. Freewheeling of ideas is welcomed—the wilder the ideas the better.
3. Quantity rather than quality of ideas is emphasized.
4. "Hitchhiking" or modification of ideas is encouraged.

A great deal of the success or failure of such a technique is directly attributable to the leader. The leader should exercise very little control, but at the same time must create an atmosphere in which ideas will flow easily. The format for brainstorming would look like the following:

Steps in the Session	Conference Leaders Are Responsible for
1. Define the problem	Defining the problem or setting up the specific objectives.
2. Discussion	Stimulating the flow of ideas.

The buzz session

A buzz session is really a number of meetings within a larger meeting. For example, a company is holding a sales meeting in which 50 people are present. This is too large a group for any really solid participation. If, however, the conferees were divided into ten groups, and a leader were appointed for each group, it would be possible to have full participation. This is a buzz session. The follow-up will probably be in conjunction with the objectives of the larger meeting, and it is normally the responsibility of the chairperson, not the group conference leader.

Steps in a Buzz Session	The Chairperson and Leader's Responsibilities
1. Define the topic of discussion	The chairperson of the meeting divides the participants into small groups, appoints a leader for each group, and defines the topic of discussion.
2. Discussion	Each group conference leader is responsible for taking notes and guiding the conferees to discuss the topic. Each participant should be allowed to give their opinion at least once.
3. Summary	Each group leader summarizes the group findings before the larger meeting.

Conferences, then, are an important internal communication function in an organization and managers will usually find themselves in some sort of conference leadership role. Often the middle and lower-range manager will be participating in conferences in the form of a lecturer, a trainer, and/or a speaker. But very little has been written or taught about this type of communication.

PUBLIC COMMUNICATION

Communicating in public is something that seems ultimately always to affect careers at one point or another. The inability to speak at least fairly well before a sizable audience and communicate with it has thrown a serious barrier in the path of many management careers. Public communication of this type may be either internal, such as to a mass organizational session, or external, such as a speech to an audience of people outside the organization.

Most of what has been written and taught in speech classes about such public communication has been public speaking oriented. That is, we train our public speakers in the skills of extemporaneous speaking. Extemporaneous speeches are those made from a skeletal outline and/or note cards. The problem here is that many large firms, in fact most firms, seem to be reluctant to turn their young managers loose as extemporaneous speakers. Instead they seem to take the less risky option of having them speak from a prepared manuscript.

The manuscript speech

The manuscript speech has many communicative disadvantages but is normally used for its single major advantage. The advantage is that a speech that is written, edited, and read is concise, virtually error free, and always under control. There is an obvious advantage here for the speaker whose main concern is accuracy.

Often these manuscripts in business firms are written by someone in the home office, distributed around to the branches of the firm, and read by some local managers at a public meeting. The writer and the reader of the speech, more than likely, have never met. Reading such a speech effectively and sincerely is a highly theatrical business which bears more resemblance to an interpretative reading than it does to a speech. Small wonder, then, that manuscript speeches are usually poorly read, given the fact that even people trained in public speaking are not usually trained to read from a manuscript.

Before we can understand how to communicate a manuscript written by another person, we must first understand how a manuscript should be prepared. As already mentioned, there are some communicative disadvantages to a manuscript speech. We can almost surely expect a lessening of important factors such as eye contact, informality, conversational quality, animation, and colloquial language—to name just a few. The aim, then, in constructing and delivering a manuscript speech should be to minimize the communicative losses.

The most important pitfall to avoid is the failure to prepare a *speech* properly. Most of the poorly read papers and manuscript presentations which we endure as receivers were originally written to be published in a written form. The manuscript speech should be a speech that has been put in a written form, *not* in the form of a piece of prose that is read. The differences between the written and oral style are many, and either form appears and/or sounds ridiculous when used in the other setting.

In their book, *Business and Professional Speech Communication,* Zelko and Dance point out that some distinguishing characteristics of oral communication are:

1. Short and simple words
2. Short and simple sentences and paragraphs
3. More use of rhetorical questions
4. More personal pronouns
5. More contractions and colloquial expressions
6. Clearer transitions and connectives
7. Repetitive language
8. Internal summaries
9. Direct audience adaptation[6]

All these characteristics of oral communication are essential for effective, quality communication; however, they are unique to oral communication. If these characteristics were applied to a written piece of work it would be just as unacceptable as prose is when presented as a speech.

Zelko and Dance further point out that an excellent way to insure the success of a public presentation is to make out a speech that is complete with a speaking outline on note cards, and practice the speech that way.[7] After the speech is sufficiently polished, put it one more time through a tape recorder and *then* write the spoken speech by transcribing it from the tape recording.

One vital communicative factor, which is most likely to be hampered in a manuscript speech, is eye contact. It has been said that manuscript speaking is like making love through a hedge; they can hear you but the contact is bad. Practice can help this eye contact problem, of course; however, proper preparation of the manuscript will also help. We have already pointed out that short paragraphs and short sentences should be used. The manuscript should be typed using only one side of the paper and with wide margins all around, triple spacing between lines, and upper-case letters throughout. A primary typewriter, if one is available, is even more effective than upper-case letters. Punctuation is relatively unimportant because the speaker will want to handmark the manuscript with the pause and emphasis marks that have particular meaning for him. To avoid a lot of distracting page turning and paper rattling, do not fasten the pages together.

The above is a brief—but hopefully helpful—guide to better manuscript speaking. Not only is most public communication done in this style in most organizations, but oral reporting (discussed earlier) also follows the same style; the objective of the speakers should always be to regain as much as possible of what they have lost through the comparative disadvantages of using the manuscript style.

ADVERTISING, PROMOTION, AND PUBLIC RELATIONS

Advertising, promotion, and public relations are the three communication techniques, along with sales, that tie the organization most closely to its external environment. An industrial firm, for instance, depends upon advertising, promotion, and public relations as its channels of outgoing communication to keep the system open with the external world, and depends upon things like market research as a feedback channel from that external world. Although there is no space in this book for an exhaustive treatise on promotion and public relations, it will be helpful to examine advertising, promotion, and public relations and see how each of them fit into the total external communication system of an organization.

Advertising

Whether the organization is selling a product or simply providing a service it must advertise in order to communicate its very existence to the external world. From the very first awareness by the social system that the organization even exists, to its continued survival in that social system, the onus is on the advertising programs to be communicating continually. Advertising produces sales potential and stimulates interest in the organization and/or its products. Advertising paves the way for the salesman or organizational representative. In a smoothly operating organization where all communication subsystems are functioning properly, the advertising and sales teams are linked together inextricably and work almost as one.

Promotion

The other member of the marketing team which generally provides that strong link between advertising and sales, or field representation, is promotion. The basic functions of promotion, according to Charles Kirkpatrick,[8] are to tie the other marketing functions together and handle such things as dealer relations, providing hardware and software sales tools, and perhaps consumer relations and services. It is the business of a promotion subsystem to create tools such as point-of-sale display racks, customer give-away items, sales kits, and market and pricing information. They must keep the field representative informed about the advertising program and how best to use it. They also must keep advertising informed about what sort of advertisement-backing the competition and the field representative call for. In other words, the promotion subsystem provides the organization with a two-way linking system similar to the type we prescribed as being needed for adequate research utilization.

Public relations

As we pointed out at the beginning of this chapter, the public relations functions in an organization are functions that have come into much greater prominence in the 1960s and 1970s as an external communication channel for organizations. Even though tangible results from public relations work is rarely obtainable, the function is still considered indispensable in most modern organizations. There is, at the very least, a strong feeling that the image-building functions of public relations people is an important adjunct and helping-hand for all the other external communication people in the organization.

For instance, all the expensive advertising, promotional tools, and persuasive sales strategies would be worth little if the members of the social system had a poor image of the organization and generally held it in low esteem. It is the job of the public relations people, then, to "gatekeep" and control the flow and type of information directed toward the outside environment. The control consists of what and how much is communicated and what channels are used. Sometimes, as pointed out earlier in this chapter, control consists of employees who are satisfied with the internal organization because they are all public relations people in their own right. Pragmatically, public relations may range all the way from a news release, to the sponsorship of athletic teams, to an antipollution campaign.

All these forms of external communication working together should present the organization to its environment in a manner in which that organization would like to be viewed.

SUMMARY

In Chapter 9 we have seen that such managerial functions as leadership, motivating and change management, important as they are, are only a part of the total organizational communication responsibilities of managers. Modern managers will certainly find themselves dealing with routine messages of both an oral and a written nature as they handle the usual multitude of reports, interviews, conferences, and public speeches.

Managers must be responsible for, or at least responsive to, communication needs both within and outside the organization. Total organizational communication includes both internal and external communication, which we have found to be inextricably interrelated. A great portion of this book has already been devoted to the internal communication facets of an organization. In Chapter 9 we added the concerns of external communication functions, such as advertising, promotion, and public relations. We also noted the advantages and disadvantages of both the oral and the written communication styles.

We have examined the communicative act known as *interviewing*. Within that framework we have concerned ourselves with *personnel interviews* used in employee hiring and termination, *evaluation interviews*, which are used to inform subordinates of their performance progress, and *persuasive interviews* as used in sales.

The manager who is concerned with total organizational communication must understand the management of conferences. Conferences may involve groups of varied sizes and purposes. We have concerned ourselves primarily with conferences focusing on problem solving, information dissemination, and the changing of attitudes. The planning and execution of such communicative conferences is a vital and important managerial function.

Another important communication function for today's manager is public communication, which often involves public speaking from a manuscript. This chapter explained that the prepared speaking manuscript is neither a piece of written prose nor a casual extemporaneous speech from note cards. Public communication on behalf of the organization requires special methods of preparation and delivery.

Of course, most organizations have special people or departments to handle external communication functions such as advertising, promotion, and public relations. The modern manager, however, still needs to understand how these communication functions fit into the total communication of the organization, and must be prepared to make full use of such external communication.

NOTES

1. Thomas L. Dahle, "Transmitting Information to Employees: A Study of Five Methods," *Personnel* (November, 1954), 243–246.
2. John Powell, S. J., *Why Am I Afraid to Tell You Who I Am,* Niles, Ill., Argus, 1969, p. 13.
3. John Fielden, "What Do You Mean I Can't Write," *Harvard Business Review,* 42 (May–June, 1964) 144.
4. James M. Lahiff, *Readings in Interpersonal and Organizational Communication* (2nd ed.), ed. Richard C. Huseman, Cal M. Logue, and Dwight L. Freshley, Boston, Holbrook Press, 1973, pp. 333–337.
5. Alex Osborn, *Applied Imagination* (3rd edn), New York, Scribner, 1963.
6. Harold Zelko and Frank E. X. Dance, *Business and Professional Speech Communication,* New York, Holt, Rinehart and Winston, 1965, pp. 191–194.
7. Ibid., p. 191.
8. Charles A. Kirkpatrick, *Salesmanship,* Cincinnati, Ohio, South-Western Publishers, 1966, pp. 120–124.

10 the analyst and teacher

> Learning is such a common phenomenon that we tend to take it for granted. It is no exaggeration, however, to state that past learning is responsible for virtually every act of behavior in which you are now engaged.
>
> Bernard M. Bass and James A. Vaughan

OBJECTIVES for Chapter 10

After reading the chapter you should be able to:

1. Develop a suitable assessment tool for the analysis of organizational training needs.
2. Demonstrate knowledge of the questionnaire, interview, critical incident, and network analysis methods of organizational analysis.
3. Demonstrate the ability to state organizational training needs in terms of behavioral objectives.
4. Demonstrate an understanding of the on-the-job training method.
5. Design a complete training program based upon predetermined needs.
6. Demonstrate the various off-the-job training methods available to us.
7. Discuss the motivational factors that might make trainees want to learn.

8. Demonstrate the ability to prepare, administer, and communicate an instructional program, including the use of various training methods.

9. Design an evaluation program for the purpose of giving the feedback necessary for the upkeep of an ongoing training program.

Just as we have suggested the merit in strategically managing and controlling the inevitable processes of communication and of change, so might we suggest the planned, strategic control of the inevitability of learning described in the opening quotation. The Bass and Vaughan quotation points out clearly that human behavior is learned. It further points out that, just as we seem to take communication and change processes for granted, we often take the process of learning for granted instead of controlling it.

Learning is in essence a change in behavior of some kind. Controlled learning and its accompanying goal of efficiency through planned strategy is really a definition of *training*. Training, in the organizational sense, is the strategically planned, finely designed tool by which the organization can change and grow under the control of management in a predetermined desired direction. Organizational subordinates will learn new behaviors every day. Management must decide whether or not it wants those subordinates to learn haphazardly and without control of the behaviors that are learned. If such random learning experiences are not desired, then management must see to it that learning is controlled by an ongoing training which is well researched, well planned, and constantly under evaluation.

We are speaking now of the sort of training program that is a vital part of the total organizational plan and strategies of the management. Gerald Goldhaber has suggested a general training model that seems to place a training program in just such an organizational position.[1] He states that a complete training program should include pretraining analysis, designing the training program, conducting the training program, and post-training evaluations which include feedback loops from the evaluation state back to the first three stages. The feedback loops are, of course, a necessity if the evaluation is to have any effect upon continuing improvement of the training program.

Our major concern in this book is communication, so communication in a training program will be our major focus in this chapter.

In Chapter 2 a statement was made concerning the advisability of an organization hiring "a communication expert" as a panacea answer to its communication problems. Recall that we pointed out the probable uselessness in the long run of one expert trying to troubleshoot all the communication problems arising in an organization because every member of the management team is really a communication manager whether they like it or not. At this point it seems clear that when an organization hires a communication expert, the most productive, forward-looking job description for that expert would be the training of all managers, especially as communication experts. In other words, instead of trying to handle all the training and communication from one office, the communication expert, as a trainer and linking pin, would provide all managers with the research information and strategic tools to head off organizational problems before they begin thus creating a team of far more efficiently communicating organizational managers at all levels. Ideally, the trained managers would themselves act as trainers to their own subordinates.

In Chapter 10, then, we will approach the manager as an organizational analyst and trainer. Before we begin close scrutiny of the manager in this role, it will be useful for us to examine the available training materials, concepts, and methods of communicating by taking a retrospective look at the manager communication strategist we have been describing in the last few chapters.

RECAPITULATION

We have seen that an organization must be an open system, which means that the organization is constantly interacting with its environment, transforming inputs into outputs that are exported to the environment, and maintaining some sort of dynamic equilibrium. Further, the organization is a system made up of mutually dependent subsystems. Perhaps most important of all, we have found that the system is linked to its environment and the subsystems are linked to each other by communication networks.

In Chapter 5 we described the problem of research utilization in which we have research systems doing communication research and client systems made up of practitioners who have daily communication needs. It seems that the research system cannot determine what client system questions need answering and the client cannot locate and/or make use of the research in its present form. We have, then, identified the need for a third system called a *linking system* to tie research and client systems together with a two-way communication network. A training program provides an excellent example of a linking system. A trainer fulfills Likert's "linking pin" function very well.

Since the communication trainer or training department is our organizational linking system, we must examine the sort of material and concepts that would be a part of this training program. We are speaking of the communicatively strategic considerations described in Chapters 6, 7, 8, and 9, and included in the following list of organizational communication assertions:

1. The formal organizational chart rarely resembles the informal structure.
2. The informal organizational structure cannot be ignored or destroyed. If it is ignored, the informal organization will continue to flourish—only less obviously—and become much harder to control.
3. Communication is never perfect and often is distorted. The distortion is apt to increase as it moves upward through the organization.
4. The amount and accuracy of upward communication depends largely upon the interpersonal trust between subordinate and superior and upon overtly established and maintained upward communication channels.
5. The formal bureaucratic organization seems to have difficulty in communicating and absorbing planned change.
6. Lower and middle-range managers are examples of "change agents."
7. A manager change agent must develop strategies for planning change and communicating that change to the organization.
8. The managerial change plan must take into account both the technical and social aspects of a given change.
9. Interpersonal communication relationships directly affect managerial effectiveness in an organization.
10. Persuasion is a part of all communication.
11. Attitudes and beliefs are blueprints for behavior and tend to cluster within each individual in the form of an interrelated system of beliefs.
12. A key managerial function is the creation of a work climate based upon high morale and interpersonal trust.
13. To be a really effective motivator, a manager must be perceived as a credible source by the subordinate receivers.

14. Effective messages must be created with the receiver in mind.
15. Every manager is basically in the sales business, selling ideas and policies.
16. An effective motivational strategy must be based upon purposes and goals, familiarity with subordinate belief systems, establishment of subordinate needs, creation of a research-based communication plan and a method of evaluation.
17. Small groups can normally accomplish more work and can normally better fulfill individual social needs than large complex organizations.
18. The most effective, long-range leadership style is a democratic, participative one.
19. A middle or lower-range manager is the leader of a small task-oriented group and most task group research applies to the management of such a group.
20. Managers who wish to be considered total organizational communicators must also develop facility in interviewing, conference management, and public speaking.

Although the foregoing list is by no means a totally exhaustive one, it does provide us with a retrospective look at some key assertions covered in this book. These assertions should provide us with the content focus we need as communication trainers. The problems and strategic principles set down in the first nine chapters are very likely to be the communication materials upon which a manager trainer will draw.

COMMUNICATION OF A TRAINING PROGRAM

Because communication and training are such pervasive and important parts of organizational functioning, every manager is at one time or another a communicator of training programs as well as the receiver of training messages. Certainly, as we have already pointed out, a modern organization may hire a communication or training specialist who fulfills a legitimate training role. But, as we also pointed out, if that specialist trains the managers to be communication and training specialists themselves, then in time each manager may become a communicating trainer. It is toward both types of trainer roles that this section of the text is directed. This section, in fact, is a pragmatic presentation of the total training function, whether it is performed by designated trainers or managers serving a training function with their own subordinates.

The organizational function most apt to provide the learning for growth and necessary organizational change is training. An overt effort to train managers as communicating trainers is probably the largest single step toward the guarantee of controlled managerial successes and the elimination of trial and error. The new thinking of top management seems to be to give more and more attention to formal training for managers, particularly middle and lower-range managers. Such new thinking is heartening because it represents a recognition of the importance of one of the primary aspects of good human relations in organizations. It offers definite promise that there is a trend toward regarding training as the essence of management. However, it is, or should be, a first principle of training that the means fit the end, that the techniques be appropriate to the needs. We must, therefore, first examine the present demands upon management before we can identify its training needs.

A fault of training programs—in fact of education in general both on and off the campus—has been that we have provided the "right" training for the "wrong" era. We have often trained our people to operate in the new world of the future by providing them with the old skills so valid in the past. In a world involved in minute-to-minute change, we have almost unwittingly taught our trainees how it used to be or, almost as uselessly, how it is. By the time in the near future when the trainees apply what they have learned, knowledge of the present will be of little use. The trainees need future-oriented tools to control the environment they will face in the future, especially considering Toffler's predictions in *Future Shock*.

This sort of planned, future-oriented training requires some prediction of what the future will in fact hold for us. Warren G. Bennis attempts such a prediction in his book, *Changing Organizations,* where he forecasts what organizational life may be like in the next 25 to 50 years.[2]

Bennis predicts that the *environment* around the organization will be characterized by even more rapid technological change, diversification, and increased partnerships between industry and government. The three basic features of this new environment will be interdependence rather than competition, turbulence rather than stability, and large rather than small enterprises. Any of these characteristics, not to mention all of them at once, will certainly place heavy demands upon the improvement of communication systems.

The Bennis prediction for future organizational life goes on to consider *aggregate population characteristics*. Two-thirds of the aggregate population in the next few years will be made up of college-educated people. Further, this population will have greater job mobility and will shift from job to job as they are needed, with far fewer occupational roots than presently exist.

Bennis also predicts changes in *work relevant values*. Research indicates that, because of the increased education level, people will be more intellectually committed to their jobs, which in turn will require more personal involvement, participation, and autonomy. Also, workers will be more "other directed" and dependent even though their colleagues are more temporary.

The *tasks and goals of the firm* will be more technical, complicated, and unprogrammed which will call for more brains and less brawn. Goals will be far more complicated; we will feel the need for a set of priority goals against which we may measure other goals. There will be more conflict over which goals and tasks are appropriate for each organization.

Bennis further predicts changes in *organizational structure*. The word best describing structures in the future is "temporary." The system will be far more flexible and adaptive with the executive becoming more of a coordinator or linking pin. Teams of specialists will be common. Bureaucratic management will definitely be rare and many such jobs may simply disappear. Such organic-adaptive structures will obviously bring about changes in *motivation*. These better-educated workers will find greater job satisfaction in the organic-adaptive structures and so motivation should increase toward work in general even though commitment to specific work groups will decrease. Group cohesiveness will decrease but the need for improved interpersonal communication will increase. The tasks of the future seem to guarantee enough problems and involvement to be far more captivating to the worker than today's tasks.

While in many ways the organizational life of the future Bennis is describing sounds like an improvement over the organizational life we presently know, it does present some problems as well. For instance, Bennis concludes his predictions by pointing out that:

> Coping with rapid change, living in temporary systems, and setting up (in quickstep time) meaningful relations—and then breaking them—all augur strains and tensions. Learning how to live with ambiguity and to be self-directing will be the task of education and the goal of maturity.[3]

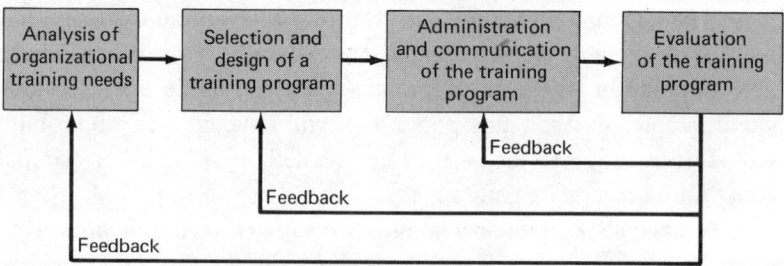

Figure 10-1 A model of a training program.

Whether the future of organizations turns out to be exactly as presented here or not, it should be obvious that the demand for improved communication systems in the future will be even greater than it is now, with training and retraining a constant day-to-day necessity.

With at least some idea of what the future might hold for us and the apparent need for more and better communication or training programs, let us now examine how we may become better managers through more effectively communicating training programs.

In light of the foregoing information and the standard training program models we can propose our own training model. The model (see Figure 10.1) follows the stages of analysis, selection, administration, and evaluation and provides feedback channels so that the program evaluation results may have an effect upon the earlier stages in the model. Let us now examine the four stages more closely.

ANALYSIS OF ORGANIZATIONAL TRAINING NEEDS

As we have already pointed out, if training is to be properly planned and effective, we must first determine what the needs of organizations are. This analysis or assessment can be as broad as an analysis of the total system or as narrow as the specific analysis of a particular problem situation. Systems analysis of this sort is really a business of inquiry. Therefore, the analysis of needs would probably be a series of questions. Basically, we are asking *who* is in need of training and *what* are their training needs. The questions involved in the actual analysis are more direct and are leveled so that the analysis can ask an initial question and then probe deeper and deeper. While it is possible that organizational problems may be obvious or that managers of subsystems may voluntarily ask for training assistance, it is unlikely. The fact is that such information will normally have to be sought out overtly.

In Chapter 3 we suggested a number of ways to analyze an organizational communication system. The communication audit procedures described briefly in Chapter 3 are appropriate tools for assessing the communication-training needs, or any other needs, in an organization because organizational problems are not always assessable without examining the basic communication problems first.

Whether we are analyzing a total system or specific subsystem there are certain types of information we will want to examine. Some of these informational types are:

1. Organizational demographics
2. Personal demographics
3. Nature of downward communication received
4. Nature of upward communication sent
5. Examination of the satisfaction level and importance of various organizational information sources and channels
6. Examination of the amount of information overload
7. Who talks to whom related to the "job" and the accomplishment of that job
8. Job satisfaction

These assessments may be accomplished through the use of a number of audit tools available to us, to be used either singly or in conjunction with one another. Let us now examine some of the more popular tools.

Questionnaires

A questionnaire is a written information-seeking device with which most of us are familiar. The questionnaire technique is effective in tapping data about a person's attitudes, beliefs, and perceptions. The main advantage of a questionnaire is the large amount of data which can be collected in a short time. The main disadvantage with such a written instrument is, of course, the lack of interaction between the researcher and the subjects.

Questions can be *closed,* such as, "Is your supervisor easy to talk to?"; *open-ended* such as, "What is your opinion of the openness of your supervisor?"; or *forced choice,* such as, "Would you prefer to communicate with your supervisor or your fellow workers concerning organizational tasks?" Responses can also be measured more quantitatively through the use of *multiple choice questions, checklists, scales,* and *semantic differentials.* Examples of these are as follows:

1. Multiple choice questions
   Do you communicate with your supervisor concerning organizational tasks:
   _____ Daily
   _____ A few times a week
   _____ Once a week
   _____ Once a month
   _____ Almost never
2. Checklists
   Please check all or any of the adjectives which apply to your supervisor:
   _____ Fair
   _____ Unfair
   _____ Understanding
   _____ Unfeeling
   _____ Open to communication
   _____ Closed to communication
3. Scales (such as Likert scales)
   To what extent does your supervisor remain open to communication with his subordinates:
   _____ To a very great extent
   _____ To some extent
   _____ To a small extent
   _____ To a very small extent
4. Semantic differentials
   Please place an X on the choice closest to the adjective which best describes your supervisor:

   Fair: ___ : ___ : ___ : ___ : ___ : ___ : ___ : Unfair
            1   2   3   4   5   6   7

   Understanding: ___ : ___ : ___ : ___ : ___ : ___ : ___ : Unfeeling
                     1   2   3   4   5   6   7

   Open-minded: ___ : ___ : ___ : ___ : ___ : ___ : ___ : Closed-minded
                1   2   3   4   5   6   7

Clearly, some of these techniques are more appropriate to gather certain types of data than the other techniques might be. Normally a combination of techniques will work best.

Interviews

Unlike the questionnaire, the interview technique is a *live* exchange technique providing a great deal of interaction; it is, however, a time-consuming technique. The interview technique can be used by itself but it is often used as a follow-up to a completed questionnaire. Interviews can be conducted individually or in groups; however, a group interview would naturally have a tendency to limit interaction. Interviews are conducted from an interview schedule with the interviewer reading questions aloud from the schedule and recording the responses of the interviewees. There should be a list of nonstandard questions from which the interviewer may choose to specifically supplement the standard interview schedule with certain individual interviewees. The style of interviewing questions should be a question and then a probe such as:

Q: Does your supervisor understand your needs?
Probe: Why?
Questions can also be probed in other ways such as:
Q: Does your supervisor understand your needs?
How do you communicate the needs to your supervisor?
Are you satisfied with your supervisor's responsiveness to your needs?

Guidelines for interviewing should include the following:

1. Interviewers must ask questions in a nondefensive manner, avoid personal biases, listen empathetically, and probe for in-depth answers to superficially discovered issues.
2. Questions should focus on the organizational issues being assesed (i.e., communication networks, job satisfaction, etc.).
3. Interviewers must be open and honest with interviewees right from the start by stating clearly who they are, why they seek the data, how the data will be analyzed, who will see the results, and "what is in it" for the interviewee.
4. Interviewers must accurately record data as it is gathered.

If the interview is a follow up to a completed questionnaire, then we should add the following items:

5. Interview results should be utilized to aid in the analysis of questionnaire items.
6. Interviewers should use the interview to aid in the improvement of the questionnaire.
7. Interviews should be held as soon after the questionnaire as possible.

Critical-incidents method

The critical-incident technique is actually a module for auditing communication in an organization. A critical incident is considered to be an organizational, job-related behavior which is critical to effective or ineffective information flows related to the performance of one's tasks.

In the critical-incident method, the data is collected by training the organizational members to record the actual critical incidents related to their own organizational function. The incidents may best be gathered in a group where the training can go on and questions can be answered. The principle advantage to the critical-incident method is that the incidents reflect actual organizational occurrences. The principle disadvantage is probably the organizational time required. According to the methodology guidelines of the International Communication Association's new audit procedures, the following are valuable tips to give the subordinates who are being asked to complete critical-incidents records:

1. You may want to sit and think about several incidents first and jot down a few key words on each to help you write them out later.
2. It may help you to think of one particular individual whom you believe is highly effective or ineffective in communicating, and think of a critical incident concerning him/her.
3. Report only actual behavior which you have observed directly.
4. Report *all* relevant factors in the situation.
5. Be specific without excessive detail; be short and to the point.
6. Work individually.
7. Try to have as many effective incidents as you do ineffective.
8. Work as rapidly as you can, at your own pace.
9. We would like to average a total of 10–15 incidents from each person. Do more or less, depending upon the quality of the incidents.
10. *Do not* mention the name of the individual involved in the incident.
11. Be careful to report only one incident at a time.
12. If you have any questions about the incidents, ask the interviewer.
13. Please write legibly.[4]

As we stated previously, any of these investigative tools could be used alone, but it does make some evaluative sense to use them all whenever possible. For instance, the critical-incident method can be used serially as one module with the questionnaire and the interview methods. A set of completed questionnaires might provide general information concerning organizational problem spots. Interviews would then zero-in more specifically on these problems. Finally, the critical incident data would provide for still more specific pinpointing of problems.

Network analysis

The subject of network analysis was discussed in some detail in Chapter 3. Network analysis is an advantageous method because it can describe statistically and/or graphically the actual flow of communication in a network. Analytically, then, we can compare the formal and informal organizational network by matching "what is" with "what we *think* is" concerning communication patterns. The ECCO analysis spelled out in Chapter 3 is a popular example of a network analysis instrument.

Other types of network analysis approaches are a "diary," or "tally sheet," or specifically designed questionnaires. In the diary approach the respondents are given instructions which would look something like the following:

> At the beginning of each day, you will be issued a tally sheet for your workspace, and a tally card for your pocket. These are to be used to record each communication event in which you participate, as it occurs, and wherever it occurs, during the day.

In other words, every communication event, large or small, is recorded; all face-to-face contacts, all telephone calls, all written material is recorded. The only exceptions might be the supertrivial such as "hello" and "good-bye."

Summary of analysis methods

We have not only pointed out the need for thorough and proper assessment of organizational training needs, we have also attempted to point out some commonly used methods of organizational analysis. Once an organization has been analyzed and the training needs have been identified, we must examine the available training techniques and design a training program suitable to these identified needs.

SELECTION AND DESIGN OF A TRAINING PROGRAM

In order to fulfill the training needs with programs that teach people effectively, we must first understand how they learn. We are not born with knowledge. As we have already pointed out, we learn behaviors along the way as we mature. We gain new sets of behaviors as we grow and experience the world around us through our various senses: sight, hearing, touch, smell, and taste. Recall that Berlo pointed out that we communicate, hence learn, best when we use the senses in combination rather than singly. All of this leads us to an important rule. *To be effective, we must teach in ways that allow the trainees to use as many of their senses as possible.*

If our senses were our only means of learning, however, the animals with their keener sensory development would rule the world. In addition to the senses, human beings have the ability to reason. The ability to reason enables us to learn things we could never learn by our senses alone, and enables us to move from the known to the unknown. In other words, we learn something new by starting with something we already know. Reasoning, then, is one of the most important learning processes because, when we learn by reasoning, our mind sees an important relationship between what we already know and what we are trying to learn. We are then able to take knowledge that we already have and apply it to new situations. Here are three examples of ways in which trainees can be taught to learn by reasoning:

1. Show them how their present knowledge is related to what they are trying to learn. Point out the important similarities.
2. Show them how *you* work out solutions to problems.
3. Encourage them to think out solutions by themselves.

So we train through the senses and the human power of reasoning. We still must select from the myriad training methods at our disposal the training program that is just right for our specific needs. There obviously must be some criteria developed to determine what training methods are best in a given situation. According to Bass and Vaughan, a technique will be judged adequate to the degree that it appears likely to:

1. Provide for the learner's active participation.
2. Provide the trainee with knowledge of results about his attempts to improve.
3. Promote by means of good organization, a meaningful integration of learning experiences that the trainee can transfer from training to the job.
4. Provide some means for the trainee to be reinforced for appropriate behavior.
5. Provide for practice and repetition when needed.
6. Motivate the trainee to improve his own performance.
7. Assist the trainee in his willingness to change.[5]

Through the use of such criteria and through understanding both the information to be transferred and the individuals to whom it is being transferred, it is possible to select the proper training and methodology.

Probably the first step, however, in attempting to design an appropriate training program is to have some understanding of teaching by behavioral objectives.

Training objectives

Behavioral training objectives can serve two purposes. First, the obvious purpose served is to better enable us to design a sensible, appropriate learning experience. Secondly, and perhaps not so obvious, is the purpose of building-in, before the training even begins, appropriate evaluative measures by which we may judge the trainees' degree of success. Behavioral objectives are really predictions of what the trainees will be able to do after participating fully in the training. The objectives at the beginning of each chapter in this book are similar to such behavioral objectives, though they are not quite as explicit as a true behavioral objective would be.

Behaviorally predicted outcomes such as these enable both the trainer and the trainee to evaluate the progress being achieved at any point during the training period. Robert Mager[6] in his book, *Preparing Instructional Objectives,* points to three criteria necessary in writing a set of behavioral objectives. They are:

1. *Observable behavior* such as a demonstrated accomplishment. Written into the objectives these accomplishments would take the form of verbs, i.e., to write, to identify, to solve, to list.
2. *Important conditions* such as time limits, materials, and the place.
3. *Criteria for success* such as minimum standards for acceptable performance.

Taking these factors into account we might find ourselves with a written behavioral objective like: To train workshop participants in the skills required for producing machine screws as evaluated by a practical examination.

With the training needs established through organizational analysis and assessment, as well as the establishment of a set of behavioral objectives, we are now ready to consider the major training methods available to us.

On-the-job training

Since it requires no particular extra space, equipment, and probably not even a special trainer, on-the-job training is undoubtedly the most common type of training. Of course, additional advantages of such training are that no time away from the job is required and the trainees earn and produce work while they learn.

The main disadvantage is that there is rarely any attention given to pretraining analysis or any sort of designed training curriculum. The training usually falls, then, upon whoever is in charge, usually the supervisor. If this supervisor trainer is an authoritarian with little communication skill, the training program is probably in trouble from the start. There is no better moment than the development of an on-the-job training program for a practical application of the Berlo notion of source-receiver characteristics. If the trainer encodes the training message from the point of view of source factors instead of receiver communication skills, knowledge level, attitudes, and social cultural background, the training is almost sure to be ineffective.

The author recalls just such an incident when, at age 18, he was being broken in on his first drilling machine in an auto plant. The foreman said, "You put the part in here, secure this lock, and push this button." The foreman then ran through one part of the drilling operation and walked away. Having graduated from the foregoing training course, the author began to run the machine on his own. The author is a totally nonmechanical person, the machine turned out to be a very old, temperamental one, and the result was a series of spoiled parts and broken drills. Although the result was predictable, given the combination of the circumstances and the training method, the foreman did not see it that way. He made it amply clear that he could not see why any fool could not operate the machine successfully. After all, he had trained the operator himself, hadn't he? That foreman was totally oblivious to the learning needs of the trainee and totally unaware that he had encoded the training message from his own knowledge level and sociocultural background rather than those of the receiver. We can see from this personal story that the very nature of on-the-job training makes the one-to-one communication relationship between the trainer and the trainee extremely important. It is possible, on the other hand, to create individualized tailormade training situations through on-the-job training that are second to none, if the trainer is an effective communicator.

On-the-job training may take several forms, ranging all the way from orientation training to the cross-training required by job rotation. Orientation training sets out initially to familiarize the new or transfer subordinate with the new work environment. Orientation training includes such specialized information as an introduction to the people with whom they will work, organizational benefits, and organizational policies and objectives. Although this type of training message may seem simple, it can set the tone for the subordinate's entire tenure in the organization.

Another common type of on-the-job training is the sort that trains people to do a specific job described in the foregoing personal story. If the training message is to be communicated properly rather than in the way it was described in the story, there must be an experienced trainer, a training schedule, and a pretraining analysis of what the trainee already knows about the job. A similar type of on-the-job training is an apprentice program. An apprentice program, however, is normally formalized, spread over more time, and very well supervised.

Many organizations have a policy of cross-training, or job rotation, which requires a continuous program of on-the-job training. The systematic rotation of people from job to job enables all people to be more broadly trained in the organization and hence much more likely to see the "big picture." Such a rotation of personnel must be systematic, however, which is the business of the trainer and must be very carefully tailored to the needs of both the trainees and the organization.

On-the-job training in general, then, does have some advantages since, in theory, it is possible to create maximally favorable conditions with this type of training. In practice, creating such theoretically ideal conditions is extremely difficult. This difficulty is pointed out clearly by Bass and Vaughan when they say:

> The chief reason militating against such ideal conditions is that on the job the primary function is *production,* not *training*—which, under the circumstances must take second place.[7]

Let us now examine the organizational setting where training *is* the primary function.

Off-the-job training

The type of situation that we usually think of as off-the-job training is a formal training program where a designated trainer is most apt to be found. This type of training situation usually finds the trainee taken away from the job and placed in a classroom setting for anywhere from a few hours to a few months.

Off-the-job training is advantageous in several ways. First, as already pointed out, being away from the job puts the emphasis on training and away from a task orientation temporarily. Further, off-the-job training enables the organization to bring in experts as instructors, to gain the comparatively undivided attention of the trainee, and generally presents the trainee with a personal challenge to learn and excel.

The major disadvantage of off-the-job training is that it may be difficult to transfer the learned material back to the job, especially if the rest of organizational management is not behind the training program 100 percent. One way to resolve, or at least reduce, this problem is to provide a mixture of on-the-job training and off-the-job training so that practical application of newly learned material may be made immediately. For instance, the author recalls an encounter with one training program that consisted of a formal program and an exchange of ideas between participants all day, one Saturday per month. Of course, the advantage here was that the practical experience on the job between training sessions provided a good pragmatic testing ground for the training. Another organization which comes to mind puts its new sales people in the field, selling, with the manager providing on-the-job training, for several months before they are brought in for classroom training. The obvious advantage here is that the trainees have made mistakes and encountered problems which give them good questions to ask and enable them to get the most out of the training classes. The trouble with new trainees, sometimes, is that they know so little about the practical tasks to be accomplished that they cannot even ask a good question, let alone understand what is being presented to them.

With these advantages and disadvantages in mind, let us now turn to the following helpful methods for the conduct of off-the-job training.

1. Use a seating arrangement that allows as much face-to-face contact as possible. The least desirable seating arrangement is parallel rows of chairs all facing the instructor. When chairs are movable, move them into the optimum possible arrangement.
2. Say what you have to say simply and directly. Do not talk down.
3. Minimize the use of terms and examples pertaining only to private industry.
4. Stimulate discussion and group interaction—that is one of the program goals. Break up cliques. The trainees dislike sessions consisting of nothing but lecture. Use simulations, role-playing, and games. Try to keep the group identity building continually throughout the session.
5. Use visual aids during training and handouts after training to complement the discussion.
6. Stress the basic points in class, then apply them to the trainees' specific needs via examples or answers to questions. For details that supplement basic points, use handouts. This will also provide the trainees with reference material in the future. If immediate application is not seen, apathy results.
7. Prepare and hand out a list of resource or supplemental materials that can provide additional information to those who want or need it.

8. Teaching methods: do what you feel most comfortable doing. Feel free to use whatever technique you believe is best suited to the topic. Just remember that one of the major aims of such programs is to provide specific methods, techniques, and ideas that can be used. Everyone receiving training should be able to clearly identify the "take-home" from each session.

To supplement such basic off-the-job training advice we must examine the various training methods. Normally, a training program would probably consist of a combination of methods rather than the choice of one method exclusively.

Lecture. The lecture method is a frequently used technique; however, it is often not used very well. Probably the greatest single reason for using the lecture method is that large amounts of information can be disseminated to a sizable number of trainees simultaneously. The faults in the lecture method basically hinge on the unnatural behaviors surrounding one-way communication. The lecture method is quite apt to be one-way communication and, from our discussion in the earlier chapters, we have learned that such communication tends toward ineffectiveness. If we are going to use the lecture method in our training programs, then, we must be careful to use it properly.

Once we understand the drawbacks of the lecture method, we must set out strategically to reduce those drawbacks. Much of the public communication material discussed in Chapter 9 will be helpful in creating relevant, effective lecture techniques in our training programs. Additionally, we can advise the lecturer to begin the lecture strongly so that the trainees understand that:

1. The training period will be interesting.
2. They have something to gain by learning what we plan to teach them.
3. We know our material and know how to present it.

Holding the attention of the trainees over a lengthy training period is particularly difficult, especially if the room is hot, they have just finished a big meal, or have a headache. If the lecturer hears snoring or detects other forms of negative feedback, there are ways to mediate these problems such as:

1. See that the room is well ventilated.
2. Avoid a hypnotic monotone.
3. Put some life into the presentation. Move around. Do purposeful things that complement the lecture.

4. Get the trainees to participate. Give them problems to work out. Ask them questions.
5. Take a break. There is an old saying that, "The mind can only absorb what the other end can endure." Let the trainees stretch and come alive.

In short, lecturers can spot-check themselves to make sure they are minimizing the drawbacks of the lecture method by asking themselves:

1. *Am I lecturing too much?* The lecture method can be mixed in with other techniques to help keep the trainees involved.
2. *What is the take home?* In other words, as pointed out earlier, can the trainees apply what I am saying in their practical world and how?
3. *How can I get feedback from them so that I can match my ideas to their needs?* There must be enough feedback to keep the training message relevant and worthwhile.
4. *Am I on the subject?* It is important to be sure that the material being presented and the presentation itself are pertinent to the stated goals of the training, including the examples given.
5. *Have I provided resource or reference material for the trainees' further study?* As we pointed out earlier, it is helpful to provide material for further study and some steps toward enhancing the training that the trainee can follow later.

Group Discussion. The major advantage to the group discussion technique is its participative interactive nature. In research that has compared the discussion method with the lecture method, the discussion method has nearly always proven to be the most effective in training. The interaction possible between the trainees in discussion is a decided advantage when the material is more difficult and needs further clarification. It is also an advantage when the trainee class is large and needs to be split into subgroups, perhaps to discuss lecture material for further clarification. The participative nature of discussion is clearly an advantage for the management reasons already discussed in Chapters 6 and 8.

The major disadvantage to the discussion training method is the potential loss of control brought about by the informality. Informality would seem to be an advantage but, without expert leadership, the training group can wander off the subject and get hopelessly lost. In small-group leadership, the wisdom of using the discussion method depends on the education, preparation, and skill of the trainer. Rereading the small-group leadership material in Chapter 8 could be helpful here. For the moment we should simply heed the warning of Bass and Vaughan when they speak of the discussion technique and point out that:

> It requires skill, ingenuity, and above all, careful preparation. In fact, it often requires more time to prepare than a good lecture, since the leader must be ready for a variety of unknown eventualities that would not occur, for example, in a lecture.[8]

Case Study. The case study is an attempt to add enough realism to off-the-job training to make it seem situationally more like on-the-job training. In a case study, the trainee is provided with a set of givens that make up a situation they are likely to find on the job. The trainees must then call upon their management and communication training and ability to solve the problem just as they would in the real world.

The case study method is advantageous because of its participativeness, its realism, and the fact that trainees are given a chance, within the comparatively sterile confines of the training room, to see how they would handle such a situation and to make whatever mistakes they are apt to make on a first attempt without "real world" consequences. Tremendous additional advantage can be gained from the case study method if it is followed immediately by the discussion method. A discussion follow-up provides the trainees with an opportunity to discuss the various solutions to the case and the good and bad points of each.

Role Playing. The role-playing technique is similar to the case study technique in that the trainees are placed in managerial positions and act out the situations in which they are placed. Role playing is a common technique in sales-training classes, with one trainee playing the customer role, the other playing the role of the salesman, and then reversing the roles.

In a management-training situation there is great psychological merit in role playing both the manager's and subordinate's role. It does no harm for a manager to see various situations through the eyes of a subordinate.

Since changing attitudes is part of the business of training, role playing can prove to be a further advantage. Classic research by Janis and King points out that when asked to play a role and verbalize a set of opinions, the subjects will shift their opinions in the direction of the role.[9]

The role-playing technique is far more effective if each role is openly criticized after the performance. In fact, a recent media method used in conjunction with role playing is videotape. Playing the tape back to the trainee is an effective critique method.

Programmed Learning. Programmed instruction is a self-instructional method that can be accomplished in a small group; however, normally it is an individual training method. Customary programmed instruction has been presented in the form of instructional or informational frames. The frames are progressively sequenced and immediate feedback is provided following each trainee response. The trainees do not advance to the next frame until they have proven their proficiency in the present frame.

An advantage of programmed instruction is that each trainee may move at their own pace. A subsequent disadvantage, then, would be the lack of group, classroom, or trainer pressure to motivate the trainee toward completion of the training program in a quick and nonfragmented fashion.

Programmed instructional material has traditionally been presented in the written form and often by correspondence. In the past few years, however, electronic programmed training devices have been developed which involve taped lessons projected on a TV-type screen and all the trainee has to do is to read the screen and push the appropriate buttons.

Simulation and Gaming. In the search for new and more effective training methods, an increasing number of firms have turned to simulation and gaming. Why has this training method gained in popularity? Why has it often provided what the training people are looking for? To answer these and other important questions we need to answer a more primary question, one dealing with a definition of simulation and gaming.

In *Game Theory and Related Approaches to Social Behavior,* Guetzkow points out that "simulation is an operating representation of central features of reality."[10] Some writers have made a distinction between simulation and gaming. In this regard, Shubik states:

> Computer simulation, man-machine simulation, and gaming are often all classed as simulation. It is important to clarify the distinctions between these very different methods designed for different purposes. Our major distinction is between gaming and simulation. Gaming is an experimental, operational, or training technique which may make use of a simulated environment, but is invariably concerned with studying human behavior or teaching individuals. In a simulation, the behavior of the components is taken as given. The actual presence of individuals is not necessary to a simulation, but it is to a gaming exercise.[11]

This writer would define gaming, then, as a laboratory operationalization of similar decision situations to those one might encounter on the job in the field. It is a training device in which the setting is simulated in that it is representative or symbolically imitated; however, the actions taken in the game are real actions taken by real people. Perhaps to define simulation or gaming fully we should consider some requirements for a game as an effective training device. This list of requirements might include:

1. A game should be typical of situations the trainee is likely to face in the future.
2. A game should present a challenge and offer the trainee sufficient motivation to think.
3. A game should provide two or more intelligent answers. We should seek solutions, but not *the* solution.
4. A game should be sufficiently meaningful to permit the trainee to perceive principles and theories as he participates. These principles and theories can be implicit, but they should be there.
5. A game involves a narrative account of a situation, as in a case problem, and should be relevant to the trainee and to the real situations in which he operates.

After this brief look at gaming theories, what games are, and what the potentialities might be for their use, we should see how such a game operates. Shubik describes the gaming factors as including the players (or individual decision makers), the payoffs (or the values assigned to the outcomes of the game), and the rules which specify the variables that each player controls, the information conditions, and all other relevant aspects of the environment.[12] Also included are strategies, general plans of action containing instructions on what to do in every contingency, and the outcomes of a game, which will depend on the strategies employed by every player and possibly on events beyond the control of any player, such as a natural disaster.

These are the basic building blocks of game development; there are, however, some other second-level considerations which normally should be built into a game. As indicated earlier in our list of suggested attributes for an effective training game, it is clearly desirable for the game to possess some degree of *overdetermination*. Overdetermination, in this case, means offering a multiplicity of variables which can tend to act in the same direction, providing the players with multiple routes to the same general end and a simulation of the law of equifinality. Another important consideration is the evaluation and critique method used. Clearly, a great deal of thought must be given to a proper critique method in order to maximize the effectiveness of the game as a training device.

If a game involves multiple plays with free time between them, brief critiques after each play may be more desirable than one big session at the end of the game; this approach permits the participants to deal with issues while they are fresh and thereby maximizes the reinforcing and corrective values of feedback. Here again, the skill of the person conducting the critique is very important. Most trainees want the instructor to evaluate their behavior in the game—to tell them "how they did"—but the most fruitful critiques are probably those in which the instructor simply directs attention to certain important issues that he observed and then lets the trainees process and evaluate what happened and why.

We have seen in our brief examination of the game as a training method that it has practical advantages for us. Foremost among these are probably the facts that a game provides the trainee with a fairly accurate replication of a situation he has found and will find in his own real world, and that he may take experimental chances not possible in his real world, gaining immediate feedback on their effectiveness. The concepts, methodologies, and uses surrounding gaming should be still clearer if we take a look at some different applications that have been made of it.

As previously mentioned, games of all kinds have become increasingly popular in the past few years. Games presently in use span such subjects as economics, urban planning, management training and many others. These games carry titles ranging from such straightforward ones as "UCLA Executive Decision Games" and "Kroger Supermarket Simulation" to more descriptive and clever ones like "Prospectville," "Metro Game," and "Change Agent." The games are being used by a variety of reputable organizations such as Kroger, Burroughs, Remington Rand, McKesson and Robbins, as well as most of the country's major universities.

Games are played in small groups and by hand on paper. In the past few years computerized simulations have come into use. The overdetermination and "real life" factors possible on a computer are nearly endless.

Another popular type of simulation used in management-training programs is known as the in-basket technique. The in-basket technique is a relatively simple form of simulation which can be done with a paper and pencil. The trainees are given a descriptive managerial situation in which they are asked to assume they are replacing the present manager. They are then given a packet of materials resembling the contents of an "in" basket on a manager's desk. The packet might include memos and letters to be answered and a series of problems to be prioritied and solved.

Summary. We have taken a quick look at on- and off-the-job training and some of the major training methods available. We have further examined some advantages and disadvantages of each technique and, it has emerged perhaps more clearly than any other single fact, that usually we can maximize the effectiveness of a training program by utilizing a combination of methods.

ADMINISTRATION AND COMMUNICATION OF THE TRAINING PROGRAM

Having examined the process of analyzing an organization to discover its training needs and the training techniques available to us, we must now explore ways to administer and communicate the training program. Designing a viable, relevant training program is certainly important to an organization but the best program in the world is useless if it cannot be administered properly and communicated to the trainees.

A major concern in the actual administration of a training program is motivating the trainees to want to learn. People do things to gain some benefit or satisfaction. Sometimes the satisfaction consists in doing the thing itself but most of the time the satisfaction or benefit people hope to gain by performing a certain activity lies outside the activity itself. For instance, most people do not work simply because they enjoy working. They work in order to earn a living and provide for their families.

Learning is an activity. When you ask trainees to learn, you are asking them to do something. But, sooner or later, trainees are bound to ask themselves, "Why should I?" By first motivating trainees—that is, by making them want to learn—you help both the trainees and yourself. You help the trainees by making it easier for them to learn, which automatically makes your job easier because the trainees will learn with less effort.

What motivates a person to want to learn? People are moved to action by basic desires which manifest themselves differently in different people. However they manifest themselves, these desires are in all of us to some degree and are the mainsprings of all human action. Examples of these human desires are:

1. *Security.* A trainee who feels that his training will provide job security, for instance, will be eager to learn.
2. *Group Approval.* Most people will be more willing to be trained if the training can help win the approval and acceptance of colleagues.
3. *Individual Approval.* Sometimes the approval of an important individual such as a supervisor, parent, or wife can be a strong motivating factor.
4. *Interest.* If the trainees can become interested in their own training, learning should be much easier. We learn things more easily when we are interested in them.
5. *Curiosity.* The curiosity of trainees can be aroused by the right kind of questions and genuine curiosity can make them want to learn.
6. *Challenge.* Most people with the potential to be trained in the first place are motivated by competition and challenge.

Although the foregoing list of motivational factors is by no means exhaustive, it does suggest some emotional reasons why people want to learn. Trainees should bear in mind that they should tap into as many motivational factors as can be found in each individual. Trainers should also remember that not all trainees are motivated by the same factors and therefore motivational attempts must be adapted to each individual whenever possible.

Instructional techniques

With the trainees properly motivated to learn, we must be certain that we are ready to present the material in the most effective manner possible. The first step in insuring the success of any public communication, including training, is preparation. No matter how well managers or trainers know their subject matter, they should not count on being able to conduct an effective training session without preparing for each training period. For instance, a trainer might want to consider the following suggestions:

1. Review the training needs being answered by the training program.
2. Study the material you plan to cover.
3. Make a brief outline of your material so that all points get covered and the points are covered in order.
4. Plan to give special attention to clarifying difficult points.

Having examined this all-important factor of preparation, we

should pause to look at an example of a total technique of instruction. An outline for a total instruction session might look like the following:
- A. Beginning
    1. Welcome the trainees.
    2. Be sure they are comfortable.
    3. Motivate them toward learning.
- B. Instruction
    1. Tell the trainees what you are going to teach them.
    2. Tell them that you expect them to learn the material.
    3. Teach them by:
        a. Telling
        b. Showing
        c. Letting them do the operation themselves
    4. Remind the trainees of what they have learned.
- C. Practice
    1. Have the trainees practice what they have learned.
    2. Give them feedback on how they are doing.
    3. Gradually decrease the amount of supervision.
    4. Continue the practice.

It might be useful to break down the outline of point B-3 to a more specific description of the actual instructional process. That might be outlined as follows:
- A. Telling
    1. Communicate *what* must be done.
        a. Cover one point at a time
        b. Teach the rule, not the exception
    2. Communicate *why* it must be done that way.
        a. Give as many reasons as possible
    3. Communicate your explanations clearly.
        a. Start with what the trainee already knows
        b. Use examples
        c. Use understandable, meaningful language:
            i) Short, simple sentences
            ii) Everyday words
            iii) Explanation of necessary, new, technical terms
        d. Use drawings, pictures, charts, or any other kind of *training aids* which are appropriate and available
- B. Showing
    1. Show them the various methods available but only one at a time.

2. Show them one step at a time.
3. Communicate to them the purpose of each step.
C. Letting them do the operation themselves
1. Let the trainees try the operation.
2. Have the trainees tell what they are doing and why.
3. Correct the mistakes of the trainees.

The foregoing information about instructional techniques is certainly the real hub of a training program and the very reason for all the rest of the analysis and planning. We might add a reminder about breaks. Learning uses up energy and a tired mind simply cannot learn as well as a refreshed one. A trainer must be alert to feedback signaling fatigue and be prepared to stop for a brief break when it occurs.

Training aids

In the sample outline of an instructional plan we mentioned using various training aids to assist in the communication of the training message. It is true that training aids are a vital link in the totally effective communication of a training message. Training aids can:

1. Create a more vivid impression upon the senses of the trainees.
2. Force the trainees to use more of their senses in receiving the training message. Recall that in Chapter 2 we pointed out that Berlo tells us that the communication channels available are the five senses and normally the more of them we use, the more effective will be our communication.
3. Simplify material if used appropriately and properly.
4. Improve the quality of the entire training program.

However, there are two important things to keep in mind in connection with training aids. First, we must always remember that they are only tools for training and nothing more. They *cannot* take the place of an effective trainer. Second, to be effective, training aids must be used intelligently. Used carelessly or without understanding they can do more harm than good. We must *never* let the training aid become so important that it obscures the original training message instead of enhancing it. The very words, "training aid" indicate a device that directly helps, not hinders, the trainee to learn. Recall that some of the common training aids mentioned in Chapter 9 were:

Overhead projectors
Chalkboards

Feltboards or flannel boards
Charts, graphs, and posters
Manuals and booklets
Film strips and slides
Movies
Audiotape and video tape

Specifically we should point out the obvious potential for disaster in relying solely upon a piece of hardware such as a projector of some kind. Smart trainers will not only check such equipment thoroughly before using it, they will also have an alternative training plan should the equipment fail at the last minute.

Here are some things to remember when you use film strips or slides in a training room:

A. Physical arrangements
   1. Have the room dark and well ventilated.
   2. Arrange the seats so that they will all be as close to the projector beam as possible without crowding.
B. Training preparation
   1. Familiarize yourself thoroughly with the film.
   2. Put the trainees at ease. Tell them about the film. Show how its contents relate to the training program.
   3. Let the trainees know that questions are welcome.
C. Showing the film
   1. Allow plenty of time for each picture.
   2. If you are commenting on the film, speak slowly and distinctly.
   3. Use a pointer if necessary.
   4. Answer any questions that come up but save the long-answer questions until after the showing. They might break up the continuity of the film.
D. After the showing (a very crucial time in training)
   1. Ask the trainees if they have any questions and have other trainees answer those questions if possible.
   2. Review the contents of the film, clearing up any difficulty or confusion. If your experience tells you that certain points are more difficult to grasp, give special attention to these points.
   3. A short test on the material covered in the film can help, especially if you then give the correct answers to the test.

Summary

We saw that in order to properly administer and communicate a training program, we must first motivate the trainees to want to learn. We then examined instructional techniques through some sample outlines and took a brief look at some of the more common training aids. Now it remains only to plan the effective evaluation of our training programs.

EVALUATION OF THE TRAINING PROGRAM

No training system can function and grow without proper evaluation through feedback from the trainees themselves. As we have pointed out several times, an efficient, open system will be self-corrective. We further pointed out, however, that self-correction is nearly impossible without feedback, particularly negative feedback, to point out errors in the system. Feedback from trainees is also a form of upward communication. You should also recall our earlier discussion concerning the difficulty in obtaining useful upward communication. We can therefore probably assume that evaluative feedback from the trainees will not come automatically or voluntarily but rather will have to be elicited in some planned way.

The training program results may, of course, be evaluated by measuring the overall growth of the trainee, be evaluated by the training staff itself, or there may be long-range, objective measurement of trainee behavioral change. All of these evaluative methods are valid, however, we will still want the trainees' opinion of their training experiences, and we will no doubt have to ask for it. Bass and Vaughan offer the following guides for eliciting such information from trainees:

1. Determine what you want to find out beforehand and design a written comment sheet covering these items.
2. Design the form so that the trainees' reactions can be easily recorded, tabulated, and quantified.
3. Do not ask the trainees to sign their names if you want them to be frank.
4. Allow space for the trainees to write in comments that are not covered by the items designed to be tabulated and quantified.
5. Provide adequate time for the trainees to complete the form; do not surprise them with it five minutes before they must leave the training site.[13]

In determining what information we want to find out from the trainees, we would probably want to include some of the following:

1. Was effort made to make the trainees, particularly the new people, feel at home?
2. Was the room arrangement effective?
3. Were the arrangements comfortable?
4. Did the meeting open on time and follow the schedule? If not, what delayed it?
5. Was the meeting clear and interesting to the audience?
6. Was each speaker introduced?
7. For each presentation:
    a. Could everyone hear?
    b. Could everyone see?
    c. Did the presentation arouse interest?
    d. Did it accomplish its purpose?
    e. Did the speakers stay within their allotted time?
    f. Is there any way it could be improved?
8. Were there any outside distractions? If so, how could they have been avoided?
9. Were breaks given and did they end on schedule?
10. Were there effective summaries?
11. Did the meeting end on time?

Just as a pretraining analysis of needs, the design of the training program, and the eventual administration and communication of that program are important managerial functions, so it is with the constant evaluation of those programs. As previously mentioned, without evaluation and the interpretation and adjustment which follows that evaluation, there would soon be no program.

SUMMARY

We have seen that, just as communication in general and organizational change are inevitable, so is learning. The objective for organizational management, then, is to gain control of organizational learning through well-planned training programs.

After reviewing some organizational communication facts of life for managers pointed out in the first nine chapters, we examined the communication procedures involved in organizational training programs. Before considering the training programs themselves we must analyze the actual training needs of the organization at any given time. We may make these organizational assessments by such measurement tools as questionnaires, interviews, the critical-incident method, and the various methods of network analysis.

After analyzing the training needs, it is possible to call upon the many teaching methods available to us to select and design the most appropriate training method, or combination of methods, to fulfill the discovered needs. We may select from such methods as lecture, group discussion, case study, role playing, programmed learning, and simulations.

Administration and communication of the training program we have designed is a particularly crucial part of the total program. The most appropriate, uniquely designed training program will be worthless if a well-planned instructional program is not presented to trainees who have been motivated to want to learn. The instructional program can be enhanced considerably by the judicial use of the myriad of training aids available.

Finally, we have pointed out that there is little use in analyzing, designing, and communicating a training program until we have developed effective means of evaluating the outcomes of the programs. The evaluation provides the feedback necessary for the training subsystem to self-correct, change, and grow.

NOTES

1. Gerald M. Goldhaber, *Organizational Communication,* Duboque, Iowa, Brown, 1974, p. 325.
2. Warren G. Bennis, *Changing Organizations,* New York, McGraw-Hill, 1966, pp. 10–13.
3. Ibid., p. 14.
4. International Communication Association pilot audit procedure guidelines, 1974.
5. Bernard M. Bass and James A. Vaughan, *Training in Industry: The Manageagement of Learning,* Belmont, Calif., Wadsworth, 1966, p. 86.
6. Robert Mager, *Preparing Instructional Objectives,* Palo Alto, Calif., Fearon, 1962.
7. Bass and Vaughan, op. cit., p. 87.
8. Ibid., p. 99.
9. I. L. Janis and B. T. King, "The Influence of Role Playing On Opinion Change," *Journal of Abnormal Social Psychology, 49* (1954), 211–218.
10. Harold Guetzkow, In Martin Shubik (ed.), *Game Theory and Related Approaches to Social Behavior,* New York, Wiley, 1964, p. 274.
11. Martin Shubik (ed.), *Game Theory and Related Approaches to Social Behavior,* New York, Wiley, 1964, p. 71.
12. Ibid.
13. Bass and Vaughan, op. cit., pp. 142–143.

APPENDIX
case situations

The following dilemmas are included in the book to provide students with a chance to put themselves into management situations and communicate their way out. Hopefully, students will be able to make strategic use of the material in the book to solve these sample problems. The situations are short and varied. Some of them are situations already cited in the book. All of them are either actual organizational happenings or they are based upon real organizational experiences. The students should feel free to fill in any additional assumptions needed to solve the problems but be sure to state what these assumptions are.

Situation #1

You are a regional training manager. The company has come out with a new product line which will enable its salespeople to sell to markets from which they have never received business before. This new line is quite highly priced but it has a smaller commission percentage than the salespeople are used to, plus a tricky flat surcharge rate that goes to them. There are 600 retail salespeople in your region, which covers four states.

Your job here is to plan the best method for making the salespeople in your region aware of, and interested in, the new product. You must also devise the most complete training program possible and have all 600 people trained within 20 days.

Situation #2

Within a large corporation there is a new research subsystem created which has about 250 employees and is, naturally, vital to the corporate future. The employees of this subsystem are 95 percent technical people, two-thirds of whom have advanced degrees. There are 90 people with a Ph.D. degree. You get the managerial assignment here because you are a proven manager with presumably enough managerial experience to handle this difficult task. However, your background in scientific and technical work is limited. Some things to consider are:

1. Such structural items as working hours etc.
2. On-going training programs
3. What the perceptions of the rest of the corporation toward this "special" subsystem will be and what can you do about them
4. An internal and external communication system

Situation #3

You are the general manager of a local manufacturing firm which employs about 300 people. Everyone knows everyone else and the company provides a company picnic in the summer and a family Christmas party. In short, the firm is just one big, happy family.

The system has always operated on a hand-to-hand or person-to-person basis; however, it becomes obvious that such an operating base is no longer feasible. The only way the company can grow is to computerize across the board, involving all departments (sales, accounting, production, drafting and design, and office management).

Considering the typical fear and trauma that frequently accompany automation attempts, how are you going to introduce, communicate, and train people for the computerized system that is coming their way? Your job is to gain maximum acceptance and implementation of this organizational change.

Situation #4

You are named manager of a department which has had an interesting history over the past eleven years. For eight years the manager managed the way he wanted to manage. He always kept a lid on disagreeable subjects and pushed for a constant state of consensus at all costs. Agreement was king and ironically was accomplished through a peculiar sort of amiable authoritarianism. It should be noted at this point that the entire organization was managed in much the same manner.

After this eight-year period, a new manager was brought in who was much younger, a politician, and very keen at least to give the impression of an open democracy and fair play. A basic strategy involved in this effort was a steady bombardment of information through meetings, word of mouth, and a constant flow of dittoed memos. At this point, subordinates who formerly were told only what was necessary and sometimes less, were put in a state of information overload and asked to vote on everything. As in the case of the eight years of information drought, the subordinates more or less got used to being overloaded with information.

Now you are appointed manager of this department. What will be your management style and communication methods, considering the managerial history that preceded you?

Situation #5

You are considered to be a classic, textbook example of a Theory Y type manager. You have just been transferred to manage a department that has been managed for the past three years by a totally Theory X manager.

What are the management communication problems you would expect to encounter and how will you strategically handle each of these problems?

Situation #6

You are a design department manager in a large engineering job shop which has a number of sizable contracts with major automobile firms. Your department, which consists of 30 draftsmen and designers, is presently working on a project for one of these firms. Since the auto firm is paying the bill, their project engineers sometimes hang around and make themselves a general nuisance.

Suddenly, a project engineer from the auto firm bursts into your office, says that one of your promising young designers has called him a nasty name, and he demands that the designer either apologize or be fired. Quick investigation proves that the engineer badgered the designer and then called him a nasty name first. It is fairly clear that the young designer is not very likely to apologize and it is equally clear that the insulted engineer is going to insist on some action on the grounds that the contract with his company is paying the salaries.

What will you do, both in the long and short run, to solve this dilemma?

Situation #7

You are the manager of a department which includes 50 employees. These 50 employees work in 10-person units which are directly supervised by five foreman.

Several months after you are put in charge, it becomes apparent that all of the policies and directives that you set down are not being implemented immediately. It becomes further apparent that there is a worker somewhere in the middle of one of the 10-person units with whom a vast majority of the other 49 employees is checking out your decisions before making an innovation-decision. In other words, without seeking out such a role, this individual seems to have the power to make or break your implementations by his approval or disapproval. This undesignated leader is a top-notch worker and a loyal employee; however, he is sitting in a position of power or potential power. How will you handle the situation and maintain some kind of organization equilibrium?

Situation #8

You are put in charge of an 80-member department which includes ten subunits, each with its own supervisor. There is a morning and an afternoon coffee break schedule which enables the people to go across the street in small groups to buy the only available cup of coffee in or around the plant without everyone being absent at the same time.

It alarms you somewhat that the people must take that much time, money, and energy to get their coffee. In what you feel is both a magnanimous gesture and a bright idea, you suggest to your boss that these outside breaks be replaced by sending a coffee cart around twice a day through each department. The proposal calls for coffee to be served free at each desk. It would be handy and free. Wow! What a great idea!

But wait a minute. The supervisors and workers are not so thrilled with the idea and, when asked by your boss, they indicate their disapproval.

1. What could be some reasons for their lack of enthusiasm for the idea?

2. Are there really some advantages to the present system?
3. What will you do now?

Situation #9

The superintendent of the production department in a middle-sized manufacturing firm complains to the company president that he feels his subordinates are about to scream "unfair." It seems that a production worker gets docked 15-minutes-worth of pay for every five minutes he is late for work. At the same time these unionized production workers complain that they see salespeople and engineers coming and going at all hours and also that the salespeople and engineers seem to have unrestricted coffee breaks. The production superintendent suggests that the president should call in the sales manager and the chief engineer and tell them to "get their house in order" before there is union trouble.

The president, himself a former production superintendent, is always at his desk by 8:00 A.M. and is initially sympathetic to the argument. He is about to call in the sales manager and chief engineer. But then, the president also realizes that the reason salespeople work late, irregular hours and engineers also keep irregular hours is because of their project-oriented work.

To help solve this dilemma, he calls you, the personnel manager, in to help.

1. What are the differences in working styles?
2. What is really fair? Is it equal treatment for all?
3. What are some solutions and how would you communicate your decision to the people involved?

Situation #10

You accept a field management position with a firm that has undergone a traumatic scare over a recent employee vote on whether or not to unionize. The employee force of about 100 voted down the collective bargaining issue by a scant six votes and there was considerable divisiveness, bitterness, and rancor accompanying the decision. The union scare was followed by a TLC (tender loving care) period which was characterized by an open-door policy between these employees and top management, a "hands-off" management style, and no real hiring and firing power for the bottom-level, field managers. The open-door policy, for instance, means that the employees frequently get information before the managers do.

1. What are the communication problems created for a field manager by such a system?
2. What are the management problems created for a field manager by such a system?
3. What do you think should be done about the situation, if you had the power to do it?

bibliography

ALLPORT, GORDON, W. *Psychology of Rumors.* New York, Holt, Rinehart and Winston, 1948.
AMSDEN, FORREST M., and NOEL D. WHITE. *How to Be Successful in the Employment Interview: A Step-By-Step Approach for the Candidate.* Cheney, Washington, Interviewing Dynamics, 1975.
ARGYRIS, CHRIS. *Understanding Organizational Behaviors.* Homewood, Ill., Dorsey Press, 1960.
ARGYRIS, CHRIS and ROGER HARRISON. *Interpersonal Competence and Organizational Effectiveness.* Homewood, Ill., Dorsey Press, 1962.
ARONSON, ELLIOTT. "Who Likes Whom and Why." *Psychology Today 4,* no. 3 (August, 1970), 48–50.
BALES, ROBERT. *Interaction Process Analysis.* Reading, Mass., Addison-Wesley, 1950.
——— "Task Roles and Social Roles in Problem-Solving Groups," in T. M. Newcomb and E. L. Hartley, *Readings in Social Psychology* (3rd edn.). New York, Holt, Rinehart and Winston, 1958.
BARKER, LARRY L. and ROBERT J. KIBLER. *Speech Communication Behavior: Perspectives and Principles.* Englewood Cliffs, N.J., Prentice-Hall, 1971.
BARNLUND, DEAN. *Interpersonal Communication: Survey and Studies.* Boston, Houghton Mifflin, 1968.
BASS, BERNARD M. and JAMES A. VAUGHAN. *Training In Industry: The Management of Learning.* Belmont, Calif., Wadsworth, 1966.
BAVELAS, ALEX. "Communication Patterns in Task-Oriented Groups." *Journal of the Acoustical Society of America, 22* (1950).
BAVELAS, ALEX and DERMOT BARRETT. "An Experimental Approach to Organizational Communication." *Personnel, 27,* no. 5 (March, 1951), 366–371.
BECKER, SELWYN W. and FRANK STEFFORD. "Some Determinants of Organizational Success." *Journal of Business,* 40 (1967).
BECKER, SELWYN W. and THOMAS L. WHISLER. "The Innovative Organization: A Selective View of Current Theory and Research." *Journal of Business, 40* (1967).
BENNE, KENNETH D. and MAX BIRNBAUM. "Chicago Does Not Have to Be Haphazard." *The School Review,* University of Chicago, *68,* no. 3 (1960), 283–293.
BENNIS, WARREN G. *Changing Organizations.* New York, McGraw-Hill, 1966.
——— "Leadership Theory and Administrative Behavior: The Problem of Authority." *Administrative Science Quarterly, 4,* no. 3 (December, 1959), 299.
BENNIS, WARREN G., KENNETH D. BENNE, and ROBERT CHIN (eds.). *The Planning of Change.* New York, Holt, Rinehart and Winston, 1969.

BERELSON, BERNARD and GARY A. STEINER. *Human Behavior.* New York, Harcourt Brace Jovanovich, 1964.

BERG, THOMAS L. and ABE SHUCHMAN (eds.). *Product Strategy and Management.* New York, Holt, Rinehart and Winston, 1963.

BERLO, DAVID K. *The Process of Communication.* New York, Holt, Rinehart and Winston, 1960.

BERLO, DAVID, JAMES B. LEMERT, and ROBERT J. MERTZ. "Dimensions For Evaluating the Acceptability of Message Sources." *Public Opinion Quarterly, 33* (Winter, 1969–1970), 562–576.

BETTINGHAUS, ERWIN P. *Persuasive Communication.* New York, Holt, Rinehart and Winston, 1960.

BLAU, PETER. "Patterns of Interaction Among a Group of Officials in a Government Agency." *Human Relations, 7,* no. 3 (1954), 337–348.

BLAU, PETER M. and W. RICHARD SCOTT. *Formal Organizations: A Comparative Approach.* New York, Intext, 1962.

BORMANN, ERNEST G. *Discussion and Group Methods: Theory and Practice.* New York, Harper & Row, 1969.

BORMANN, ERNEST G., WILLIAM S. HOWELL, RALPH G. NICHOLS, and GEORGE L. SHAPIRO. *Interpersonal Communication in the Modern Organization.* Englewood Cliffs, N.J., Prentice-Hall, 1969.

BRYSON, LYMAN. *The Communication of Ideas.* New York, Harper & Row, 1948.

BURNS, TOM and G. M. STALKER. *The Management of Innovation.* London, Tavistock, 1961.

CAPLOW, THEODORE. *Principles of Organizations.* New York, Harcourt Brace Jovanovich, 1961.

CARTWRIGHT, DARWIN and ALVIN ZANDER. *Group Dynamics: Research and Theory.* New York, Harper & Row, 1968.

CARZO, ROCCO, JR. and JOHN N. YANOUZAS. *Formal Organizations: A Systems Approach.* Homewood, Ill., Irwin, 1967.

CLEVENGER, THEODORE, JR. "What is Communication," Taskgroup Letter no. 2, NSSC Committee on Extant Theory. *Journal of Communication 9* (March, 1959), 5.

COCH, LESTER and JOHN R. P. FRENCH, JR. "Overcoming Resistance to Change." *Human Relations 1,* no. 4 (1948), 512–532.

COHEN, ARTHUR R. *Attitude Change and Social Influence.* New York, Basic Books, 1964.

COLLINS, BARRY E. and HAROLD GUETZKOW. *A Social Psychology of Group Processes for Decision-Making.* New York, Wiley, 1964.

CYERT, RICHARD and JAMES G. MARCH. *A Behavioral Theory of the Firm.* Englewood Cliffs, N.J., Prentice-Hall, 1963.

DAHLE, THOMAS L. "Transmitting Information to Employees: A Study of Five Methods." *Personnel, 31,* no. 3 (1954), 243–246.

DANCE, FRANK E. X. (ed.). *Human Communication Theory: Original Essays.* New York, Holt, Rinehart and Winston, 1967.

DAVIS, KEITH. *Organizational Behavior.* New York, McGraw-Hill, 1974.

——— "Communication Within Management." *Personnel 31,* no. 3 (November, 1954), 212.

——— "The Organization That's Not on the Chart." *Supervisory Management* (July, 1961).

ETZIONI, AMITAI. *A Comparative Analysis of Complex Organizations.* New York, Free Press, 1961.

FARACE, R. VINCENT and J. A. DANOWSKLEY. "Analyzing Human Communication Networks in Organizations: Applications Management Problems." Paper presented to the International Communication Association, April, 1973.

FESTINGER, LEON. *A Theory of Cognitive Dissonance.* New York, Harper & Row, 1967.

FESTINGER, LEON, STANLEY SCHACTER, and KURT BECK. *Social Pressures in Informal Groups.* New York, Harper & Row, 1950.

FIELDEN, JOHN. "What Do You Mean I Can't Write." *Harvard Business Review, 42* (May–June 1964), 144.

FISHER, B. AUBREY. *Small Group Decision Making: Communication and the Group Process.* New York, McGraw-Hill, 1974.

FOTHERINGHAM, WALLACE. *Perspectives on Persuasion.* Boston, Allyn & Bacon, 1966.

FRENCH, JOHN R. P. JR. and RICHARD SNYDER. "Leadership and Interpersonal Power," in Dorwin Cartwright (ed.), *Studies in Social Power.* Ann Arbor, Institute for Social Research, University of Michigan, 1959, pp. 118–149.

GALLUP, GEORGE. "The Absorption Rate of Ideas." *Public Opinion Quarterly, 19* (1955).

GOLDHABER, GERALD M. *Organizational Communication.* Dubuque, Iowa, Brown, 1974.

GOLDNER, FRED H. "Demotion In Industrial Management." *American Sociological Review, 30* (1965), 714–724.

GORDON, THOMAS. *Group-Centered Leadership.* Boston, Houghton Mifflin, 1955.

HAIMAN, THEO and RAYMOND L. HILGERT. *Supervision: Concepts and Practices of Management.* Cincinnati, Ohio, South-Western Publishing, 1972.

HALL, JAY. "Decisions, Decisions, Decisions." *Psychology Today, 5,* no. 6 (November, 1971), 88.

HANEY, WILLIAM V., *Communication and Organizational Behavior* (3rd edn.). Homewood, Ill., Irwin, 1973.

HARE, A. PAUL, *Handbook of Small Group Research.* New York, Free Press, 1962.

HARRIS, THOMAS A. *I'm OK—You're OK.* New York, Harper & Row, 1967.

HEIDER, FRITZ. *The Psychology of Interpersonal Relations.* New York, Wiley, 1958.

HOMANS, GEORGE C. *The Human Group.* New York, Harcourt Brace Jovanovich, 1950.

——— "The Western Electric Researchers." *Bobbs-Merrill Reprint Series,* S-123.

HOSLETT, SCHUYLER DEAN (ed.). *Human Factors in Management.* New York, Harper & Row, 1946.

HOVLAND, CARL I., IRVING L. JANIS, and HAROLD H. KELLEY. *Communication and Persuasion: Psychological Studies of Opinion Change.* New Haven, Yale University Press, 1953.

HUSEMAN, RICHARD C., CARL M. LOGUE, and DWIGHT L. FRESHLEY. *Readings In Interpersonal And Organizational Communication.* Boston, Holbrook Press, 1969.

JANIS, IRVING L. "Groupthink." *Psychology Today, 5,* no. 6 (November, 1971), 43.

JANIS, IRVING L. and SEYMOUR FESHBACK, "Effects of Fear-Arousing Communications." *Journal of Abnormal and Social Psychology, 48,* no. 1 (1953), 78–92.

JANIS, IRVING L. and CARL I. HOVLAND (eds.). *Personality and Persuasibility.* New Haven, Yale University Press, 1959.

JUDSON, ARNOLD S. *A Manager's Guide to Making Decisions.* New York, Wiley, 1966.

KAST, FREMONT and JAMES ROSENZWEIG, *Organization and Management: A Systems Approach.* New York, McGraw-Hill, 1970.

KATZ, DANIEL and ROBERT L. KAHN. *The Social Psychology of Organizations.* New York, Wiley, 1966.

KATZMAN, NATAN. "Social Entropy And Communication Systems," ICA paper. Minneapolis (May, 1970).

KELMAN, HERBERT. "The Process of Opinion Change." *Public Opinion Quarterly, 25* (1961).

KILLIAN, RAY. *Managing by Design . . . For Executive Effectiveness.* American Management Association, 1968.

KING, I. L. and B. T. KING. "The Influence of Role Playing On Opinion Change." *Journal of Abnormal Social Psychology, 49* (1954), 211–218.

KIRKPATRICK, CHARLES A. *Salesmanship.* Cincinnati, Ohio, South-Western Publishers, 1966.

KNIGHT, KENNETH E. "A Descriptive Model of the Intra-Firm Innovation Process." *Journal of Business, 40* (1967).

LAWRENCE, PAUL R. "How To Deal With Resistance To Change." *Harvard Business Review, 32* (May–June, 1954), 49–57.

LEARY, TIMOTHY. *Interpersonal Diagnosis of Personality.* New York, Ronald Press, 1957.

LEMERT, JAMES B. "Dimensions of Source Credibility." Paper presented to the Association for Education in Journalism, August 26, 1963.

LEWIN, KURT. *Field Theory In Social Science.* New York, Harper & Row, 1951.

——— *Resolving Social Conflicts.* New York, Harper & Row, 1948.

LIKERT, RENSIS. *New Patterns of Management.* New York, McGraw-Hill, 1961.

LINDH, A. W. "Plain Talk About Communicating in Business." *Business Management, 26* (April, 1964), 91–95.

LIPPITT, RONALD, JEANNE WATSON, and BRUCE WESTLY. *The Dynamics of Planned Change.* New York, Harcourt Brace Jovanovich, 1958.

LUFKIN, JAMES M. "Cultural Barriers to Interprofessional Communication." *IEEE Transactions on Professional Communication, PC-15,* no. 2, (June, 1972), 26–29.

MCCORMICK, JAMES S. "Communication and the Organization." *Advanced Management Journal, 33* (January, 1968), 63–67.

MCCROSKEY, JAMES C. "Scales for the Measurement of Ethos." *Speech Monographs, 30* (1966), 65–72.

MCGRATH, JOSEPH E. *Social Psychology: A Brief Introduction.* New York, Holt, Rinehart and Winston, 1964.

MCGREGOR, DOUGLAS. *The Human Side of Enterprise.* New York, McGraw-Hill, 1960.

MCGUIRE, WILLIAM. "Inducing Resistance to Persuasion: Some Contemporary Approaches." *Advances in Experimental Social Psychology, 1* (1964), 191–229.

MAGER, ROBERT. *Preparing Objectives for Programmed Instruction,* Palo Alto, Calif., Fearon, 1962.

MARCH, JAMES G., and HERBERT A. SIMON. *Organizations.* New York, Wiley, 1958.

MARTIN, HOWARD H. and KENNETH E. ANDERSON. *Speech Communication: Analysis and Readings*. Boston, Allyn & Bacon, 1968.
MASLOW, ABRAHAM H. *Motivation and Personality*. New York, Harper & Row, 1954.
MERRIHUE, WILLIAM V. *Managing by Communication*. New York, McGraw-Hill, 1960.
MEYER, H. H. "Factors Related to Success in the Human Relations Aspect of Work Group Leadership." *Psychological Monographs, 63,* no. 3 (1951).
MILES, MATTHEW. *Learning to Work in Groups*. New York, Bureau of Publications, Teachers College, Columbia University, 1967.
MILES, MATTHEW B. (ed.). *Innovation in Education*. New York, Bureau of Publications, Teachers College, Columbia University, 1964.
MILLER, J. G. "Information Input Overload and Psychopathology." *American Journal of Psychiatry, 116,* no. 8 (February, 1960), 695–704.
MOORE, LEO B. "Too Much Management, Too Little Change." *Harvard Business Review, 34* (January–February, 1956), 41–48.
NEWCOMB, THEODORE M., RALPH H. TURNER, and PHILLIP E. CONVERSE. *Social Psychology*. New York, Holt, Rinehart and Winston, 1965.
OSBORN, ALEX. *Applied Imagination* (3rd ed.). New York, Scribner, 1963.
PIGORS, PAUL. *Effective Communication in Industry*. New York, National Association of Manufacturers, 1949.
PLANTY, EARL and WILLIAM MACHAVER. "Upward Communication: Project in Executive Development." *Personnel, 28* (1952), 304–319.
POWELL, F. A. "The Effects of Anxiety-Arousing Messages When Related to Personal, Familial, and Impersonal Referents." *Speech Monographs, 32* (1965), 102–106.
POWELL, JOHN, S. J. *Why Am I Afraid to Tell You Who I am*. Niles, Ill., Argus Communications, 1969.
REDDING, W. CHARLES and GEORGE A. SANBORN. *Business and Industrial Communication: A Source Book*. New York, Harper & Row, 1964.
REVANS, REGINALD W. *Developing Effective Managers*. New York, Praeger, 1971.
RICHARDS, WILLIAM D., JR. "An Improved Conceptually Based Method For Analysis of Communication Network Structures of Large Complex Organizations." Paper presented to the International Communication Association, April, 1971.
ROETHLISBERGER, F. J. *Management and Morale*. Cambridge, Harvard University Press, 1950.
ROGERS, EVERETT M. and F. FLOYD SHOEMAKER. *Communication of Innovation: A Cross-Cultural Approach*. New York, Free Press, 1971.
ROKEACH, MILTON. *The Open and Closed Mind*. New York, Basic Books, 1960.
ROSNOW, RALPH L. and EDWARD J. ROBINSON. *Experiments In Persuasion*. New York, Academic Press, 1967.
SAPOLSKY, HARVEY M. "Organization Structure and Innovation." *Journal of Business, 40* (1967).
SCHEIN, EDGAR H. *Organizational Psychology*. Englewood Cliffs, N.J., Prentice-Hall, 1970.
SCHOLZ, WILLIAM. *Communication in the Business Organization*. Englewood Cliffs, N.J., Prentice-Hall, 1962.
SCHREIMAN, D. BRUCE and J. DAVID JOHNSON. "A Model of Cognitive Com-

plexity and Network Role." Paper presented to the International Communication Association, April, 1975.

SCOTT, WILLIAM G. "Communication and Centralization of Organizations." *Journal of Communication, 8* (March, 1963), 3–11.

SHEPARD, HERBERT A. "Innovation-Resisting and Innovation-Producing Organizations." *Journal of Business, 40* (1967).

SHEPHERD, CLOVIS R. *Small Groups: Some Sociological Perspectives.* New York, Intext, 1964.

SHERIF, MUZAFER. *The Psychology of Social Norms.* New York, Harper & Row, 1936.

SHUBIK, MARTIN (ed.). *Game Theory and Related Approaches to Social Behavior.* New York, Wiley, 1964.

SIMON, H. A. *Administrative Behavior* (2nd ed.). New York, Macmillan, 1957.

SMITH, CLARENCE. "Closing the Gap Between Communication Researchers and Practitioners." Research conducted on behalf of Division IV of ICA, 1972.

STODGILL, R. M. "Personal Factors Associated With Leadership: A Survey of the Literature." *Journal of Psychology 25,* (1948), 35–71.

SUTERMEISTER, ROBERT A. *People and Productivity.* New York, McGraw-Hill, 1969.

TANNENBAUM, ROBERT and WARREN H. SCHIMIDT. "How To Choose A Leadership Pattern." *Harvard Business Review, 36,* no. 2 (March–April, 1958), 95–101.

THAYER, LEE. *Administrative Communication.* Homewood, Ill., Irwin, 1961.

THIBAUT, JOHN W. and HAROLD H. KELLEY. *The Social Psychology of Groups.* New York, Wiley, 1959.

THOMPSON, JAMES D. *Organizations in Action.* New York, McGraw-Hill, 1967.

THOMPSON, WAYNE. *Quantitative Research in Public Address and Communication.* New York, Random House, 1967.

TOFFLER, ALVIN. *Future Shock.* New York, Random House, 1970.

TOWNSEND, ROBERT. *Up the Organization.* New York, Knopf, 1970.

TUBBS, STEWART L. and SYLVIA MOSS. *Human Communications: An Interpersonal Perspective.* New York, Random House, 1974.

WATSON, GOODWIN. "Resistance to Change," in Goodwin Watson (ed.), *Concepts for Social Change.* Vol. 1, Cooperative Project for Educational Development Series, Washington, D.C., National Training Laboratories, 1966.

WENBURG, JOHN and WILLIAM WILMOT. *The Personal Communication Process.* New York, Wiley, 1973.

WESTLEY, BRUCE H. and MALCOLM S. MACLEAN, JR. "A Conceptual Model for Communication Research." *Journalism Quarterly, 34* (1957), 31–38.

——— "A New Breed of Men Will Call the Shots." *Business Week* (December 6, 1969), 144.

WHITE, RALPH and RONALD LIPPITT. *Autocracy and Democracy.* New York, Harper & Row, 1960.

WHYTE, WILLIAM H., JR. *The Organization Man.* New York, Simon and Schuster, 1956.

WEINER, NORBERT. *The Human Use of Human Beings: Cybernetics and Society.* New York, Avon, 1967.

ZELKO, HAROLD and FRANK E. X. DANCE. *Business and Professional Speech Communication.* New York, Holt, Rinehart and Winston, 1965.

index

Action skills, 152
Advertising, 259
Anchoring, 192–193
Anxiety-arousing cues, 191–192
Attitude management, 184–186
Attitudes, 44, 178–179
Audiovisuals, 252
Authoritative approach, 110, 112
Authority, 26, 216
Authority innovation decisions, 148

Balance theories, 195
Behavioral communication, 192
Belief, 178–179
Belief systems, 179–180
Bridges, 65

Change, 90–92, 135–137
   barriers to, 94–100
   communication of, 104–110
   planning of, 111
   types of, 106–107
Change agent, 148, 151
Change resistance, 100–103, 160–163
Change strategies, 156–157
Channel variables, 190
Channels, 44
Climate development, 131
Clique groups, 208
Cognitive dissonance, 100, 195–196
Communication
   barriers to, 74–77
   downward, 72–73
   ethics of, 140–141
   external, 40, 232–234
   face-to-face, 56–57
   formal, 40
   horizontal, 77
   informal, 40
   integration, 70–71
   internal, 40, 231–232
   mass, 58
   models, 41–46
   nonverbal, 39–40
   oral, 40, 234–235
   process, 41
   selectivity, 46–48
   skills, 44
   small groups, 57–58
   speaker-audience, 58
   unintentional, 39
   upward, 73
   written, 40, 234–235
Communication networks, 63–71, 93
Communication plan, 121–123
Communication roles, 129–135
   controlling, 130
   decision-making, 131
   delegation, 131
   directing, 130
   leadership, 130
   organizing, 130
   planning, 130
   recognition and participation, 131
   staffing, 130
   teamwork, 131
Compatibility, 155
Complexity, 155
Complexity and technology, 119
Conference management, 249–252
Conferences, types of
   brainstorming, 255–256
   buzz session, 258
   change of attitude, 254–255
   informational, 253–254
Conflict management, 133
Conflict reduction, 131–133
Conformity, 211–212
Consequences, change, 163–165
Counseling, 131

Decentralization, 30–33
Decoder, 43, 44
Delegation, 26
Dynamic equilibrium, 22

Encoder, 43, 44
Entropy, 20–21, 23
   negative, 22
Equifinality, law of, 18, 21

Error, 83
Escaping, 83
Esteem, 214

Fayol's bridge, 78
Feedback, 3-4, 72
Field theory, 211
Filtering, 83
Formal communication networks, 65-67
Freezing and unfreezing, 112-113

Gatekeeper, 83
Goal achievement, 24-25
Grapevine, 67-68
Grievance settlement, 133-134
Group
  composition, 208
  development, 208
  dynamics, 204
  leadership, 139-140
  process, 208
  size, 206
  structure, 208
Groups
  deliberately formed, 205
  externally designated, 205
  spontaneously formed, 205
Groupthink, 212

Hetrophily, 105-106
Homophily, 105

Information overload, 80-86
Innoculation, 193
Innovation decision process, 109, 154-155
  action, 155
  decision, 154-155
  knowledge, 154
  persuasion, 154
Innovation decisions
  authoritative, 108-109
  collective, 108, 110
  optional, 107-108, 110
Instructional techniques, 288-292
Interaction, 67
Interpersonal trust, 138, 180-184
Interviews, 238-249
  evaluation, 245-248
  personnel, 241-245
  persuasion, 248-249

Knowledge level, 44

Leadership
  appointed, 215
  emergent, 215
  great man theory, 216
  leader influence, 216
  selected, 215
  trait approach, 216
Leadership
  and cohesiveness, 224-225
  group success, 226-227
  interpersonal attraction, 224
  patterns of, 219-221
  productivity, 225-226
  satisfaction, 226-227
  styles of, 219-221; authoritarian, 220, 222; democratic, 220; laissez-faire, 220
Learning, 264, 279, 287-288
Learning motivation, 287-288
Liaison, 65, 128
Linking pin role, 65
Linking system, 128-129
Logical vs. emotional appeals, 191

Managerial motivation, 175
Managerial style, 27-30
Manuscript speech, 257-259
Meaning, 189-190
Message, 44
Message variables, 189-190, 191-193
Morale, 24, 138, 180-184
Motivation, 137-139
Motive patterns
  instrumental satisfaction, 184
  internalization, 184
  legal compliance, 184
  self-expression, 184
Multiple channels, 83

Network analysis, 68-70
  cross-sectional analysis, 68, 69, 125
  duty study, 68, 69
  ECCO analysis, 69, 125
  participant analysis, 68, 69, 125
  resident analysis, 68, 69, 125
Nonverbal channels, 190
Norms, 97, 210-212
  modern, 97-98
  traditional, 98

Observability, 156
Off-the-job training, 279-287
Omission, 83
On-the-job training, 277-279
Opinion leader, 159
Optimization, principle of, 18-19
Organizational analysis, 270-275
  critical incident method, 273-274
  interviews, 272-273
  network analysis, 274-275
  questionnaire, 271-272
Organizational climate, 70-71
Organizational goals, 9
Organizational health, 23
Organizational stability, 95

Organizational theory
  classical theory, 5
  human relations theory, 5–6
  structuralist theory, 6–7
Organizations, 9
  coercive, 10
  formal, 11–15
  informal, 15–17
  normative, 11
  utilitarian, 10–11

Participation, 221–224
Participative approach, 110
Performance measurement, 132
Persuasion, 176–178
Power, 26–27, 212–213
Private commitment, 48
Public acceptance, 48
Public communication, 257–258
Public relations, 260–261

Queuing, 83

Receiver, 44
Receiver variables, 193–194
  dogmatism, 193–194
  intelligence, 194
  sex, 194
Relative advantage, 255
Reporting, 236–238
Research utilization, 125–129
Resistance to counter-persuasion, 192–193
Roles, 213–215

Self-appraisal, 134–135
Self-persuasion, 194–195
Social and cultural systems, 44
Social exchange theory, 206–207

Source, 44
Source credibility, 186–188
Stability, 24
Status, 214
Steady state, 21
Subsystems
  adaptive, 19
  maintenance, 19
  managerial, 19
  productive, 19
  supportive, 19
System
  cybernetic, 17
  input, 17, 21
  leading, 20
  output, 17, 21
  throughput, 17, 21
Systems
  open, 20–23
  theory, 17–19

Task and environment, 208
Task performance, 208
Theory X and Y, 28–29, 53
Training, 264–270
  aids, 290–292
  objectives, 277
  methods, case study, 283; discussion, 282–283; gaming, 284–287; lecture, 281–282; programmed training, 284; role playing, 283–284; simulation, 284–287
  program, communication of, 267–270; evaluation, 292–293
Trialability, 155–156
Two-step flow, 157–160

Written report inventory, 239

77 78 79 80 9 8 7 6 5 4 3 2 1